Ethnic Monitoring and Data Protection
The European Context

Edited
by

ANDREA KRIZSÁN

IN
DOK
HUMAN RIGHTS INFORMATION
AND DOCUMENTATION CENTRE

CEU PRESS

CPS BOOKS

CENTRAL EUROPEAN UNIVERSITY PRESS – INDOK

The publication of this volume was made possible by a grant from the Open Society Foundation.

© 2001 Central Eeuropean University and INDOK Human Rights Information and Documetation Center

English text revised by *Mark Zimmermann*
Cover design and typesetting by *József Pintér*

English edition published in 2001 by

Central European University Press
An imprint of the
Central European University Share Company
Nádor utca 11, H-1015 Budapest, Hungary
Tel: +36-1-327-3138 or 327-3000; *Fax:* +36-1-327-3183
E-mail: ceupress@ceu.hu; *Website:* www.ceupress.com

400 West 59th Street, New York NY 10019, USA
Tel: +1-212-547-6932; *Fax:* +1-212-548-4607
E-mail: mgreenwald@sorosny.org

and by

INDOK Human Rights Information and Documentation Center
József krt. 30-32, H-1085 Budapest, Hungary
E-mal: indok@indok.hu, *Website:* www.indok.hu

Distributed
in Hungary by
INDOK Human Rights Information and Documentation Center
József krt. 30-32, H-1085 Budapest, Hungary
E-mal: indok@indok.hu; *Website:* www.indok.hu

in the United Kingdom and Western Europe by
Plymbridge Distributors Ltd., Estover Road, Plymouth PL6 7PY, United Kingdom
Tel: +44-1752-202301; *Fax:* +44-1752-202333
E-mail: orders@plymbridge.com

in the USA by
CEU Press *c/o Books International*
P.O. Box 605, *Herndon, VA 20172, USA*
Tel: +1-703-661-1500; *Fax:* +1-703-661-1501
E-mail: mgreenwald@sorosny.org

in Canada by
CEU Press *c/o University of Toronto Press Inc.*
5201 Dufferin Street, Toronto, Ontario M3H 5T8, Canada
Tel: +1-800-565-9523; *Fax:* +1-800-221-9985
E-mail: utpbooks@utpress.utoronto.ca

ISBN 963-9241-34-2
ISSN 1587-6942

Library of Congress Cataloging-in-Publication Data
A CIP catalog record for this book is available upon request

Printed in Hungary by
László és Társa, Budapest

Ethnic Monitoring
and Data Protection
The European Context

CPS BOOKS

Forthcoming:
Reinventing Media. Media Policy in East-Central Europe
(Spring, 2002)

CENTER (P FOR POLICY STUDIES
C E U Central European University

Contents

It is a pleasure to launch this book as the first in a new series sponsored by the Center for Policy Studies at the Central European University and to be known as CPS BOOKS.

The purpose of the series is to provide a vehicle for the publication of monographs and collections of essays dealing with issues of public policy.

The present volume provides an excellent start to the series. It is a well-researched and stimulating comparative analysis of the social and legal aspects of ethnic record-keeping. The book examines the need for ethnic statistics; it also analyses the compatibility of the collection and recording of ethnic data with the principles governing the protection of personal data.

I expect this to be the first of many publications in this impressive new series.

D.J. Galligan

Centre for Socio-Legal Studies
Wolfson College, Oxford
Center for Policy Studies,
Central European University

Preface

Dimitrina Petrova

Human rights ought to be enforceable. If a right can't be defended in court, then it is little more than rhetoric. With this simple assumption in our heads, we crashed against the wall we later came to describe as indirect discrimination. We were human rights defenders working at the European Roma Rights Center, and the year was 1997. From the numerous cases of abuse of Roma rights, we could see clear patterns emerging: Roma suspects were more likely to be held in deten-tion than non-Roma for the same offences; Roma were more likely to have their complaints unanswered and more likely to be beaten at the moment of arrest or in detention; Romani children were more likely to be sent to sub-standard schools for the mentally disabled; Roma residents were more likely to be victims of urban planning projects that would result in their displacement. More likely: a mathematical probability that reveals a discriminatory effect, whether intend-ed or not, if race-neutral factors fail to account for the disparity.

Of all rights abuses, discrimination is among the most difficult to prove. But absent proof, the right to equality of treatment, irrespective of race or ethnicity, can't be vindicated. Anti-discrimination litigation- especially when challenging systemic inequalities- needs statistics as evidence. Designing social policies, too, is hazardous without more or less accurate quantitative predictions. How can a budget aimed at compensating structural disadvantages be developed if the num-ber of persons in the disadvantaged category is unknown? But finding reliable race- or ethnic-coded data has been a frustrating experience. Answers, even by experts, have bordered on statistical agnosticism.

The United Nations Committee on the Elimination of Race Discrimination and other international bodies have repeatedly urged governments to provide in their reports demographic, economic, health, educational, employment and other data broken down by ethnicity, but few governments have been willing to do so in sufficient detail. Data protection laws are often cited as the main obsta-cle to collecting ethnic statistics, even though the ethnic statistics in question would contain no information about any single individual.

When in Hungary data protection laws were enacted, the Roma leaders cel-ebrated a victory: from that moment on, the press would stop circulating police statements about the proportion of Roma crime. However, what was difficult to realize at that point, was that the "struggle against discrimination," which they had chosen as the banner of the movement, could from now on be confined to the realm of political slogans, very much in the interest of any future govern - mental demagogue.

This volume is floating in the turbulent space created by three focal human rights issues: the right to access to information, the right to privacy, and the right to equal treatment irrespective of race or ethnicity. But the careful reader of the analyses offered here will see that the tension between these rights is discursive: defense strategies with a view to these different rights appear as conflicting only at the level of political debate, which is of course historically rooted. Racial profiling has served genocidal purposes. Ethnic statistics has been, and- indeed- continues to be abused for anti-minority purposes. But generalized data are impersonal, and there are ways to ensure that abuse would not be tolerated; there are even ways to store data so that it would rule out abuse. It is a matter of laws and regulations of data collection, storage, and use. Absent the political con- troversy, it is possible, and indeed necessary to defend these rights simultane - ously. While asserting our right to be free from discrimination, we at the same time want to have our privacy rights intact; to enjoy both, we need to exercise our right to obtain information from public bodies. Moreover, our right to be free from racial or ethnic discrimination should be interpreted to imply a right to obtain statistical data broken down by ethnicity, if such data would be critical evidence proving that we have been victims of indirect discrimination.

This book touches upon the right to cultural and ethnic identity as a matter of free choice. It relates thus to the paradox of disadvantaged identity: to chal - lenge anti-Romani prejudice and the reduction from a universal human being to a particular human being, a "Roma," one first has to say she is "Roma." To chal - lenge this type of reduction from the universal to the particular (which I think is the essence of phenomena such as prejudice and discrimination), one has to assume and for some time dwell in the reduced identity, in a somewhat self- defeating manner. In order to attack a reality in which there are "Roma" opposed to "non-Roma," one has to construct the dichotomy first. The claiming of that identity excludes others and at least partially opposes them. We then encounter a curious performative contradiction: those who want to end the racist distinc - tion first have to define and measure the racial group, at the risk of essentializa - tion.

It is perhaps the instinctive protest to this reduction that has made many minority activists hostile to racial statistics. "It is not important whether I am Roma, we are all citizens of the country," they say. The second and more important reason for the suspicion to ethnic data is the memory of the Holocaust and other historic forms of persecution: people of Jewish and Romani ethnicity have been first singled out and then destroyed. Understandably, hiding one's ethnicity has become a tool of survival. This book is a modest contribution to the realization that stating one's ethnicity and using racial or ethnic statistics can be a tool of reaching genuine racial equality and justice.

About the Background of the Volume

The Ethnic Statistics and Data Protection project, which stood as the basis of this volume, was directed by the Hungarian Human Rights Information and Documentation Center (INDOK) and funded by the Center for Policy Studies of the Central European University, Budapest. The project was proposed by a group of experts (lawyers, human rights activists, NGO representatives) in early 2000 as a response to Roma rights lawyers working at and with the European Roma Rights Center, who routinely noted that one of the most significant obsta - cles to effective anti-discrimination litigation was the absence of statistics show - ing disparate treatment of Roma and other minorities in most spheres of public life. This group, together with representatives from the Open Society Institute, Budapest, the Constitutional and Legal Policy Institute and other NGOs, later served as the Steering Committee of the project.

Hence the selection of countries to be examined in the project was based, on the one hand, on special characteristics and conflicts arising in the area of ethnic discrimination, and, on the other hand, on the activities of some committed col - leagues or civil rights organizations that had comprehensive knowledge of the subject and were involved in handling these problems and making them public. The sample of countries examined in the project cannot be seen as either com - prehensive, or representative.

The country reports written for the project were originally formulated on the basis of a questionnaire consisting of more than forty questions compiled by the project leaders. The first group of questions was related to the legal framework of rights and freedoms of information and communication, especially regarding per - sonal and ethnic data. The second group comprised questions relating to data on individual members of minority groups and minority groups as a whole and the uses of such data and statistics in practice. The third group consisted of questions regarding methods and means of collecting and processing data on minorities. [1]

The first version of country reports — prepared from the answers to the questionnaire — served as discussion papers at the Conference on Ethnic

---

1. See Appendix for the questionnaire.

Statistics and Data Protection, organized by INDOK in Budapest, 15-17 December 2000, where participants — authors and the public alike — exchanged information and ideas in this area. The reports also served as the starting point for the studies published in this book.

However, the studies included in this volume went on to develop the reports written for the project. In some cases new in others second authors were com- missioned for the writing of the country studies to be included in the volume. The new studies already reflect the Editor's expectations, the claim for a more or less coherent set of reports and consequently, the results of the authors' revi- sion.

Comprehensive country studies are included on Bulgaria, the Czech Republic, Germany, Hungary and Spain. The studies on Latvia and Romania are much shorter and cannot be seen as comprehensive. They only describe some important aspects of the legal framework and the practices related to the issues our project was concerned with.

Michael Banton's paper on ethnic monitoring in Britain is somewhat differ- ent from the other country analyses. Unfortunately the project could not com- mission a country report from Britain, despite the importance of the British case as far as ethnic monitoring practices are concerned. Banton's paper has been written for purposes different than our project. Thus the paper is not following the structure of the other country reports. Its scope is not so much to address the data protection concerns connected to the collection of ethnic data, but to deal with debates that occurred in Britain connected to the application of ethnic monitoring practices. Yet the issues raised by this paper are very much of con- cern for most of the countries which the volume has reports on. It shows that an agreement in principle over the necessity and legality of ethnic monitoring for anti-discrimination policy purposes is just a first step in the process of imple- mentation of a useful, efficient, legally and socially acceptable ethnic monitor- ing system.

The volume also includes two studies on international practice and norms connected to the collection of ethnic data and its relation to data protection con- cerns. The UN Commission for the Elimination of all Forms of Racial Discrimination and the Council of Europe were selected because the norms and practices prescribed and recommended by these two international organizations are equally valid for all the countries on which the reports were written.

The introductory study at the beginning and the comparative study at the end of the volume phrase the context of the issue this volume is intended to address: the necessity of ethnic statistics and the compatibility of collection of ethnic data with the principles of data protection. Whereas Goldston's introductory study approaches the issue from the perspective of minority rights and in particular the right not to be discriminated against on grounds of national, ethnic or racial origin, Székely approaches the issue from a data protection perspective. The two studies together convey the message and aim of this volume: which is that the principles of minority protection and collection of ethnic data for its purposes, on the one hand, and the principles of data protection and informational self-determination, on the other hand, are not inherently incompatible.

Andrea Krizsán and Iván Székely

Contributors

MICHAEL BANTON was Professor of Sociology in the University of Bristol, UK, between 1965-1992 and a member of the *Commission for the Elimination of all Forms of Racial Discrimination* between 1986-2001.

BARBORA BUKOVSKA (Kvocekova) is staff attorney for the *Counselling Centre for Citizenship, Civil and Human Rights*, Prague, Czech Republic.

ALEXANDER DIX is Commissioner for Data Protection and Access to Information, State of Brandenburg, Germany.

ISIL GACHET is Executive Secretary to the *European Commission against Racism and Intolerance* (ECRI).

JAMES GOLDSTON is Deputy Director of the *Open Society Institute*, and Senior Counsel of the *European Roma Rights Center*.

KRASSIMIR KANEV is Director of the *Bulgarian Helsinki Committee* and member of the Executive Committee of the *International Helsinki Federation*.

ALEXANDER KASHUMOV is a lawyer working at the *Access to Information Program Foundation*, Sofia, Bulgaria.

BORIS KOLTCHANOV in Director of the Latvian non-profit organization *Baltic Insight*.

ANDREA KRIZSÁN is a Ph.D. candidate at the Political Science Department of the *Central European University*. She is currently working on issues related to anti-discrimination policy.

FLORIN MOISA is Executive President of the *Resource Center for Roma Communities*, Cluj Napoca, Romania.

DIMITRINA PETROVA is the Executive Director of the *European Roma Rights Center*.

IVÁN SZÉKELY is a social informatist; former Chief Counsellor of the Parliamentary Commissioner for Data Protection and Freedom of Information in Hungary; at present Counsellor at *Open Society Archives* at Central European University, and Associate Professor at *Budapest University of Technology and Economics*.

DANIEL WAGMAN is coordinator of the Barañi project, Madrid.

INA ZOON is a human rights advocate who works as consultant for interna-tional organizations such as the *Council of Europe* and the *Open Society Institute*. She is member of the Board of the *European Roma Rights Center*.

I.

Introduction

Race and Ethnic Data:
A Missing Resource in the Fight against Discrimination

James A. Goldston

The tension between the right to information and the right to privacy has been widely recognized, if not definitively resolved. Nowhere is the difficulty of reconciling these interests more pronounced than in the field of race relations. Fundamental to the task of promoting civil rights and non-discrimination throughout Europe is accurate documentation of the subordinated position of racial and ethnic minorities in many areas of public life. Statistical information is a prerequisite for the formulation of government policy. It is particularly crucial in addressing, and providing evidence to support, claims of racial discrimination. And yet, if statistics are needed to document the condition of minorities and prove legal violations, many understandably fear the abusive purposes to which statis-tics have been — and can be — put. Some actively oppose renewed efforts to gather information on the number of ethnic minorities in schools, courthouses and prisons. Others, mistrustful of the willingness and/or capacity of government and other officials to maintain the confidentiality of collected information, coun-sel non-cooperation with surveys and census counts. Some data protection laws are interpreted so as to hinder the collection of race- or ethnic-coded statistics. [1] The unfortunate consequence is that non-discrimination advocates are handi-capped by scarce reliable information, and allegations of racial discrimination often lack the persuasive power which statistical evidence would provide. [2]

In seeking to obtain such statistics, rights advocates typically confront, on the one hand, a widespread belief that international law and/or the domestic legis-

---

1. The term "race statistics" is somewhat controversial. Throughout my paper, I will employ the phrases "race- or ethnic-coded statistics," "race or ethnic statistics," "race statistics," "race- or eth-nic-coded data," and "statistics broken down by race or ethnicity" to refer to information that is dif-ferentiated as to the race and/or ethnicity of the persons to whom it pertains. These terms are not intended to suggest that "races" as such exist. [The same terminology will be used throughout the volume. The Editor]

2. "While Roma are considered to be among the poorest and most marginalized minorities in Central and Eastern Europe, information on their living conditions and the characteristics of their poverty is scarce, fragmented, and often anecdotal. Measurement problems are daunting and include undersampling in censuses and household surveys, privacy legislation in many countries that pro-hibits the gathering of data by ethnicity, the reluctance of many Roma to identify as Roma, and the incredible diversity of Roma groups and subgroups." D. Ringold (2000) *Roma and the Transition in Central and Eastern Europe: Trends and Challenges*. The World Bank. pp. vii.

lation of numerous countries in Europe prohibit the gathering and maintenance of race statistics; and, on the other, a fear, among racial minorities and others, that — regardless of their legal status — race statistics will be misused to the detriment of minorities, and/or that the very effort to gather statistics on the basis of race reinforces negative racial stereotypes. The project of which this publication is a part is an effort to address those obstacles, in part, by undertaking studies about the law and the practice in several countries.

As initially conceived,[3] this project is not primarily about data protection. It is about the need for evidence to prove and combat racial discrimination, and about how those concerned to address racial discrimination can overcome the obstacles to obtaining such evidence to which data protection laws — and/or misunderstandings of those laws — sometimes give rise. Thus, at its start, it was hoped that the project might contribute to the following actions:

a) clarify the present availability — or lack thereof — of race statistics in European countries — to what extent are they used? By governments? By anti-discrimination advocates?

b) clarify the legal status of race statistics in Europe under both international and domestic law to determine which, if any, legal prohibitions limit their collection and maintenance

c) where law is an obstacle, recommending legal reforms

d) where law is not the problem, but public understanding is, educate public and policy-makers that the law does not bar them from gathering such information, and

e) in all places, (i) make clear the costs of the absence of statistics (i.e., advocates cannot prove, and governments cannot monitor or combat, discrimination), and (ii) suggest practical steps that might be taken to permit the gathering and collection of such statistics with safeguards which address the legitimate concerns that have been raised.

Since the commencement of this project, I have become only more convinced that the importance of the law as a bar to, or restriction upon, the collection and maintenance of race statistics, is often overstated. Indeed, perhaps the most significant legal development over the past 12 months in this field has been the adoption in June 2000 by the Council of the European Union of the

---

3. The first collaborative meeting which led to the research done for the project was held in February 2000. The second meeting in which the results of the research were presented was the INDOK-organized "Workshop on Race Statistics and Data Protection" at the Central European University, Budapest, December 16-17, 2000.

Directive implementing the principle of equal treatment between persons irre-spective of racial or ethnic origin[4]. The Directive constitutes a major step for-ward in the fight against racial discrimination, as it provides the first European Union-wide legal prohibition. The Directive must be transposed into domes-tic legislation in each of the EU member states within three years. It will become part of the Community acquis, which all candidate countries must adopt as well.

The Directive prohibits both direct and indirect indiscrimination. While "direct discrimination" requires the existence of a law or practice, which treats people differently on its face ("no blacks may apply"), "indirect discrimination" is more subtle. Indirect discrimination, as defined by the Directive, occurs "where an apparently neutral provision, criterion or practice would put persons of a racial or ethnic origin at a particular disadvantage compared with other per-sons, unless that provision, criterion or practice is objectively justified by a legit-imate aim and the means of achieving that aim are appropriate and necessary." [5] The very notion of indirect discrimination implies a need for data. A showing of a disadvantage "compared with other persons" requires information about how other persons have been treated. Indeed, the Race Directive expressly authorizes the use of statistical evidence to prove indirect discrimination. "The apprecia-tion of the facts from which it may be inferred that there has been direct or indi-rect discrimination is a matter for national judicial or other competent bodies, in accordance with rules of national law or practice. *Such rules may provide in par-ticular for indirect discrimination to be established by any means including on the basis of statistical evidence.*" [6]

Without such statistics, many victims of racial discrimination are unable to pursue and obtain redress for legitimate claims. Moreover, as noted above, gov-ernments can hardly be expected to comply with international obligations to eradicate racial discrimination without data showing the racial impact of poli-cies in the fields of, inter alia, employment, housing, education, and criminal justice.

At an official level, race- and ethnic-coded data are comparatively rare across much of Europe. Fifty percent of all member states of the Council of Europe "do not collect data of an ethnic nature because their constitutions prohibit it." [7] Of 37 countries which took part in a comprehensive Council of Europe survey two

---

4. Council Directive 2000/43/EC of 29 June 2000. (Race Directive in the following).
5. Race Directive, Article 2(2)(b).
6. Race Directive, Preamble, paragraph 15 (emphasis supplied).
7. *Roma and Statistics: Strasbourg, 22-23 May 2000.* (2000). Council of Europe. Paragraph 41 (sum-marizing the contribution of F. Millich, principal administrator, Population Division, Council of Europe).

21

years ago, [8]only four — Bulgaria, Cyprus, the Netherlands, and United Kingdom — included information about ethnicity in the last census or in the official population register.[9] Only in the Netherlands and the United Kingdom were surveys containing information on ethnicity common[10]An additional eleven countries — all in Central and Eastern Europe and the Balkans — asked about "national group" at the last census: Russia, Ukraine, Romania, Belarus, Hungary, Slovak Republic, Latvia, Estonia, Croatia, the Former Yugoslav Republic of Macedonia, Slovenia. Lithuania asked about "nationality." [11]

And yet, though race statistics may be rare at the official level, they are by no means absent. Indeed, many institutions — local governments, individual government ministries, social service and law enforcement agencies — collect and maintain race statistics. The report on Spain prepared for this project indicates that a wide range of ethnic statistics are maintained by schools, police, social service and welfare offices. [12] This evidence and other examples cited below suggest that the practice is far more widespread than is officially acknowledged.

The experience of the European Roma Rights Center in building a case to challenge racial segregation in schools in the Czech Republic is emblematic. At first, when our representatives from Budapest went to the schools and asked for information about how many Roma and how many non-Roma were in each class, they were told, simply, we don't have that information. Subsequently, local Czech Roma leaders with connections to local officials went back to the schools and asked for the same information and, miraculously, the schools suddenly produced signed, stamped, certified statistics of their students, broken down by ethnicity.

Indeed, as technology expands and increasing amounts of information (ethnic-coded and other) are collected and circulated in computerized databases, the choice that is so often posed — that is, whether advocates of non-discrimination

8. Werner Haug, Youssef Courbage, Paul Compton (1998) *The demographic characteristics of national minorities in certain European states.* Council of Europe. The data contained in this work was derived from a "survey to determine the statistical sources of information, existing or potential, concerning religion, language, national group and ethnic group" sent to the Statistical Offices of 43 European countries in 1995. The Council of Europe Group of Specialists prepared the survey on the demographic situation of national minorities, with the aid of Eurostat and the United Nations Economic Commission for Europe. Ibid. pp. 23.
9. Ibid. pp. 54-55.
10. Ibid. pp. 55. United Kingdom surveys including information on ethnic groups addressed households and the working population, among other sectors. In the Netherlands, information concerning the place of birth of father/mother may be found in the population register, employment surveys, and immigration and vital statistics. Ibid. pp. 55-56.
11. Ibid. pp. 42-47.
12. See Ina Zoon and Daniel Wagman "The Case of Spain" in this volume.

should or should not support the collection and maintenance of ethnic-coded data — may seem quaint, if not false. Increasingly, it may well be that the choice is not whether to have such data — it exists whether we want it or not — but rather how to democratize access to data which is often monopolized by the discriminators. In order to end discrimination, the victims too will have to lay claim to this controversial, but essential information.

The report on Spain for this meeting observes that the data protection "legislation is almost universally misunderstood to prohibit any kind of ethnic data gathering, storing or use. However ... the law does not prohibit gathering ethnic data; it only imposes special guarantees for its processing and transfer. Thus, new proposals for further ethnic data gathering can be carried out without legal reforms." [13] I think this observation is likely true for other countries as well. Which suggests that, in this field as in others, it is important not to mis-characterize as problems of law, what are often questions of changing attitudes.

As part of this effort to address popular misunderstanding, we must highlight the need for rational discourse and reasoned approaches. Some persons concerned about past and present abuses of race statistics have advocated their complete prohibition. Apart from this notion's inconsistency with international law, a complete ban on all race statistics would be like barring all speech about race or ethnicity, simply because some hateful statements intentionally incite violence and discrimination against minorities. It would be overreaching and counter-productive to ban all use of race statistics simply because some uses are objectionable. Like taking a hammer to kill a mosquito, a total ban on race statistics is far too broad a remedy for those genuine abuses, which can be adequately addressed through effective enactment and enforcement of privacy controls on government data.

In this vein, I think that our goals for this project should be, on the one hand, to identify legal lacuna — where they exist — which unfairly bar the collection of race statistics, and which may need to be changed; and on the other, and no less importantly, to identify strategies for collecting race data which are consistent with privacy standards and which overcome the objections and fears which are so prevalent.

At present, the victims of racial discrimination are at an enormous disadvantage — there is all too little information with which to describe and document the extent of their discriminatory treatment. One of the reasons that Roma have had such difficulties in challenging racist myths is the paucity of statistics which might prove what they allege — their over-representation in prisons, in schools for the mentally retarded, in sub-standard housing. Of course, such statistics are

13. Ibid. pp. 212.

not a panacea. It is still possible to argue that the number of Roma in prison sim-ply reflects the penchant for Roma to steal, or that the number of Roma in spe-cial schools shows that Roma are genetically more stupid than everyone else. But statistics are a crucial first step in the battle against racism, without which the victims of discrimination stand helpless against a mountain of prejudice.

And still, numerous concerns about race- or ethnic-coded data collection per-sist, often within the very minority communities on whose behalf the supporters of such data purport to advocate. Among the most commonly voiced objections are: a) the inherent inaccuracy of racial classifications and the data upon which they are based; b) the history of abuse of race statistics in the past, and the risk that continuing abuses will only reinforce negative stereotypes about minorities; c) the purported infringements of the rights to privacy and self-determination; and d) the barriers to the collection and maintenance of race statistics posed by international and/or domestic legislation.

Let me try to address each of these briefly.

A. Inaccuracy

Race statistics, it is commonly argued, are inherently inaccurate. First, such statistics are necessarily based on racial categories, which are themselves unsci-entific and unreliable. Race cannot be defined scientifically, because there exist no objective biological boundaries to divide one sub-group of the human species from another. The categories are "determined by the cultural practices of the classifiers." [14] Indeed, it has long been accepted that "pure races — in the sense of genetically homogeneous populations — do not exist in the human species.... Many anthropologists, while stressing the importance of human variation, believe that the scientific interest of [racial] classifications is limited, and even that they carry the risk of inviting abusive generalizations." [15] Even governments

14. James C. King (1981) *The Biology of Race*. University of California Press. pp. 157 (quoted in Paul Knepper (1996) "Race, Racism and Crime Statistics," 24 *Southern University Law Review* 71, 77). "All the attempts during the past 150 years to bring greater refinement and precision to the delineation of human races have only led to greater and greater complication and confusion for the simple rea-son that the problem is insoluble.... No system of classification, no matter how clever, can give [sub-species] a specificity they do not have."
15. *Proposals on the Biological Aspects of Race* (1964) UNESCO, see also *Statement on Race and Racial Prejudice* (1967) UNESCO ("The division of the human species into 'races' is partly conventional and partly arbitrary"); *Legal Measures to Combat Racism and Intolerance in the Member States of the Council of Europe* (1996) Council of Europe, European Commission Against Racism and Intolerance (ECRI). pp. 437 "It seems that in biological terms there is very little, if any, distinction between what are commonly called the races of human beings" summarizing United Kingdom court decision in *Ealing London Borough Council v. Race Relations Board* (1972) Appeal Cases 342

which regularly collect and make use of race statistics acknowledge that, as the U.S. government's *Statistical Policy Handbook* notes, officially-designated racial categories are based on "social identity, what's commonly accepted by the public, not science." [16]

In addition to the above problems, race statistics may be distorted by identification and/or perception bias. Thus, race statistics may be based upon self-identity, social (community) identity, or official (government-imposed) identity, and each of these may differ. Moreover, if observation is the basis of a racial designation, the designator may rely on skin color, language, the subject's last name — all of which, again, may yield a different racial categorization. In the field of criminal justice, the vagaries of perception distortion are heightened by factors such as the emotional state of a crime victim, the fact that many crimes occur quickly and/or in situations of less-than-perfect visibility (i.e., at night), and the efforts of perpetrators intentionally to disguise their identity.

Third, racial categories have powerfully negative legacies in different countries. In Europe, of course, Nazi-era racial classifications as a prelude to mass extermination are well known and rightly feared. But in the United States too, racial categories have a sorry genesis in slavery and the "Jim Crow" racial segregationist laws, which perpetuated second-class citizenship for many African Americans into the mid-20th century. More particularly, the use of race-based crime statistics in the U.S. stems from discredited theories of scientific racism, which sought to link ethnicity with biologically determined criminal propensity.[17] Influenced by such notions, between 1911 and 1930 thirty-three states enacted laws requiring sterilization for a variety of behavioral characteristics believed to be genetically determined.[18] The FBI's first quarterly Uniform Crime Report, in 1933, made reference to race-coded crime statistics to show that a "correspondingly high proportion" of "Negroes" and "colored" persons were arrested for assault, weapons charges, and gambling.[19]

Finally, since they are socially constructed, racial categories change over time. In Europe, notwithstanding the continuing reluctance of many to self-identify as "Roma," many persons who 20 years ago defined themselves as "Romanian", "Czech", or "Hungarian" today consider and call themselves "Roma" or "Tsigan". In the U.S., official categorizations have changed over time, complicating any effort to compare data. Thus, in the 1930s, the FBI's Uniform Crime

16. *Statistical Policy Handbook* (1978) Office of Federal Statistical Policy and Standards. pp. 37.
17. See, e.g., Earnest A. Hooton (1939) *The American Criminal*. Greenwood Publishing; Gina Lombroso-Ferrero (1911) *Criminal Man According to the Classification of Cesare Lombroso*. London: Putnam.
18. Knepper op.cit. pp. 92.
19. Quoted in ibid. pp. 102.

Reports considered "Mexicans" a separate race. In 1942, the Reports dropped the "Mexican" category and grouped arrests of such persons together with other "Whites." This practice continued until 1980, when "Mexicans" were re-classified as "Hispanics." [20]

And yet, the above-cited flaws, however real, have not impeded the use of race statistics to document discriminatory patterns and highlight abuse. Thus, governmental and non-governmental bodies in the United States have employed analyses of race statistics to document pervasive disparities of treatment accorded racial minorities in the criminal justice system. One report by the U.S. Department of Justice showed that "[b]lack and Hispanic youths are treated more severely than white teenagers charged with comparable crimes at every step of the juvenile justice system" and noted that, "for those charged with drug offenses, black youths are 48 times more likely than whites to be sentenced to juvenile prison." [21] A report by Human Rights Watch found that, although five times as many whites use drugs as blacks, black drug offenders are imprisoned at far higher rates than whites. [22] These and similar studies[23] correct popular misperceptions about race and crime, and may lead to reforms of law and practice essential to equal justice.

B. Legacy of Abuse/Reinforcing Stereotypes

The history of intentional misuse of race- and ethnic-coded data to the detriment of minorities and the continuing potential for abuse — perhaps most evident in the field of crime statistics — mandates caution in the collection and dissemination of such information. Closely related to the foregoing is the concern that the very effort to gather and publish race statistics reinforces negative stereotypes about minorities.

20. Ibid. pp. 98-99. It has also been argued that the 1980 U.S. census classifications violated "'elementary rules for constructing a taxonomy — that the classes be mutually exclusive, that all the classes add up to the whole of the population, and that they be of roughly the same order of importance and magnitude.' The logical absurdity of the classification project is exposed by demands for a 'multiracial' category, open to all of 'mixed race' (the closest option in previous censuses has been 'Other'). These have been met with objections from African Americans who point out that almost all of their community is, in the sense of ancestry, multiracial." Marek Kohn, (1995) *The Race Gallery: The Return of Racial Science*. London: Jonathan Cape, pp. 22-23 (quoting the sociologist William Petersen).
21. Fox Butterfield "Racist Disparities are Pervasive in Justice System, Report Says" *The New York Times*, April 26, 2000.
22. *Punishment and Prejudice: Racial Disparities in the War on Drugs.* (2000) Human Rights Watch.
23. See, e.g. B. Whitaker, "San Diego Police Found to Stop Black and Latino Drivers Most" *The New York Times*, October 1, 2000. Survey conducted for San Diego Police Department "found that African-Americans and Hispanics have a much greater chance of being stopped by the police in San Diego than whites and Asian-Americans."

Those concerned about race statistics point to the legacy of abuse of such data in Nazi-era Europe and by some of the Communist regimes in power before 1989 in Central and Eastern Europe. Indeed, the stereotyping of one pan-European minority — the Roma — as an "asocial" or "criminal" group formed the intellectual underpinning of the Porraimos, or Romani Holocaust, during the Second World War. And there are some indications that controversial prac-tices continue. Thus, the annual report for 2000 of the United Nations Special Rapporteur on Racism noted information from Germany

"that Sinti and Roma minorities are being specially registered in the data-bases and records of the Bavarian police as Roma/Sinti type, gypsy type or the old Nazi term *Landfahrer* (vagrant). The Central Council of German Sinti and Roma has been informed of the report of the Bavarian Data Protection Commissioner of 16 December 1998 which states that Sinti and Roma are being registered generally on special police files without reason or legal basis by their personal details and even the number plates of their cars and further data. The police justify this storage as supposed-ly *vorbeugende Verbrecenbekampfung* (preventive crime combat) and explain that Sinti and Roma could be a public danger." [24]

Others have claimed that customs officers have employed the practice of racial profiling to identify and deport members of certain ethnic minorities. Czech Airlines was discovered to have been identifying Roma with the letter "R" on their records, in order to assist this process of sifting out "unwanted" migrants.[25] It has recently been revealed that the Czech Ministry of Interior maintains records of criminal suspects, including Roma, who are considered to be "statistically significant." [26]

A recent survey of media coverage of Roma in Slovakia reported several examples in which race statistics were used to document an alleged Romani propensity to commit crime. Thus, one cited article from the local press noted, "... [S]ince 1994 Romani criminality accounted for 22 percent of the total num-ber of investigated offences.... Romani youth account for more than 30 percent

24. E/CN.4/2000/16, 10 February 2000, paragraph 37. The UN Report goes on to note that, in December 1996, when a question was raised in the German Bundestag about racial classifications in police records, the "Federal Government stated that ... doing away with such classifications alto-gether does not come into consideration because of their indispensable nature for police work...." Ibid. paragraph 39.
25. *Roma and the Law: Demythologizing the Gypsy Criminality Stereotype* (1999) Project on Ethnic Relations. pp. 12.
26. Interview with human rights researcher, Czech Republic, November 2000 (documents on file with author).

of investigated criminal offences committed by young people." [27] And, "Of all morality-breaking offenders Roma comprised 56 percent." [28]

The legacy of misuse of ethnic and race-coded data is such that even actions with apparently well-intended motives have fallen under the suspicion of their ostensible beneficiaries. Thus, in November 1999, the Ministry of Education in the Czech Republic sent a letter to elementary and special schools nationwide, asking that files be maintained on the educational achievements of Roma students. The government said that special monitoring was needed to improve the education of Roma. The reaction among some Roma leaders was hostile. "If somebody wants to differentiate people according to the color of their skin, that's clear discrimination, even if made for good purposes," one Roma activist was reported to have commented. "We have a certain historical experience with genocide, and have no guarantee democracy will stay here forever. What if neo-Nazis take over?" [29]

And yet, race statistics are not a necessary pre-condition to prejudice, discrimination, or the fostering of negative stereotypes. Thus, for example, statistics are not needed for negligent and/or consciously biased authors to selectively note and publish the ethnicity of persons arrested for alleged criminal activity.[30] Nor are they required for political leaders to inflame racial prejudice through insensitive and/or openly hostile public statements.[31]

Indeed, some purported abuses of "statistics" seem more made up than grounded in the reality of authentic data.[32] The alleged abuse is often more accu-

---

27. *Praca*, 25 August, 1998, pp. 4, quoted in *Image of the Roma in Selected Slovak Media* (2000) Slovak Helsinki Committee. pp.19-20.

28. Ibid. pp.20.

29. *Associated Press*, "Controversy flares over Gypsy lists in Czech schools," 3 November, 1999.

30. Numerous examples are cited in *Image of the Roma in Selected Slovak Media*, op.cit. pp. 20-21.

31. Thus, in early August 2000, a parliamentary deputy representing the Slovak National Party publicly declared that "unadaptable Roma" must be placed in "reservations" to reduce the crime rate, CTK reported. The deputy reportedly said that 1) the state must stop providing social benefits to "people who harm it," deeming the payment of such benefits to Roma "inhumane to the rest of the population"; 2) placing Roma in reservations would be "completely normal" as "in America there are also reservations for the Indians"; and 3) if Slovakia does not place "unadaptable Roma" into reservations now, "they will place us there 20 years from now." Three days later, the chairwoman of the Slovak National Party (SNS) said that she saw no need to apologize for the deputy's comments, since, in her view, the failure to solve the "genuine Roma problem" suits those Roma activists who "should come up with some proposals instead of strong words that solve nothing." The chairwoman added that "the SNS is interested in a thorough solution of the problem of the Romany ethnic group, because it is not the Gypsies, but the rest of Slovakia's population that is discriminated against." RFE/RL *(Un) Civil Societies*, Vol. 1, No. 13, 10 August 2000.

32. The same Slovak National Party parliamentary deputy referred to in footnote 32, supra, was further quoted as saying it has been "statistically proven" that most "retarded people" come from among the Roma and as asking, "What is humane about morons being allowed to give birth to more morons and raise the percentage of morons and crazies in the nation?" See also *Slovenska Republika*, 12 December, 1998, pp. 3, quoted in *Image of the Roma in Selected Slovak Media* op.cit., pp. 23 ("There are crimes 95 percent of which are committed by our fellow Romani citizens. It is not just specific sexual crimes, incest or sex abuse of the under-aged").

rately a reflection of the absence of statistics, which provides a vacuum to be exploited by creative, often malign, invention.

Some observers have noted what they perceive is a "double standard" with regard to race statistics. Thus, on the one hand, when advocates of non-discrimination ask for data concerning, inter alia, the number of Roma and non-Roma children in certain schools, or the number of ethnic minorities represented in the police force, government officials not uncommonly claim that such information does not exist.[33] On the other hand, this alleged non-existence of such data has not prevented even officials representing governments with restrictive data protection laws from on occasion citing a broad range of race- or ethnic-coded statistics.[34]

At their worst, some governments appear willing to use and/or publicize ethnic- and race-coded data when it serves the purpose of highlighting what is alleged to be disproportionate criminal activity on the part of certain ethnic minorities. Thus, Bulgarian authorities have told the Council of Europe Monitoring Committee that data show "more than 30% of all crimes in the country are perpetrated by Roma."[35] And information provided by Romanian police about a series of raids in the spring of 2000 raised similar concerns:

"In the last five days, police have raided Bucharest's seediest areas, in a crackdown on violent crime. Of 2,000 people arrested, police have said, most of them were Roma."[36]

33. Thus, the 1999 Progress Report of the European Commission on Hungary observes: "According to the Hungarian Government, identifying the ethnicity of offenders is not allowed under the data protection law and thus no statistical evidence on discrimination is available." In *Regular Report from the Commission on Progress on Accession* (13 October 1999) European Commission.
34. At a meeting in Bucharest in January 2000 sponsored by the Embassy of Finland, a representative of the Hungarian government's Office for National and Ethnic Minorities offered a range of statistics concerning the Roma. Among the data provided were the following: "some 60 percent of the Roma live in rural areas, about 30 percent in towns and the remaining 10 percent in Budapest"; "more than 70 percent of Roma children finish the eight classes of primary school"; "[o]nly one-third of all Roma children attend secondary education"; the unemployment rate within the Roma community "is about five times higher" than for others. Judith Solymosi, "Roma Policy in Hungary between 1998 — 2000," in Embassy of Finland in Romania. *International Expert Symposium on Roma Questions* (28-29 January, 2000) pp. 98.
35. See *Honoring of Obligations and Commitments by Bulgaria: Information Report* (September 1998) Council of Europe Doc. 8180, paragraph 107.
36. *Associated Press*, "Gypsies march to protest racism," 23 March 2000. Indeed, racial stereotyping is not unique to Europe. A United States police-training manual states that it is "structured to provide police personnel with Gypsy lifestyle and criminal activities which contribute to effective investigative and enforcement techniques." The manual suggests how physical characteristics may be used to identify "European Gypsies." B.H. Carter (1987) *Gypsies, Travelers and Thieves*, South Carolina Criminal Justice Academy, see: *Roma and the Law* (2000) Project on Ethnic Relations. pp. 12.

C. Privacy/Choice of Identity

Among the most fervent objections to race statistics is the threat they are said to pose to individuals' rights to choose whether- and how- they publicly identify themselves. On the one hand, ethnic data collection is said to interfere with the right to privacy, understood to encompass freedom to decide what kinds of information are collected and maintained about oneself. On the other, it is claimed, data collection may compromise the exclusive right of an individual to choose and express— or not— his/her ethnic identity. The very question of ethnic identity (who is "Roma"; who is "Hungarian") can only be answered by each individual, rather than by independent investigators or the state.

These are real concerns and they must be addressed with care. This is particularly so, given the traditional reluctance of members of some minority groups to endure the prejudice and hostility to which self-identification might subject them.[37] Indeed, the desire to redress- and/or not to repeat— the long history of privacy violations under previous authoritarian regimes, particularly in a technological environment which renders more data about each individual potentially available, has been one of the principal factors underlying the adoption of increasingly comprehensive data protection laws in Europe over the past three decades.[38]

And yet, it would be strange if, taken to extremes, the new data protection norms were interpreted so as to prohibit the gathering of ethnic data essential to document and challenge discrimination against these same minorities. Limited to the use of collective, anonymous data capable of showing discriminatory patterns and trends, the use of statistics ought not implicate the rights of individuals to privacy or self-determination. Indeed, for the purposes of making out a legal claim of racial discrimination, it is important to determine, not only whether the alleged victims *in fact* belonged to a particular minority group, but also whether the challenged action or decision was grounded *in the belief* that they so belonged. In this sense, a discrimination claim may say nothing about the self-proclaimed ethnicity of the alleged victims, and hence need not implicate their rights to privacy or self-determination.[39] This reality appears to

37. A participant in the 1991 Czechoslovak census explained, "At the census I declared myself a Slovak because being a Gypsy is reason enough to have other people hate you." C. Powell (1994) "Time for Another Immoral Panic? The Case of the Czechoslovak Gypsies," 2 *International Journal of Sociology and Law*, vol.2, 105-21, quoted in Kohn op.cit., pp. 189.
38. See, e.g., D. Banisar and S. Davies (1999) "Global Trends in Privacy Protection: an International Survey of Privacy, Data Protection, and Surveillance Laws and Developments," 18 *J. Marshall J. Computer & Info. L.*1.
39. A recent World Bank study of Roma in Central and Eastern Europe defines Roma "broadly to include those who identify themselves as Roma and those who are identified by others as Roma. This

be reflected in the international legal regime governing the use of race- and eth -
nic-coded statistics.

D. Legal Barriers

Some of the resistance to intensified collection and maintenance of race- and
ethnic-coded data is premised on the understanding that European regional law
and the domestic law in a number of countries prohibit or severely restrict such
activities. A number of surveys of domestic legislation prepared for this project
suggest that the picture is somewhat mixed. Additional research on domestic leg -
islation in other countries is needed. For now, I limit myself to noting that
regional data protection regulations in Europe reasonably distinguish between
individual, identifiable data and collective, anonymous data in ways which safe -
guard privacy and do not impede the good-faith collection and dissemination of
race statistics for legitimate governmental, scientific, and/or public interest
objectives.

Thus, the Council of the European Union Directive on the protection of
individuals with regard to the processing of personal data and on the free move -
ment of such data[40] expressly exempts from its application anonymous statistical
information of the kind needed to document and prove racial discrimination. [41]
Article 2 defines "personal data" as "any information relating to an identified or
identifiable natural person ('data subject'); an identifiable person is one who can
be identified, directly or indirectly, in particular by reference to an identification
number or to one or more factors specific to his physical, physiological, mental,
economic, cultural or social identity." Moreover, even if the data at issue were
considered "personal data" under the terms of the Directive, processing of that
data would still be permissible where "b) processing is necessary for the purpos -
es of carrying out the obligations and specific rights of the controller in the field
of employment law in so far as it is authorized by national law providing for ade -
quate safeguards; or ... e) the processing relates to data which are ... necessary
for the establishment, exercise or defence of legal claims.". Thus, the Directive

is both because of the collection of data sources used and because of the policy focus of this paper —
if policies affect ethnic minorities, they may do so regardless of personal identity." Ringold, op.cit.
pp. 3 (emphasis supplied).
40. 95/46/EC, of 24 October 1995 (EU Directive on Data Protection in the following).
41. See EU Directive on Data Protection, paragraph 26 ("the principles of protection must apply to
any information concerning an identified or identifiable person"; and "the principles of protection
shall not apply to data rendered anonymous in such a way that the data subject is no longer iden -
tifiable").

ought not bar the collection of race or ethnic data necessary to challenge discrimination in court.

The Council of Europe's Convention for the Protection of Individuals with Regard to Automatic Processing of Personal Data[42] is in accord.[43] Indeed, the Council of Europe has made clear that the principle of data protection is not an absolute. To the contrary, the Committee of Ministers has pronounced itself "[a]ware of the needs in both the public and private sectors for reliable statistics for analysis and understanding of contemporary society, and for defining policies and strategies for making arrangements in practically all aspects of daily life," and has suggested that "a balance should be struck between the need for research and statistics, on the one hand, and the necessary protection of the individual, especially when automatic data processing is involved, on the other." [44] To that end, Recommendation No. R (97) 18 distinguishes between "personal" and "anonymous" data (as to which "identification requires an unreasonable amount of time and manpower"), [45] and notes that "statistical results ... are not personal data, as they are not linked to an identified or identifiable natural person." [46] It also makes clear that "sensitive data" — including "personal data revealing racial origin" — may be processed automatically where domestic law provides for the data to be "collected in such a way that the data subject is not identifiable." [47]

Even where the data subjects are identifiable, "an important public interest" may justify the collection or processing of sensitive data absent the consent of the data subjects, where such consent would ordinarily be required. [48] In this regard, the Explanatory Memorandum to the Recommendation notes that an

---

42. 1981 (Convention in the following).

43. See, e.g., Article 2(a) "'personal data' means any information relating to an identified or identifiable individual"; Explanatory Report on the Convention, paragraph 28 ("'Identifiable persons' means a person who can be easily identified: it does not cover identification of persons by means of very sophisticated methods").

44. Recommendation No. R (97) 18 of the Committee of Ministers Concerning the Protection of Personal Data Collected and Processed for Statistical Purposes (1997), preamble.

45. Recommendation No., R (97) 18, Appendix, Principles 1, 8.1.

46. Explanatory Memorandum to Recommendation No. R (97) 18, paragraph 58.

47. Article 6, Convention for the Protection of Individuals with Regard to Automatic Processing of Personal Data; Recommendation No. R (97) 18, Appendix, Principle 4(8); Explanatory Memorandum to Recommendation No. R (97) 18, paragraph 76(a). Moreover, the Convention expressly exempts from the requirement of "additional safeguards" certain "automated personal data files used for statistics or for scientific research purposes when there is obviously no risk of an infringement of the privacy of the data subjects." ETS 108, Art. 9(3). The Convention's Explanatory Report notes that this exemption "leaves the possibility of restricting the exercise of the data subjects' rights [to additional safeguards] with regard to data processing operations which pose no risk. Examples are the use of data for statistical work, insofar as these data are presented in aggregate form and stripped of their identifiers." ETS 108, paragraph 59.

48. Recommendation No. R (97) 18, Appendix, Principle 6.2.

exception to the consent requirement for the collection and processing of "sen-sitive data" for statistical purposes might be "justified by major public interest, as where statistical information is needed to, [inter alia] ... develop aid to social groups in difficulty. Such examples, to which many more might be added, relate to matters which affect society's essential interests and in which the state has responsibilities. In such cases, the guarantees on protection of sensitive data must be adapted to the objective information needs arising from the public interest."[49] It seems plausible that the governmental obligation to eradicate racial discrimi-nation might, under some circumstances, qualify as such a "major public inter-est."

These principles, which seem consistent with the use of collective, anony-mous data to document racial discrimination, are bolstered by the practice of European and international bodies in repeatedly encouraging governments to gather and provide race- and ethnic-coded information necessary to measure compliance with international anti-discrimination law.

European Union

The EU Race Directive, discussed above, offers perhaps the most recent and clearest statement that race- and ethnic-coded statistics are useful tools in the combat of discrimination. However, European Union organs have on previous occasions made clear that such information is, not only permissible, but indeed desirable. Thus, the European Parliament's most recent Resolution concerning racism in the context of accession "calls on the candidate countries to collect, as a basis for policy action, reliable monitoring data on ethnic, linguistic and reli-gious minority groups including immigrants and refugees, the number and out-come of racist acts reported and prosecuted, and the performance of minority groups in the economic and social spheres." [50] The Regulation establishing the European Union Monitoring Centre on Racism and Xenophobia authorized the Centre, inter alia, to "collect, record and analyze information and data, includ-ing data resulting from scientific research," to "build up cooperation between the suppliers of information and develop a policy for concerted use of their databas-es in order to foster ... the wide distribution of their information," and to "devel-op methods to improve the comparability, objectivity and reliability of data at Community level by establishing indicators and criteria that will improve the

49. Explanatory Memorandum to Recommendation No. R (97) 18, paragraph 85(b).
50. *Report on the communication from the Commission countering racism, xenophobia and anti-semitism in the candidate countries* (28 February, 2000) European Parliament (COM(1999)256-C5-0094/1999-1999/2099(COS)), paragraph 13.

consistency of information." [51] And the 1998 Annual Report of the European Union Monitoring Centre stated that, in certain countries, such as the United Kingdom, "As far as the public authorities and public opinion are concerned, the best means of combating racist and xenophobic acts and attitudes is to start with a clear picture: in other words, to compile statistics based on the best possible criteria so as to obtain a close-up view of the real nature of these phenomena. The aim is not to compare such figures between different countries, but to be able to approach them on the basis of the same definitions, something that has yet to be done." [52]

European Commission against Racism and Intolerance

The European Commission against Racism and Intolerance (ECRI), a mon-itoring organ of the Council of Europe, has consistently sought statistical infor-mation from governments on the effects of government policies on different racial and/or ethnic groups. ECRI's General Policy Recommendation No. 1 on "Combating Racism, Xenophobia, Antisemitism and Intolerance," recommends that, "since it is difficult to develop and effectively implement policies ... with-out good data," governments should "collect, in accordance with European laws, regulations and recommendations on data protection and protection of privacy, where and when appropriate, data which will assist in assessing and evaluating the situation and experiences of groups which are particularly vulnerable to racism, xenophobia, anti-Semitism and intolerance." [53]

A subsequent ECRI recommendation "stress[es] that statistical data on racist and discriminatory acts and on the situation of minority groups in all fields of life are vital for the identification of problems and the formulation of policies," and notes ECRI's "convi[ction] that such statistical data should be supple-mented by data on attitudes, opinions and perceptions." [54] The Recommendation goes further to "recommend" that "governments of member States ... take steps to ensure that national surveys on the experience and per-ception of racism and discrimination from the point of view of potential victims are organised," and sets forth guidelines for the conduct of such surveys, which note the importance of "[g]ood population statistics including information

51. Council Regulation (EC) No. 1035/97, of 2 June 1997, Articles. 2(a), 2(b), 2(f). The Regulation further notes that the "Centre shall apply to its processing and exchange of data under this Regulation the provisions laid down in Directive 95/46/EC [the European Union's data protection directive]." Ibid. Article 5(1).
52. *Annual Report 1998* European Monitoring Center on Racism and Xenophobia, pp. 11-12.
53. ECRI, General Policy Recommendation No. 1, 4 October 1996.
54. ECRI, General Policy Recommendation No. 4, 6 March 1998.

about variables such as place of birth, ethnic origin, religious confession, mother tongue, citizenship, etc." [55]

ECRI's Country-by-Country Reports have specifically suggested that authorities gather statistical information on racial and ethnic minorities for the formulation and evaluation of government policies. In considering Poland, ECRI noted:

> "There is a system of data collection on ethnic and national groups in Poland, based on individual declarations of persons belonging to minority groups. However, most sources indicate that it is impossible to determine accurately the size of any ethnic or national group in Poland, since post World War II censi have not included questions pertaining to ethnic identity. Without accurate and up to date statistics in this field, it is impossible to draw up suitable policies or evaluate their effectiveness. Therefore, an absolute priority must be the establishment of a reliable system of data-collection in this field, in accordance with European laws, regulations and recommendations on data-protection and protection of privacy, in order to determine the real figures of ethnic and national minorities, immigrant groups, etc." [56]

Reports on other countries have evinced similar concerns. [57]

Finally, ECRI has urged even those countries whose data protection legislation purportedly prohibits the dissemination of race or ethnic statistics to pur-

---

55. Ibid. Appendix, paragraph 6.
56. *ECRI's Country-by-Country Approach: Volume 1* (1997) ECRI. pp. 86.
57. For the ECRI country-by-country reports see Isil Gachet "The Issue of Ethnic Data Collection from the Perspective of Some Council of Europe Activities" in this volume. Also see Report on the Netherlands ("ECRI's Country-by-Country Approach: Volume III", 1998, pp. 47) "Despite the widespread collection of statistics in a number of areas, there seems to be a lack of reliable, harmonized and comparable statistics as regards the situation of minority groups in all areas of social and economic activity.... Further efforts should be made to collect more comparable and reliable statistics, using a standard national form of categorization of ethnic origin as the basis of all relevant studies, after full consultation about its acceptability and in full accordance with European laws, regulations and recommendations on data protection and protection of privacy"; Report on Russia (ECRI, "ECRI's Country-by-Country Approach: Volume IV", 1999. pp. 41) noting that existing data "do not include statistics on the condition of ethnic minorities or the extent to which they are affected by social and economic policies — for example, in the shape of breakdowns of the experience of the various ethnic minorities in respect of employment, housing, health, social services, education and law and order. Experience in other countries has demonstrated the usefulness of such statistics in monitoring the relative position of minorities in society and in constituting policies which might affect them"; Report on Spain (ECRI, "ECRI's Country-by-Country Approach: Volume IV," 1999. pp. 75) saying "One statistical area which should be improved is data concerning the Roma/Gypsy community. Consideration should be given to various ways of obtaining information about the size and situation of the Roma/Gypsy community at national and regional/local level"; Report on United Kingdom (ECRI, "ECRI's Country-by-Country Approach: Volume IV," 1999. pp. 89) endorsing as "valuable and important" the collection of information "on ethnic origin as such," including a question in the 1991 census on "respondents' ethnic origin."

sue alternative avenues for the collection of such data. Thus, its Report on the Czech Republic advises: "The Czech authorities state that data on demographic composition other than census results cannot be published in the Czech Republic with regard to legislation designed to protect personal data and privacy. It is suggested that steps should be taken to improve information on the Roma/Gypsy community at the level of local authorities, research institutions and non-governmental organisations in order to facilitate the planning of social policies in relation to the Roma/Gypsy community." [58] And even Hungary, whose data protection legislation is among the most restrictive in Europe, is urged to "work towards establishing a system of collection of data and information in accordance with" European standards, "bearing in mind the importance of accurate and up-to-date statistics for drawing up policies and evaluating their effectiveness." [59]

United Nations Committee on the Elimination of Racial Discrimination

In response to widespread government refusals to provide demographic information broken down by race or ethnicity, the United Nations Committee on the Elimination of Racial Discrimination (CERD), in its "General Guidelines Regarding the Form and Content of Reports to be Submitted by States Parties under Article 9, Para. 1, of the Convention," has gone so far as to state the following:

"8. The ethnic characteristics of the country are of particular importance in connection with the ... Convention... Many States consider that, when conducting a census, they should not draw attention to factors like race lest this reinforce divisions they wish to overcome. If progress in eliminating discrimination based on race, colour, descent, national and ethnic origin is to be monitored, some indication is needed of the number of persons who could be treated less favourably on the basis of these characteristics. States which do not collect information on these characteristics in their censuses are therefore requested to provide information on mother tongues ... as indicative of ethnic differences, together with any information about race, colour, descent, national and ethnic origins derived from social surveys."

58. *ECRI's Country-by-Country Approach, Volume I*, pp. 17.
59. Ibid. pp. 44.

Similarly, CERD General Recommendation IV (1973) expressly endorses the use of race statistics by inviting "States parties to endeavour to include in their reports under article 9 relevant information on the demographic composition of the population." These general guidelines have been frequently reinforced by CERD requests to individual governments for statistical information on the racial/ethnic composition of the population.[60]

CERD's interest in obtaining race statistics — and the invalidity of commonly deployed government justifications for the failure to collect race statistics — were highlighted in a recent dialogue with the Portuguese government from 1999. In response to Committee requests for demographic information broken down by race or ethnicity, the government of Portugal maintained a) that its Constitution "prohibited the conducting of surveys on the racial or ethnic component of the population," b) that the United Nations Population Commission had recommended that the category of "race" should be optional in government censi, and c) that Portugal's "multiracial tradition and the absence of racial prejudices" made it "improper to establish statistics in terms of the race, religion … of the persons concerned." [61]

The Committee rejected all these arguments, observing that the UN Population Commission recommendation that the category of "race" should be optional in censi "concerned only the methodology of State census-taking. None of the optional categories could be a legal barrier for a State to gather information on the demographic composition of its population." [62] The Committee concluded by urging that Portugal "in its next periodic report provide detailed and relevant information on the demographic composition of the Portuguese population…."[63]

Other United Nations Organs

Although they have had less occasion to address the question, other United Nations monitoring bodies have also asked governments to provide race- or eth-

60. For state reports see Michael Banton "Ethnic Monitoring in International Law: the Work of CERD" in this volume. Also see *Concluding Observations on Poland* (15 October 1997) CERD/C/304/Add.36, paragraph 16 suggesting that "the State Party take all appropriate measures to compile more precise information" with regard to "statistical information on minorities," and "include such data in the next periodic report"; *Concluding Observations on Ukraine* (30 March 1998) CERD/C/304/Add.48, paragraph 8., expressing "concern" at "the inadequacy of demographic data on the different ethnic groups living in the State party."
61. Summary Record of the 1311th Meeting of the CERD Consideration of Portugal (4 March 1999), CERD/C/SR.1311, paragraph 14; Summary Record of the 1312th Meeting of the CERD, Consideration of Portugal (4 March 1999) CERD/C/Sr.1312, paragraph 5.
62. Summary Record of the 1311th Meeting of the CERD, supra, paragraph 14.
63. *Concluding Observations* (8 April 1999), CERD/C/304/Add.67, paragraph 15.

nic-coded information. In its Concluding Observations of 19 November 1998, the UN Committee Against Torture requested that "Hungary should include in its next periodic report all relevant statistics, data and information on: a) the number of complaints about ill treatment; the proportion they represent in rela-tion to the total number of cases investigated and, in particular, the proportion of Roma complaints, detainees and prisoners....".[64] During its consideration of Romania, the United Nations Human Rights Committee "members ... wanted to know the number of complaints lodged by Roma alleging mistreatment by authorities or private individuals." [65] And on more than one occasion, the UN Committee on the Rights of the Child (CRC) has asked for data specifically con-cerning ethnic minorities.[66]

Other Bodies

The recent *Report on the situation of Roma and Sinti in the OSCE Area* by the High Commissioner on National Minorities of the Organization for Security and Cooperation in Europe highlighted the need for race- and ethnic-coded data: "Statistical data on the ethnic composition of populations is an important tool for establishing patterns of discrimination, for facilitating efforts to enforce legal prohibitions of discrimination and for assessing the efficacy of anti-dis-crimination and other policies aimed at improving the conditions of Roma." [67]

In calling for the adoption of a directive covering non-discrimination and equal treatment, the Final Report of the Project on the European Union and Human Rights — the principle reference document used by the Comite des

64. *Concluding Observations* (19 November 1998), CAT. A/54/55, paragraph 85.
65. United Nations Press Release HR/CT/99/18, 20 July 1999.
66. See, e.g., *Concluding Observations on Bulgaria* (24 January 1997) CRC/C/15/Add.66, paragraph 9. expressing "concern about the need to strengthen the State party's capacity to collect and process data to evaluate progress achieved and to assess the impact of policies adopted on children, in par-ticular the most vulnerable groups of children"; ibid. paragraph 23 recommending that "the State party give priority give attention to the development of a system of data collection and to the iden-tification of appropriate disaggregated indicators with a view to addressing all areas of the Convention and all groups of children in society. Such mechanisms ... can be used as a basis for designing programmes to improve the situation of children, particularly those belonging to the most disadvantaged groups, including ... children belonging to minority groups, especially Roma"; *Concluding Observations on Czech Republic* (27 October 1997) CRC/C/15/Add.81, paragraph 10., expressing "concern about the need to strengthen the State party's limited capacity to develop specific disaggregated indicators to evaluate progress achieved and assess the impact of existing poli-cies on all children, in particular children belonging to minority groups"; ibid. paragraph 29., rec-ommending that priority be given to identification of "appropriate disaggregated indicators" to address this need; *Concluding Observations on Hungary* (5 June 1998) CRC/C/15/Add.87, paragraph 9., expressing "concern at the lack of disaggregated statistical data covering all children."
67. Text at note 179. in *Report on the Situation of Roma and Sinti in the OSCE Area* (10 March 2000) Organization for Security and Cooperation in Europe, High Commissioner for National Minorities.

Sages in the preparation of their Human Rights Agenda for the EU for the Year 2000 — suggested that such a provision should "require employers to monitor the composition of the workforce in terms of gender, race and disability to estab-lish a workplace equal opportunities policy." [68]

In short, while more research on the legal parameters is needed, there appears to be broad agreement among international and European expert bod-ies that, with the proper safeguards in place to protect against abuse, race and ethnic statistics are an essential component of any effective anti-discrimination policy.

Guiding Principles:
Initial Thoughts

The history of Europe in the twentieth century casts a long shadow over any discussion of race statistics and complicates efforts to extricate the issue of num-bers from broader questions of race, ethnicity, and justice. And too, the subjec-tive nature of racial and ethnic identity makes it difficult to achieve consensus on its contours. Indeed, "[i]t is one of the special features of ethnic identity that its form and expression can change and be modified. Ethnic identities alter under the influence of historical events, politics, the media, education and succeeding generations, a tendency that is encouraged by migration, mixed marriages, assimilation processes, etc." [69] One expert group has gone so far as to suggest, "Minority statistics constitute a great illusion. Under the appearance of scien-tific certainty and mathematical precision, they conceal, advertently or inadver-tently, a world of differing degrees and conceptions of identity, diverging definitions, and unstable classifications." [70] Thus, even well-intentioned efforts to count the numbers of ethnic minorities will face a number of obstacles, including the fear of some minority members to self-identify; the desire to iden-tify with another, more powerful ethnic group; the incentive of some to artificial-ly inflate or deflate counts for political purposes; and, in a number of countries, the poor quality of public databases produced by poverty and/or decades of neglect. These persistent difficulties have been complicated by political factors

68. P. Alston and J.H.H. Weiler *The European Union and Human Rights: Final Project Report on an Agenda for the Year 2000.* (1998), paragraph 205.
69. Haug, Courbage, Compton (1998) op.cit. pp. 15. The concepts of "national or ethnic groups or communities" are "multidimensional: cultural, historical and territorial. The complexity of the terms and the lack of a precise and generally recognized definition mean that it is difficult to make the con-cepts operational." ibid. pp.14
70. *Final Report of the Reflection on the Long-Term Implications of EU Enlargement: the Nature of the New Border* (1999) Robert Schuman Center for Advanced Studies, EUI, Florence and Forward Studies Unit, European Commission. pp. 81.

in much of Central and Eastern Europe.

And still, the reality of enduring racism, and the need for knowledge — cold, hard facts — to struggle against it, mandate persistence. Even if race and ethnicity are socially and historically constructed, they are living concepts which continue to affect (and distort) the distribution of resources and power in many contemporary societies. Hence, the desire to identify as "human" and no more — though admirable to some — does not erase the existence of prejudice or the need to measure its effects. To ignore racial categories — to stop asking about race — is no defense against racism.

At the same time, it is, of course, not the data themselves, which are value-laden, but their potential use or misuse by government authorities and others. Thus, the mere existence of statistics showing that, for example, fifty percent of all the prison inmates in a country are Roma, even though Roma amount to only ten percent of the nationwide population, is not prejudicial or racist. Controversy arises in the interpretation of this data, and the conclusions to be drawn therefrom. Thus, some may view the hypothetical data as evidence of the inherent criminality of the Roma. To others, however, the same statistics constitute definitive proof that the criminal justice system operates in a discriminatory manner. Often, debates which appear to be about race statistics are really about more fundamental, independent questions of racial prejudice and political power.

In seeking to develop policies capable of, on the one hand, generating reliable race- and ethnic-coded data, and, on the other, safeguarding individual privacy, the following considerations should be taken into account:

- First, it is important to distinguish between race statistics — which are social indicators — and the social and political values, which affect how they are interpreted and used.
- Second, and as a corollary to this more general observation, we must distinguish between, on the one hand, hate speech and its contribution to the perpetuation of racial stereotypes, and, on the other, the misuse of race statistics. We need to develop effective means of addressing the former, including the promulgation and enforcement of codes of conduct for police and other government authorities in labeling, referring to, and characterizing ethnic minority groups.
- Third, distinguish between, on the one hand, the *individual's* right to choose and express his/her own identity and, on the other hand, *collective* and *anonymous* race- or ethnic-coded data which, if generated and maintained in accordance with international data protection procedures, are not traceable

to any individual.[71] Thus, it should be possible for a school to maintain statistics showing that, say, 30 percent of the students are Roma, without divulging the identity of any single student reflected in the data.

- Fourth, involve members of all affected minority groups in the design, conduct and analysis of data collection from the very beginning of the process.
- Fifth, distinguish data collected and maintained by governmental bodies from that gathered by non-governmental institutions.
- Sixth, separate the issue of crime statistics from other statistics. For a variety of reasons, race-coded crime statistics often raise far more controversy than analogous statistics in the fields of employment, education or political participation. Although race-coded crime statistics are essential to document, and/or correct, systematic racial bias in criminal justice systems, the frequent misuse of race statistics in the criminal justice field may warrant a particularized approach.
- Seventh, do not confuse means and ends. Race statistics are needed not to satisfy an ideal notion of truth or science, but to assist in the achievement of very real, concrete goals: measuring and eliminating discrimination.
- Finally, recall that, necessary as they are, race statistics are not a substitute for other methods to tackle discriminatory practices, including forthright political leadership, the adoption and implementation of comprehensive anti-discrimination legislation, and public education about the extent of racism and the need to overcome it.

---

71. In this regard, see, e.g., Explanatory Memorandum, Council of Europe Recommendation No. R(97)18 concerning the Protection of Personal Data Collected and Processed for Statistical Purposes, paragraph 10. "It is therefore necessary to make a fundamental distinction between *the individual use of personal data* and their *collective use*. This is a differentiation of purpose, which is essential from the standpoint of the protection of individuals, their privacy and their rights and freedoms" (emphasis in original).

II.

The International Dimension

The Issue of Ethnic Data Collection
From the Perspective of Some Council of Europe Activities

Isil Gachet

The Council of Europe is a pan-European Organization (43 member states)[1] based on intergovernmental and parliamentary co-operation, which seeks to uphold the rule of law and pluralist democracy and to protect and promote human rights.

The issue of ethnic data collection has not, as such, been the subject of any Council of Europe initiatives specifically and exclusively devoted to this subject and to its qualitative and quantitative aspects. There is, however, a wide range of activities within the Council, particularly in the fields of legal co-operation, protection of national minorities and the fight against racism and intolerance, that are worth mentioning in connection with a study on ethnic data collection.

This paper will endeavor to examine the issue mainly from the perspective of the activities of the European Commission against Racism and Intolerance (ECRI), the work carried out under the Framework Convention for the Protection of National Minorities, and in the field of personal data protection.

It should be emphasized, however, that this study does not claim to be exhaustive and that there are other initiatives, in various areas of the Council of Europe's activity, which are connected with the matter under discussion. Of particular relevance is the work carried out by the European Population Committee on population censuses and the demography of national minorities[2] and by the Specialist Group on Roma/Gypsies[3].

---

1. Albania, Andorra, Armenia, Austria, Azerbaijan, Belgium, Bulgaria, Croatia, Cyprus, the Czech Republic, Denmark, Estonia, Finland, France, Georgia, Germany, Greece, Hungary, Iceland, Ireland, Italy, Latvia, Liechtenstein, Lithuania, Luxembourg, Malta, Moldova, the Netherlands, Norway, Poland, Portugal, Romania, the Russian Federation, San Marino, Slovakia, Slovenia, Spain, Sweden, Switzerland, "the former Yugoslav Republic of Macedonia," Turkey, Ukraine, the United Kingdom.
2. See Werner Haug, Paul Compton, Youssef Courbage (2000) *The demographic characteristics of national minorities in certain European states*, Volume 2, Population Studies No. 31, Council of Europe Publishing.
3. See *Roma and Statistics* (22-23 May 2000) document MG-S-ROM (2000) 13, Strasbourg.

The Issue of Ethnic Data Collection in the Work of the European Commission against Racism and Intolerance (ECRI)

ECRI is a mechanism, which was established by the first Summit of Heads of State and Government of the member states of the Council of Europe. The Vienna Declaration, adopted on 9 October 1993 by the first Summit, contains the decision to set up ECRI and assigns it the following terms of reference: review member states' legislation, policies and other measures to combat racism, xenophobia, anti-Semitism and intolerance, and their effectiveness; propose further action at local, national and European levels; formulate general policy recommendations to member states; study international legal instruments applicable in the matter with a view to their reinforcement where appropriate.

ECRI's task is to combat racism, xenophobia, anti-Semitism and intolerance at the level of greater Europe and from the perspective of the protection of human rights. ECRI's action covers all necessary measures to combat violence, discrimination and prejudice faced by persons or groups of persons, notably on grounds of race, color, language, religion, nationality and national or ethnic origin. ECRI's members are designated by their governments on the basis of their in-depth knowledge in the field of combating intolerance. They should have high moral authority and recognized expertise in dealing with racism, xenophobia, anti-Semitism and intolerance. They are nominated in their personal capacity and act as independent members.

As part of its program of activities[4], ECRI adopts *general policy recommendations* for the governments of all Council of Europe member states. These general recommendations cover the main areas of the fight against racism and intolerance and provide guidelines for implementing comprehensive national policies[5].

So far, ECRI has not adopted any general policy recommendation specifically concerned with ethnic data collection. However, two of its general policy recommendations are worth noting in connection with this subject. *ECRI general policy recommendation* No. 1, adopted on 4 October 1996, is a very broad recommendation, covering the legal and non-legal aspects of combating racism and intolerance[6]. In the first part of this text, on national law, law enforcement and judicial remedies, ECRI recommends that governments: "*ensure that accurate data and statistics are collected and published on the number of racist and xenophobic*

---

4. See *ECRI and its programme of activities* (CRI (99) 53 rev.). All ECRI documents referred to in this paper are accessible on ECRI's web site: *www.ecri.coe.int*
5. See *Compilation of ECRI's general policy recommendations* (CRI (2001) 7).
6. Ibid. pp. 9-13.

offences that are reported to the police, on the number of cases that are prosecuted, on the reasons for not prosecuting and on the outcome of cases prosecuted." In the second part of the text, concerning policies in a number of areas, it recommends that they *"undertake research into the nature, causes and manifestations of racism, xenophobia, anti-Semitism and intolerance at local, regional and national level."* It is worth noting, finally, that the very last recommendation in this general text concerns data collection and reads as follows: *"Since it is difficult to develop and effectively implement policies in the areas in question without good data, [ECRI recommends that governments] collect, in accordance with European laws, regulations and recommendations on data-protection and protection of privacy, where and when appropriate, data which will assist in assessing and evaluating the situation and experiences of groups which are particularly vulnerable to racism, xenophobia, anti-Semitism and intolerance."* In the absence of an ECRI general policy recommendation containing guidelines on the collection of ethnic data, the above wording is currently used to guide ECRI in its activities, in particular the conclusions and suggestions set out in its country-specific reports to which we will come back later.

The second text that is worth mentioning here is *ECRI general policy recommendation No. 4*, adopted on 6 March 1998, and which is concerned with national surveys on the experience and perception of discrimination and racism from the point of view of potential victims[7]. In this recommendation, while stressing that statistics on racist and discriminatory acts and on the situation of minority groups in all fields of life are vital for the identification of problems and the formulation of policies, ECRI contends that such statistics should be supplemented by data on attitudes, opinions and perceptions. Considering that, in addition to surveys among the general population, targeted surveys which ascertain the experiences and perceptions of potential victims as regards racism and discrimination represent an innovative and valuable source of information, and that the results of such surveys may be used in a variety of ways to highlight problems and improve the situation, ECRI recommends that member state governments *"take steps to ensure that national surveys on the experience and perception of racism and discrimination from the point of view of potential victims are organised."*

The appendix to ECRI general policy recommendation no. 4 contains a series of guidelines for the organization of such surveys. These are concerned with the general objectives, practical organization, design and follow-up to surveys.

Without going into the details of these guidelines, we will simply point out that the aim of such surveys is to form some idea of the problems of racism and intolerance as perceived by actual and potential victims. As for the design and

7. Ibid. pp. 31-35.

implementation of such surveys, these tasks may be entrusted to researchers or institutes with experience in the field of racism and intolerance, with the field-work being carried out by survey research bodies.

Another major aspect of ECRI's program of activities is its *country-by-country approach*. This is a method whereby ECRI closely examines the situation in each of the member states of the Council of Europe and draws up, on the basis of its country-specific analysis, suggestions and proposals as to how the problems of racism and intolerance identified in each country might be dealt with. The aim of the country-by-country exercise is to formulate helpful and well-founded proposals, which may assist governments in taking practical and precise steps to counter racism and intolerance.

The country-by-country approach concerns all member States of the Council of Europe on an equal footing. The work takes place in four-year cycles, covering ten countries per year. The reports of the first round were completed in late 1998. In January 1999, ECRI began work on the second stage of country reports, which will continue through December 2002. The reports of the second stage combine the monitoring of proposals contained in ECRI's first country-by-country reports, the updating of the information contained therein, and an in-depth analysis of issues of particular concern in the countries in question.

The structure of ECRI's second reports comprises a first section giving an overview of the situation in the country in question, including a sub-title on "monitoring the situation in the country." An examination of this sub-title of ECRI's country-by-country reports published to date reveals that ECRI encountered several situations where reliable statistical data are lacking.

In *Albania*[8], ECRI underlines that it is very difficult to determine accurately the size of any ethnic group, since there has not been a census registering ethnic identity in recent years. Estimates about numbers diverge considerably depending on the source. Preparations for a general census are reportedly underway. ECRI strongly urges the Albanian authorities to include a question pertaining to ethnic identity, respecting the principle of voluntary self-identification. ECRI also believes that representatives of ethnic minority groups should be involved in the various stages of this process. ECRI encourages the Albanian authorities to consider ways of establishing a coherent and comprehensive means of data collection to enable the assessment of the situation of the various minority groups living in Albania and the extent of manifestations of racism and discrimination. Such a system of data collection should be based on the voluntary self-

8. ECRI's second report on Albania, adopted on 16 June 2000 (CRI (2001) 2).

registration of the persons involved, and be designed with due respect paid to the right to privacy and to standards of data protection and free and informed consent of the persons in question.

In *Austria*[9], in its first report ECRI noted that it was difficult to obtain reliable data about the situation of all minority groups living in the country. In particular, as concerns immigrants or people of immigrant background, the main categories used appear to be based on nationality. ECRI considers that the collection of reliable and comparable data broken down by ethnic origin could help better assess and evaluate the situation and experiences of the various minority groups living in Austria in different fields, such as employment, housing, education, etc. This should of course be carried out in accordance with European laws, regulations and recommendations on data protection and protection of privacy and the principle of freedom of declaration. In addition, ECRI considers that further efforts could be made to assess the effectiveness of various measures already undertaken to combat racism and intolerance and to establish the real situation as regards discrimination and racism — for example by means of opinion polls among the majority but also among minority populations to ascertain how they perceive levels of discrimination and intolerance. In this respect, the attention of the Austrian authorities is drawn to ECRI's general Policy Recommendation No.4 on national surveys on the experience and perception of discrimination and racism from the point of view of potential victims.

In *Belgium*[10], the scarce use made of anti-racist laws and civil remedies in cases of racial discrimination is also reflected in the current lack of detailed information on complaints of racist and xenophobic acts, the number of complaints of racial discrimination filed with the courts, the results of the proceedings instituted in these cases and the compensation granted, where appropriate, to the victims of discrimination. ECRI expresses its concern at this situation, since accurate and comprehensive statistics constitute indispensable tools to plan policies and strategies in the fields of combating racism and intolerance and to monitor their effectiveness. It therefore encourages the authorities to develop an adequate system of statistical data to cover the above mentioned areas.

In *Bulgaria*[11], no official system of data collection exists to record the incidence of racist violence, harassment or discrimination. ECRI feels that the devel-

9. ECRI's second report on Austria, adopted on 16 June 2000 (CRI (2001) 3).
10. ECRI's second report on Belgium, adopted on 18 June 1999 (CRI (2000) 2).
11. ECRI's second report on Bulgaria, adopted on 18 June 1999 (CRI (2000) 3).

opment of such a system would be very valuable in view of monitoring the situation in Bulgaria. Furthermore, little information appears to be available concerning the situation of the different minority groups living in Bulgaria. ECRI is concerned that such a lack of information may make it difficult to evaluate the extent of possible discrimination faced by these groups. For example, the Turkish and Muslim minorities apparently live mainly in small isolated communities, and it is not clear to what extent they participate on an equal footing in the structures of Bulgarian society, such as education, employment and public life. ECRI therefore recommends that the authorities consider ways of monitoring the situation, with due attention to the need for the protection of data and the protection of privacy. The knowledge and experience possessed by non-governmental organizations can be a valuable resource in this respect.

In the *Czech Republic*[12], while acknowledging the fact that the collection of data on ethnic origin is prohibited out of concern for data protection and privacy, ECRI is concerned that the lack of reliable information about the situation of the various minority groups living in the country makes evaluation of the extent and causes of possible discrimination against them, or the effect of actions intended to combat such discrimination, difficult. ECRI recommends that the Czech authorities consider ways of monitoring the situation in this respect, with due attention to the need for protection of data and of privacy. For example, carefully prepared studies which respect the anonymity and dignity of persons involved may allow the situation in some areas of life to be evaluated.

In *Denmark*[13], in its first report, ECRI suggested that steps be taken to record statistics relating to complaints concerning racial discrimination. ECRI reiterates the importance of recording detailed information about the number of complaints relating to racism and discrimination in various spheres of life, the subsequent investigation by police and prosecutors where relevant, the judicial assessment of such complaints and the redress or compensation awarded to victims. This information could prove extremely helpful in improving the effectiveness of existing legislation and establishing additional legal and non-legal measures to combat these phenomena. In gathering such information due respect should be paid to the right to privacy and to standards of data protection and free and informed consent of the persons in question.

12. ECRI's second report on the Czech Republic, adopted on 18 June 1999 (CRI (2000) 4).
13. ECRI's second report on Denmark, adopted on 16 June 2000 (CRI (2001) 4).

In *France*[14], as noted in ECRI's first report, due to the French Republican egalitarian approach, there is officially no categorization of ethnic or racial groups in statistics. The main categories used are therefore "foreigners" and "citizens," while ethnic monitoring is contrary to the Constitution and expressly prohibited by the Criminal Code. ECRI emphasizes that, given the consequent difficulties to the collection of accurate data on the incidence of racial discrimination as well as on social indicators concerning parts of the French population, a reconsideration of this approach would be beneficial.

In *Greece*[15], ECRI encourages the Greek authorities to consider ways of establishing a coherent and comprehensive means of data collection to enable the assessment of the situation of the various minority groups living in the country and the extent of manifestations of racism and discrimination. Such a system of data collection should be based on the voluntary self-registration of the persons involved, and be designed with due respect paid to the right to privacy and to standards of data protection.

In *Hungary*[16], while acknowledging the fact that the collection and utilization of data on ethnic origin is restricted for valid reasons, ECRI is concerned that the lack of reliable information about the situation of the various minority groups living in the country makes evaluation of the extent of possible discrimination against them or the effect of actions intended to combat such discrimination difficult. ECRI recommends that the Hungarian authorities might consider ways of monitoring the situation in this respect, with due attention to the need for protection of data and of privacy. For example, carefully prepared studies which respect the anonymity, dignity and full consent of persons involved may allow the situation in some areas of life to be evaluated. One very positive aspect of the situation in Hungary is the presence of active and experienced bodies of civil society and the fact that an increasing collaboration seems to be developing in many fields between such bodies and the authorities. ECRI encourages the authorities to continue to build upon this co-operation, in order to profit from the knowledge of the situation and the expertise that such bodies possess.

In *Norway*[17], sensitivity about the collection of data pertaining to ethnic origin has made the monitoring of the situation of the different minority groups liv-

---

14. ECRI's second report on France, adopted on 10 December 1999 (CRI (2000) 31).
15. ECRI's second report on Greece, adopted on 10 December 1999 (CRI (2000) 32).
16. ECRI's second report on Hungary, adopted on 18 June 1999 (CRI (2000) 5).
17. ECRI's second report on Norway, adopted on 10 December 1999 (CRI (2000) 33).

ing in the country problematic. In this respect, ECRI draws attention to its gen-eral policy recommendation No. 1, in which it highlights the importance of data collection to assist in assessing and evaluating the situation and experiences of vulnerable groups, and encourages the Norwegian authorities to further consid-er ways in which such data might be collected while respecting the right to pri-vacy, data protection and free and informed consent of the persons in question. ECRI notes that the Directorate of Immigration will present reports on the type and extent of racial discrimination in 1999-2000 and that the Centre for Combating Ethnic Discrimination published its first such report in November 1999. One of the main challenges in the future is to develop a registration sys-tem that will enable the government to monitor racially motivated incidents. ECRI also feels that the monitoring and regular evaluation of the many projects and initiatives which have been set underway in recent years should be given pri-ority, in order to ascertain their effectiveness and to disseminate good practices.

In *Poland*[18], it is very difficult to determine accurately the size of any ethnic or national group in the country, since post-World War II censuses have not included questions pertaining to ethnic identity. It is foreseen that such a ques-tion may be included in the next census, due to take place in 2001, although Parliament has not as yet taken a decision on this issue. ECRI encourages the Polish authorities to consider ways of establishing a coherent and comprehen-sive means of data collection to enable the situation of the various minority groups living in Poland and the extent of manifestations of racism and discrimi-nation to be assessed. Such a system of data collection should be based on the voluntary self-registration of the persons involved, and be designed with due respect paid to the right to privacy and to standards of data protection.

In *Slovakia*[19], members of minority groups may identify themselves as such on a voluntary basis in the census. However, systematic recording of information relating to the situation of the different minority groups in various areas of life seems to be lacking. For this reason, it is difficult to evaluate the extent of dis-criminatory practices in the various fields of society, such as access to public ser-vices, housing, employment and education, or to measure the extent of racial vio-lence. While recognizing the wish to avoid an obligatory statement of ethnic identity, ECRI encourages the Slovak authorities to consider ways of monitor-ing the situation of the various minority groups in Slovakia, with due respect to the principles of the protection of data and of privacy, and based on a system of

18. ECRI's second report on Poland, adopted on 10 December 1999 (CRI (2000) 34).
19. ECRI's second report on Slovakia, adopted on 10 December 1999 (CRI (2000) 35).

voluntary self-identification. Such monitoring should also be broken down by gender. ECRI also encourages the Slovak authorities to set up a system of data collection to record incidents of violence and discrimination perpetrated against members of minority groups. In this respect, ECRI notes that in 1999 the police have introduced a system of monitoring criminal activities motivated by racism, xenophobia and intolerance or committed by members of extremist groups or by their supporters. ECRI also draws attention to its general policy recommenda-tion No. 4 on national surveys on the perception and experience of racism and discrimination from the point of view of potential victims.

In *Switzerland*[20], little information is systematically collected regarding the extent of racism and discrimination. ECRI reiterates the recommendation made in its general policy recommendation No. 1, and urges the Swiss government to " collect, in accordance with European laws, regulations and recommenda-tions on data protection and protection of privacy, where and when appropri-ate, data which will assist in assessing and evaluating the situation and experi-ences of groups which are particularly vulnerable to racism, xenophobia, anti-Semitism and intolerance." Such a monitoring task should involve the record-ing of information from the cantonal level, with collation at the federal level. ECRI also recalls in this respect its general policy recommendation No. 4 in which it calls on governments to carry out surveys into the experiences and per-ceptions of racism and discrimination from the point of view of potential vic-tims.

In the *Former Yugoslav Republic of Macedonia*[21], to plan any action program to combat discrimination and intolerance, it is necessary to identify accurately the extent and causes of the problem. As ECRI noted in its first report, there appears to be a need for comprehensive statistical information about the participation of ethnic minorities in public life and on their economic and social situation, espe-cially with regard to access to employment, health, education and housing. Information should also be collected about the effectiveness of remedies in cases of discrimination, including the number of complaints, the subsequent investi-gation by police and prosecutors where relevant, the judicial assessment of such complaints and the redress or compensation awarded to victims. This informa-tion could cover inter alia criminal and civil provisions aimed at combating racism and discrimination. In gathering such information, due respect should be

20. ECRI's second report on Switzerland, adopted on 18 June 1999 (CRI (2000) 6).
21. ECRI's second report on "the Former Yugoslav Republic of Macedonia," adopted on 16 June 2000 (CRI (2001) 5).

paid to the right to privacy and to standards of data protection and free and informed consent of the persons in question.

The key ideas to emerge from a cross-sectional study of ECRI's analysis and suggestions concerning the monitoring of the situation in the above countries may be summarized in the form of a "case-law of the ECRI country-by-country approach" as follows: Up until now, in its country-by-country activities, ECRI has generally observed that the sensitive nature of ethnic data collection poses problems with regards to monitoring the situation of the various minority groups. While recognizing that collecting data about people's ethnic origins may be restricted for good reasons, such as data protection and privacy, ECRI has nevertheless stressed that lack of information about the situation of the various minority groups makes it difficult to assess the extent of any discrimination to which they may be subjected and the effectiveness of any measures taken to com - bat this discrimination. ECRI's suggestion is thus to consider ways in which the situation can be monitored, with due regard for the right to privacy and the exist - ing rules on data protection (in particular European legislation and recommen - dations on the protection of data and privacy), and on the basis of voluntary self-identification by the persons involved. Furthermore, ECRI has encouraged ini - tiatives in the field of ethnic monitoring in those countries where it already takes place, with due regard to national and international standards.

Framework Convention for the Protection of National Minorities and the Collection of Ethnic Data[22]

The Framework Convention is the first legally binding multilateral instru - ment concerned with the protection of national minorities in general. Adopted by the Council of Europe in 1995, the Framework Convention entered into force on 1 February 1998[23]. Its aim is to protect national minorities within the respective territories of the Parties. The Convention seeks to promote the full and effective equality of national minorities by creating appropriate conditions

22. This section of the paper is largely based on the presentation made by Mr Jeroen Schokkenbroek, Head on the Human Rights Law and Policy Development Division, Council of Europe on *What kind of information do we need for monitoring the implementation of fundamental rights of minorities? — A Council of Europe experience*, at the Montreux Conference on "Statistics, Development and Human Rights," held on 4-8 September 2000.
23. To date, the Framework Convention has been ratified by 33 member States. The full text of the Framework Convention and the Explanatory Report are available through the human rights website of the Council of Europe: *www.humanrights.coe.int*

enabling them to preserve and develop their culture and to retain their identity, whilst fully respecting the principles of territorial integrity and political independence of States. The principles contained in the Framework Convention have to be implemented through national legislation and appropriate governmental policies.

The Convention sets out principles to be respected as well as goals to be achieved by the Contracting Parties, in order to ensure the protection of persons belonging to national minorities. The substantive provisions of the Framework Convention cover a wide range of issues, *inter alia*: non-discrimination, the promotion of effective equality; the promotion of the conditions necessary for the preservation and development of the culture and preservation of religion, language and traditions; freedoms of assembly, association, expression, thought, conscience and religion; access to and use of media; freedoms relating to language, education and transfrontier contacts; participation in economic, cultural and social life; participation in public life and prohibition of forced assimilation.

Monitoring the implementation of the Framework Convention takes place on the basis of state reports. The State Parties must produce within one year of the entry into force a first report on the measures they have taken to implement the Framework Convention. Subsequent reports are due every five years. The Committee of Ministers may in the interim also request ad-hoc reports. State reports are made public by the Council of Europe upon receipt. They are examined first by the Advisory Committee of 18 independent experts, which may also receive information from other sources, as well as actively seek additional information and have meetings with governments and others. The Advisory Committee adopts opinions on each of the state reports, which it transmits to the Committee of Ministers. The latter body takes the final decisions in the monitoring process in the form of country-specific conclusions and recommendations.

Following the Framework Convention's entry into force on 1 February 1998, the Advisory Committee, started its work in June 1998, when it held its first meeting. In that first period, the Advisory Committee concentrated on the necessary preparatory work, bearing in mind that the first State reports were due one year after the entry into force of the Convention, that is on 1 February 1999. In particular, the Advisory Committee drafted its rules of procedure and approved certain guidelines for States Parties on how to present the information to be submitted in their reports under Article 25.1. of the Framework Convention.

These guidelines, which were subsequently adopted by the Committee of Ministers, are in the form of an outline structure for State reports. The outline indicates that the State report is to consist of two parts: (i) a general introduction on how the State party has sought to implement the Framework Convention, and (ii) an article-by-article presentation of the measures taken to ensure implementation of each of its provisions.

It is of special interest to note that the Advisory Committee and the Committee of Ministers have acknowledged, in this outline for state reports, the relevance of statistical information and quantitative data in general.

In the first place, the outline indicates that the first, general part of the State report should contain information, not only about State policies for the protection of national minorities and information of a legal kind, but also about the demographic situation in the country and basic economic data such as the Gross Domestic Product (GDP) and per capita income.

Secondly, the specific information to be submitted in the second, article-by-article part of the report should be presented in five different categories:

– a *narrative* part, giving general information about relevant state activities;
– a *legal* part, with information on relevant legislation and legal practice;
– a part on *State infrastructure*, indicating which authorities have competence in the various fields covered by the Framework Convention;
– a *policy* part, on measures, programs and official statements etc.;
– a *factual* part.

This last rubric is the most interesting one for our present purposes. The outline states that: "under this category factual information enabling an evaluation of the effectiveness in practice of the measures taken to implement the Framework Convention should be provided, such as statistics and results of surveys. It is understood that, where complete statistics are not available, governments may supply data or estimates based on ad hoc studies, specialised or sample surveys, or other scientifically valid methods, whenever they consider the information so collected to be useful."

The detailed explanations given in the outline in respect of each provision of the Framework Convention make clear that States Parties are not requested to provide factual information under each and every article. Under some provisions, this type of information *prima facie* does not appear relevant, but States are of course free to submit such information. A clear example is Article 2, which states that the provisions of the Framework Convention shall be applied in good faith, in a spirit of understanding and tolerance and in conformity with the principles of good neighborliness, friendly relations and co-operation between States.

This contrasts with certain provisions under which statistical information is expressly requested:

– Article 3 (freedom of choice to be treated or not to be treated as member of a national minority): here, information is requested about the numbers and places of settlement of persons to whom the Framework Convention is applied (and information about how these data were collected);

– Article 6.2. (obligation to take protective measures against threats, acts of discrimination, hostility or violence as a result of a person's ethnic, cultural, lin‑ guistic or religious identity): statistics are requested of reported cases and the success-rate in prosecution of such acts of discrimination, hostility or violence.

At first sight, it might seem surprising that no such explicit request for statis‑ tics was made in respect to the above-mentioned provisions on linguistic and educational rights: Articles 10.2. and 14.2. each of which refer to "areas inhab‑ ited by persons belonging to national minorities traditionally or in substantial numbers," or Article 11.3. which refers to "areas traditionally inhabited by sub‑ stantial numbers or persons belonging to a national minority." However, the request to submit demographic information relevant for these provisions has already been made under Article 3 (see above). It is clear that such demograph‑ ic information is also relevant under Article 16, which prohibits States from altering the proportions of the population in areas inhabited by persons belong‑ ing to national minorities and are aimed at restricting their rights.

The first State reports were received in February 1999 and, to date, the Advisory Committee has received 22 reports. Having analyzed a first group of reports, the Advisory Committee is currently preparing and adopting its opin‑ ion on those States' implementation of the Framework Convention and for‑ warding them to the Committee of Ministers. It will be interesting to examine the evaluations made by the Advisory Committee under the above-mentioned provisions, for which statistical information is a priori of great importance.

Finally, it is worth quoting here from the aforementioned presentation [24]. After looking at some of the challenges facing the monitoring of the Framework Convention, with special reference to statistics, the speaker moved on to the question of the definition of "national minority," saying that no international consensus had been possible on the definition issue. He proceeded to outline the various strands of the debate, pointing out that strong arguments had been advanced in legal literature for considering that State Parties were not totally free to determine the beneficiaries of the protection of the Framework Convention, and made the following observations:

"However, there is one element in this discussion, which can be high‑ lighted as being particularly relevant for the question of minority statis‑

24. See footnote 22 (Mr Jeroen Schokkenbroek, Montreux Conference).

tics. It concerns Article 3.1. of the Framework Convention according to which every person belonging to a national minority shall have the right freely to choose to be treated or not to be treated as such and no disad-vantage shall result from this choice or from the exercise of the rights which are connected to that choice. In essence, this provision guarantees the right to self-identification, an important and well-known principle in the international standards for minority protection (see, e.g., the Copenhagen Document of the CSCE/OSCE of 1990 and the UN Declaration on the Rights of Persons belonging to National or Ethnic, Religious and Linguistic Minorities of 1992).

"This principle has two main consequences for the collection and use of statistical data. In censuses and official collections and records of data, per-sons should be free to state or not to state their belonging to a national minority. The collection of data on a person's affiliation with a particular national minority without their consent would be in violation of the right not to be treated as a person belonging to a national minority.

"Secondly, this places clear limits on the reliability and usefulness of cer-tain statistical data concerning minorities. It is well known, for instance, that official census figures concerning Roma/Gypsies are generally well below the estimated actual numbers as they result from surveys (the dif-ferences are even more striking when those figures are compared to those presented by Roma/Gypsy organizations).[25]

"This places the national authorities as well as monitoring bodies of the Framework Convention in a dilemma. On the one hand, it is clear that reliable statistics are instrumental for designing and implementing minor-ity policies by Governments. One only has to think of the question of allo-cation of financial resources. On the other hand, important human rights considerations — such as the right to self-identification but also the right to respect for private life — place limits on the quantitative precision that can be obtained."

The Council of Europe and Personal Data Protection

The *European Convention on Human Rights*[26] contains two articles that are of direct relevance here.

---

25. See Youssef Courbage, *Demographic characteristics of national minorities in Hungary, Romania and Slovakia*, in: W. Haug, Y. Courbage, P. Compton op.cit., pp. 123-156 (147, 156).
26. Consult human rights website: *www.humanrights.coe.int*

Under Article 8 of the Convention, "*Everyone has the right to respect for his private and family life, his home and his correspondence.*" The enjoyment of this right may be restricted by a public authority only in accordance with domestic law and insofar as it is necessary, in a democratic society, for the defense of a number of legitimate aims. The Convention also lays down, however, in Article 10, the fundamental right to freedom of expression. This right includes explicitly the "*freedom to receive and impart information and ideas without interference by public authority and regardless of frontiers.*" The "*freedom to receive information*" set out in Article 10 is considered as implying the "*freedom to seek information.*"

In the conceptual architecture of the Convention, Articles 8 and 10 are not contradictory but complementary. In practice, however, the exercise of one of these rights can be sometimes restricted by the exercise of the other. For this reason, the European Commission and Court of Human Rights have defined in case-law the limits to the exercise of each of these rights and, in particular, the extent to which public authorities have the right to interfere. This case-law has been — and still is — of great importance to the Council of Europe in its work on data protection as the source of criteria for the development of national regulations on data protection. In its recent case (*M.S. v. Sweden* of 27 August 1997), the European Court of Human Rights "reiterates that the protection of personal data (...) is of fundamental importance to a person's enjoyment of his or her right to respect for private and family life as guaranteed by Article 8 of the Convention." Nevertheless, in the years following the adoption of the European Convention on Human Rights, it became apparent that efficient legal protection of privacy required more specific and systematic development.

The Council of Europe Convention for the Protection of Individuals with regard to Automatic Processing of Personal Data (ETS No. 108) [27] was concluded in 1981. It was the first universal, legally binding, international instrument in the field of data protection.

Under Convention 108, the Contracting Parties take the necessary measures, in their domestic law, to implement the principles laid down in the Convention with regard to the personal data of everyone resident on their territory. These principles concern in particular fair and lawful collection and automatic processing of data, stored for specified legitimate purposes and not for use for ends incompatible with these purposes, nor kept for longer than is necessary. They concern also the quality of the data, in that they must be adequate, relevant and not excessive (proportionality); their accuracy, the confiden-

---

27. Consult the Directorate of Legal Affairs website on data protection: *www.coe.fr/dataprotection/adacs.htm* See also summary of the contribution of Ms Marie-Odile WIEDERKEHR, Director of Legal Co-operation in *Roma and statistics* (2000), pp. 13-17.

tiality of sensitive data, information of the data subject and his/her right of access and rectification.

The Convention establishes a Consultative Committee, consisting of representatives of Parties to the Convention, which is responsible for interpreting the provisions and for ensuring improvement of the implementation of the Convention.

Inasmuch as Article 4 provides that states must have enacted adequate legislation before becoming Party to the Convention, 21 member states have ratified the Convention to date. Other states have signed the Convention and some of them have passed data protection acts and are preparing to ratify the Convention. In addition, Article 23 provides for states not members of the Council of Europe to accede to the Convention.

In order to further elaborate the principles of the Convention, a series of recommendations (accompanied by ample explanatory notes) have been adopted. Although not legally binding, these recommendations are extremely comprehensive and detailed as regards the practical implementation of the various principles set out in Convention 108.

Of particular relevance to the subject that concerns us here are Articles 5 and 6 of the Convention. The former is concerned with the quality of data and states that:

"Personal data undergoing automatic processing shall be:
a. obtained and processed fairly and lawfully; stored for specified and legitimate purposes and not used in a way incompatible with those purposes;
b. adequate, relevant and not excessive in relation to the purpose for which they are stored;
c. accurate and, where necessary, kept up to date;
d. preserved in a form which permits identification of the data subjects for no longer than is required for the purpose for which those data are stored."

As for Article 6, which concerns special categories of data, this stipulates that: "Personal data revealing racial origin, political opinions or religious or other beliefs, as well as personal data concerning health or sexual life, may not be processed automatically unless domestic law provides appropriate safeguards. The same shall apply to personal data relating to criminal convictions."

One last text worth mentioning is Recommendation No. R (97) 18 of the Committee of Ministers to member states concerning the protection of personal data collected and processed for statistical purposes (adopted on 30 September 1997). This very detailed recommendation contains principles concerning respect for privacy, general conditions for lawful collection and processing for

statistical purposes, information, consent, rights of access and rectification, ren-
dering data anonymous, primary collection of personal data for statistical purposes, identification data, conservation of data, communication, transborder data
flows, statistical results, security of personal data and codes of ethics.

Closing Remarks

A few closing words, finally, to emphasize the point that this study is essentially descriptive and merely skims the surface of the complex issue of collecting
ethnic data. On no account should it be seen as an attempt to provide a comprehensive picture of what is a highly controversial and multi-faceted subject. The
debate on ethnic data collection covers a wide range of issues, from fundamental matters of principle (at present, almost half of the Council of Europe's member states do not collect ethnic data because their constitutions prohibit it) to
matters relating to concepts, definitions and terminology or to the criteria,
methods and monitoring of ethnic data collection and use, not to mention the
extremely important issue of interpretation. These key topics have been delib-
erately omitted by the author, who is not an expert either on data collection in
general or on matters relating to statistics in particular. The aim in writing the
above article was to provide a snapshot, at a particular point in time, of the way
in which the Council of Europe's human rights mechanisms operating in the
field of combating racial discrimination and of protection of national minorities
have chosen to address this issue in the course of their work.

Ethnic Monitoring in International Law: the Work of CERD

Michael Banton

International law with respect to ethnic monitoring develops incrementally, as it does with respect to many other subjects. States' parties to the International Convention on the Elimination of All Forms of Racial Discrimination (ICERD) undertake to submit reports for consideration by the Committee on the Elimination of Racial Discrimination (CERD). The Committee reports annually to the General Assembly on its activities, among which the examination of state reports is the chief priority. If the General Assembly approves the actions of the Committee, that is an indication of international approval, though, of course, it does not give Committee statements the status of law. In the event of a dispute about the interpretation or application of the Convention, a State party may refer the matter to the International Court of Justice. The Committee could request the General Assembly to refer an issue to the Court for an advisory opin ion but it does not itself have this power.

Incremental steps

At CERD's first session in 1970 it adopted, for transmission to all States' parties, General Guidelines for the Preparation of Reports. Three years later it adopted its General Recommendation IV inviting States' parties to include in their reports information on the demographic composition of the population. In its General Recommendation VIII of 1990, the Committee referred to information in State party reports about the ways in which individuals were identified as being members of particular racial or ethnic groups, and stated that it "is of the opinion that such identification shall, if no justification exists to the contrary, be based upon self-iden tification by the individual concerned." In 1993 and 1999 it adopted some additions to the Guidelines so that the relevant portions of paragraphs 8 and 9 now read:

"The ethnic characteristics of the country are of particular importance in connection with the International Convention on the Elimination of All

Forms of Racial Discrimination. Many States consider that, when con-ducting a census, they should not draw attention to factors like race lest this reinforce divisions they wish to overcome. If progress in eliminating discrimination based on race, colour, descent, national and ethnic origin is to be monitored, some indication is needed of the number of persons who could be treated less favourably on the basis of these characteristics. States which do not collect information on these characteristics in their censuses, are therefore requested to provide information on mother tongues as indicative of ethnic differences, together with any information about race, colour, descent, national and ethnic origins derived from social surveys. In the absence of quantitative information, a qualitative descrip-tion of the ethnic characteristics of the population should be supplied..."

"The inclusion of information on the situation of women is important for the Committee to consider whether racial discrimination has an impact upon women different from that upon men. Reporting officers are asked to describe, as far as possible in quantitative and qualitative terms, factors affecting and difficulties experienced in ensuring for women the equal enjoyment, free from racial discrimination, of rights under the Convention. It is also difficult to protect against racial discrimination the rights of persons, both women and men, who belong to any vulnerable groups, such as indigenous peoples, migrants, and those in the lowest socio-economic categories. Members of such groups often experience complex forms of disadvantage which persist over generations and in which racial discrimination is mixed with other causes of social inequali-ty. Reporting officers are asked to bear in mind the circumstances of such persons, and to cite any available social indicators of forms of disadvantage that may be linked with racial discrimination."

The first occasion on which the Committee made use of the verb "to moni-tor" (as meaning to maintain regular surveillance over) was in the 1993 version of paragraph 8 quoted above. It used the same word two years later in its General Recommendation XIX, which expressed the opinion that Article 3 of the Convention is not limited to the prohibition of apartheid but prohibits all forms of racial segregation in all countries. CERD observed that "a condition of par-tial segregation may also arise as an unintended by-product of the actions of pri-vate persons... It invites States parties to monitor all trends which can give rise to racial segregation, to work for the eradication of any negative consequences that ensue, and to describe any such action in their periodic reports."

The General Guidelines, the changes to them, and the General Recommendations have all been reported to the General Assembly and have attracted no criticism, either there or in dialogue with particular States parties, so it can be inferred that they are generally acceptable and relevant to any review of the position in international law.

In August 2000 the Committee held a thematic discussion on racial discrimination against Roma, at the end of which it adopted its General Recommendation XXVII. This was reported to the General Assembly in the latter part of 2000. It included a recommendation that

> "States' parties include in their periodic reports, in an appropriate form, data about the Roma communities within their jurisdiction, including statistical data about Roma participation in political life and about their economic, social and cultural situation, including from a gender perspective, and information about the implementation of this General Recommendation."

States' parties to the ICERD are obliged to undertake effective measures against racial discrimination and to ensure that everyone within their jurisdictions can enjoy their rights free from racial discrimination. Circumstances in states differ greatly. Of the 156 States' parties, 15 have populations of less than 500,000 and 3 have populations of less than 100,000 persons. The governments of small states may have direct and personal knowledge of the incidence of discrimination and of the effectiveness of any measures they have adopted to combat it. But it can be inferred from CERD's views about the reporting process that in the opinion of the Committee there are other states which cannot be sure that they are fulfilling their obligations unless they monitor the effectiveness of their measures. Their obligation is to monitor, not to collect statistics, but the collection of statistics may be a necessary means towards the discharge of their obligation.

Ways of collecting data

The three main methods for collecting population data are central records, censuses and surveys.

The most comprehensive form of record-keeping is that in which details are collected at a person's birth and then entered upon a central registry which can be used for the issue of identity documents (like passports). Sweden may offer the best example of such a system. A new-born baby there is registered by name and given a personal number, which indicates the date of birth. Boys are allotted odd numbers and girls even numbers. The place and country of birth of the parents is registered but there is no record of ethnic or national origin. The USA uses racial classifications on birth and death certificates but does not transfer them to any central registry. In the USSR, when a Soviet citizen received his or her first passport (meaning an internal passport, not a passport for foreign travel) the nationality registered had to be the same as that in his or her parents' documents. If the parents were of different nationalities, the individual could choose one or the other, but not subsequently change.[1] A nationality was ascribed, irrespective of actual individual self-identification. There was also a *propiska*, an identity document which conferred a right of residence in a particular locality; similar documents are still used in some Central and East European countries.

A census is a periodic enumeration usually designed to produce aggregate data without identifying particular individuals or their characteristics. The use of a census even to collect aggregate data on the population according to ethnic origin is often unacceptable in African states. In Europe and North America the problems are less acute, but it may still be difficult to secure agreement on the categories to be used in collecting the information. The USA has long used the census to collect data on race and ethnicity, yet some features of the classification are currently matters of controversy. One difficulty is that the group names which are used in everyday life do not combine to form a consistent system. Another is that increasing numbers of persons have multiple ancestries and some want to be accorded a "multiracial" identity.[2] A census is often expected to serve wider purposes than simple data collection.

Government departments may need to conduct surveys in order to collect more specialized statistics supplementary to the information available from any central records and census results. These too may seek to record ethnic or national origin, and give rise to problems of the acceptability of the categories used similar to those experienced with a census. The successful completion of a census or a survey depends upon the voluntary co-operation of members of the public, some of whom may not wish their ethnic origin to be recorded for fear that it could be to their disadvantage, or who may object to particular questions. The census authorities are sometimes able to estimate the extent of under-

1. Codagnone, Cristiano, & Vassily Filipov (2000) "Equity, exit and national identity in a multinational federation: the 'multicultural constitutional patriotism' project in Russia" *Journal of Ethnic and Migration Studies*, 26:262-88. pp. 264-65.
2. Edmonston, Barry, Joshua Goldstein, & Juanita Tamayo Lott eds. (1996) *Spotlight on Heterogeneity. The Federal Standards for Racial and Ethnic Classification*. Washington DC: National Academy Press. pp.38-39.

recording in different ethnic groups. Governments have on occasion conducted publicity campaigns to persuade members of such groups that it is to their shared advantage that full information on their numbers and circumstances should be available. Some governments (e.g., Finland) have reported to CERD that they have found it difficult to secure the co-operation of Roma, and that census data for this group are subject to a significant margin of error. When asked to classify themselves by their ethnic origin, some persons resist because they consider that none of the suggested categories adequately reflects their identity. It is therefore important to explain the purpose of such a question (e.g., to state that it is included in order to uncover any inequalities between groups).

Underlying the question of the acceptability of categories are differing conceptions of the nature of nationality, national origin and ethnic origin. Nationality often overlaps with citizenship, but not always. For example, the present-day Russian Federation is considered to be a multi-national federation whose citizens are of different nationalities. Passports now include no record of the holder's nationality.

National or ethnic belonging may be conceived either as an objective attribute that can be determined by an official or as a subjective identification by an individual. In Marxist social philosophy national belonging and national consciousness were seen as the products of historical development, a view which attained an extreme expression in the words of a Russian politician quoted by Codagnone & Filipov[3]: "Any nation, any people, is a manifestation of nature, which must be respected, with which we must come to terms in the same way as we do with the sun, with the water, with the air…"

In social science such a conception is often called primordialist, and contrasted with a circumstantialist view of nationalism and ethnic identification; these are then presented as social constructs.

Some of the difficulties in collecting data that reflect differences of origin and identification can be illustrated by experience in France[4]. In French statistics persons of French nationality have been distinguished from foreigners and countries of birth have been recorded. Attempts to compile data on ethnic origins have been restricted by measures for the protection of individual privacy. The French data protection law of 1978 prohibits the recording or storage in a computer memory of personal data, which directly or indirectly reflect racial origins or political, philosophical or religious opinions. The *Institut national d'études démographiques* obtained permission to conduct an interview survey based on a

3. Op. cit. pp. 265.
4. Helpfully reviewed in Simon, Patrick (1999) "Nationality and Origins in French Statistics: Ambiguous Categories", *Population: An English Selection*, 11. pp.193-220.

sample drawn from the national census; the survey distinguished French citizens according to their parents' countries of birth. *Appartenance ethnique*, or ethnic belonging, was determined by the interviewee's answer to a question about the first language spoken as a child; this then enabled the researchers to distinguish, for example, between Berber-speaking and Arabic-speaking Algerians. Whereas *origine ethnique* was equated with an ancestor's membership in the population of a state, *appartenance ethnique* was equated with membership in a subdivision of such a population.

Michèle Tribalat[5] expressed the hope that the survey's findings may have contributed, in some degree, to the lifting of a French taboo on the collection of data relating to origins. This it seems to have done, though two objections deserve attention[6]. Firstly, in practice *appartenance ethnique* results from an individual decision. The same can be said for *origine ethnique* whenever an individual can point to more than one ethnic origin. To classify ethnic belonging by mother-tongue and ethnic origin by the country of birth of just one ancestor is to take a short-cut that misrepresents the relations in question. Secondly, and more contentiously, Le Bras maintained that a state official did not have the same liberty as a research worker when classifying individuals. In France, the moment men belonged to the same nation they, by a mysterious process, became brothers. The creation of a national community rested on the right of individuals to identify themselves as they chose and differences of origin should not be open to research of any kind. The present writer finds this subjectivist approach persuasive but self-defeating, in that for the practical purposes of data collection it is necessary to rely on criteria like country of birth and mother-tongue, even if a small number of persons do not fit easily into such categories (e.g. the children of diplomats may be born abroad and sometimes children speak different languages with their two parents).

Such considerations make it more important to differentiate ethnic origin from ethnicity. In a survey individuals can be asked with which of several possible ethnic origins they identify themselves. The United Kingdom's Race Relations Acts have all recognized this by referring to ethnic origins in the plural rather than the singular. The concept of ethnicity, however, is much vaguer, being used in a great variety of ways, most of which lack the specificity of ethnic origin.

If states are to fulfil their obligations under ICERD Article, 5(a) and (b), they may need to collect statistics of the number of complaints about incitement to

---

5. Tribalat, Michèle (1995) *Faire France. Une grande enquête sur les immigrés et leurs enfants*. Paris: La Découverte. pp. 17, see also Tribalat, Michèle et al. (1996) *De l'immigration à l'assimilation: enquête sur les populations d'origine étrangère en France*. Paris: La Découverte/INED.
6. See Le Bras, Hervé (1998) *Le démon des origines, démographie et extrême-droite*. Paris: Éditions de l'aube. pp. 228-33.

racial hatred and of unequal treatment in the administration of criminal justice, the numbers resulting in prosecution and conviction, and the sentences imposed. If they are to fulfil their obligations under Article 5(e) they may need to collect statistics on differential rates of employment and complaints of discrimination in promotion and dismissal; in the field of housing they may need to collect data on the distribution of ethnic groups in different sectors of the housing market and indices of residential segregation). Different ethnic groups may have differ-ent needs in respect of health services. States may also need to monitor differ-ences in the educational attainment of pupils associated with ethnic differences and any tendencies towards segregation in the school system.

State reports

After considering an initial or periodic report from a State party to the ICERD, the CERD formulates "concluding observations" containing a collec-tive opinion about implementation of the Convention in the state during the period reviewed. The following section recapitulates, from 1994, the passages in these observations which relate to the reporting of demographic data. States are considered in alphabetical order.

Algeria

"The Committee reiterates its recommendation…that the State party pro-vide… information on social indicators reflecting the situation of the ethnic groups, including the Berbers. Such information is essential for the Government itself to detect possible patterns of discrimination and for the Committee to mon-itor effectively the implementation of the Convention" (A/52/18, paragraph 398).

Austria

"The Committee further recommends that the State party include in its next report more detailed information on the demographic composition of the Austrian population…" (A/54/18, paragraph 37).

Argentina

"The Committee… regrets the lack of information on the subject of the rep-resentation of indigenous populations and other ethnic minorities in the civil service, police, judicial system, Congress and more generally, in the socio-economic life of the country, since it hampers a full evaluation by the Committee of the implementation of the provisions of the Convention relating to such populations." (A/52/18, paragraph 545).

Azerbaijan

"The Committee suggests that the State party analyse the findings of the forthcoming census to throw light on the relatively great emigration from the Russian-speaking and Armenian minorities and on the economic and social situation of the other ethnic groups." (A/54/18, paragraph 494).

Bahrain

"While noting the extensive demographic data provided, the Committee recommends that the State party provide data disaggregated by ethnicity and nationality." (A/55/18, paragraph 49).

Belarus

"[T]he lack of information on the participation in public life of ethnic minorities and on their economic and social situation, especially with regard to access to employment, health, education and housing, is regretted, especially since this makes it difficult to evaluate the effective enjoyment by all such groups of the rights mentioned in article 5." (A/52/18, paragraph 112).

Belgium

"... include in its next report statistical data on the ethnic composition of the Belgian population... detailed information on their socio-economic situation, particularly the unemployment rate in the various ethnic communities, would be much appreciated." (A52/18, paragraph 228).

Bolivia

"The Committee recommends that information regarding the ethnic composition of the population, the geographic areas where minority communities are concentrated, the level of their standard of living and other educational and social indices be provided in the next report." (A/51/18, paragraph 282).

Brazil

"... provide precise information and 'indicators' on the social difficulties encountered by the indigenous black and mestizo populations, and in particular on rates of unemployment, imprisonment, alcoholism, drug use, delinquency and suicide. The Committee also draws the State Party's attention to the need to devise 'indicators' to assess policies and programmes for protecting the rights of the vulnerable populations." (A/51/18, paragraph 306).

Bulgaria

"The Committee recommends increased attention to the protection of the Roma's civil, political, economic, social and cultural rights... The Committee also recommends that the State party provide, in the next report, such statistical data and information as are available on the situation of all minorities on the matters covered under article 5 of the Convention." (A/52/18, paragraph 288).

Burkina Faso

"The Committee requests the State party to provide in its next report information in accordance with paragraph 8 of the reporting guidelines on the composition of the population and on the representation of ethnic groups at various levels of public life, as well as on their enjoyment of economic, social and cultural rights." (A/52/18, paragraph 632).

Burundi

"The Committee recommends that the next periodic report provide information on the representation of members of the Tutsi, Hutu, and Twa ethnic groups, in the government, the administration, the judiciary, the police and the army." (A/52/18, paragraph 581).

Cameroon

"With reference to paragraph 8 of the guidelines, the Committee requests the State party to provide information on ethnic groups' representation at the various levels of political life and the civil service and on their enjoyment of economic, social and cultural rights." (A/53/18, paragraph 270).

China

"The Committee recommends that comprehensive information regarding the composition of the population, the geographic areas where minority nationalities are concentrated, their standard of living and other educational and social indices be included in the next report. Such information should be provided not only with respect to minority nationalities living in the autonomous areas, but also as far as pos - sible with respect to those dispersed in various regions." (A/51/18, paragraph 413).

Colombia

"[T]he lack of reliable statistical and qualitative data on the demographic composition of the Colombian population and on the enjoyment of political, economic, social and cultural rights by the indigenous and the Afro-Colombian people makes it difficult to evaluate the results of different measures and poli - cies." (A/51/18, paragraph 43).

Cuba

"The Committee recommends that the State party, in its next periodic report, provide fuller information of the demographic composition of the pop - ulation in the light of paragraph 8 of the reporting guidelines. The findings of the study being conducted by the Anthropology Centre about race relations and ethnicity should be summarised in the next report." (A/53/18, paragraph 355).

Cyprus

"Concern is expressed at the insufficient information on the demographic composition of the population of the occupied part of Cyprus, due to the fact that the State party is still prevented by the Turkish army from undertaking any census or other relevant data collection on the whole of the territory of the Republic of Cyprus." (A/53/18, paragraph 339).

Czech Republic

"The Committee recommends that the State party provide, in its next peri - odic report, more specific statistical data on minority representation in local, regional, and State administrations as well as information on their situations in the fields of education, employment and health." (A/53/18, paragraph 128).

El Salvador

"The Committee recommends that reliable quantitative and qualitative information be systematically collected and analysed to evaluate progress in the elimination of racial discrimination and to monitor closely the situation of marginalized persons and groups. It recommends that detailed demographic information be submitted in the next periodic report on the categories of persons enumerated in article 1 of the Convention and in conformity with paragraph 8 of the Reporting Guidelines. The Committee specifically recommends that information be included in that report on the present situation of indigenous people…"(A/50/18, paragraph 495).

Estonia

"The State party is invited to provide further information on… Estonian birth rate trends, including separate data on the majority population and on ethnic minorities." (A/55/18, paragraph 84).

France

"While taking note of the State party's view of the importance of individual privacy when collecting information on the composition of the population, the Committee expresses concern about the paucity of information for monitoring implementation of the Convention." (A/55/18, paragraph 95).

Former Yugoslav Republic of Macedonia

"More information is requested in the next periodic report concerning the participation of the various minorities in public life…" (A/52/18, paragraph 523).

Gabon

"[P]rovide fuller information on the demographic composition of the population…" (A/53/18, paragraph 379).

Ghana

"The Committee regrets the lack of information in the report concerning the demographic composition of the country." (A/55/18, paragraph 12).

Haiti

"The Committee recommends that the State party in its next periodic report provide full information on the demographic composition of the population in the light of paragraph 8 of the reporting guidelines, together with socio-economic indicators on the situation of the various ethnic communities." (A/54/18, paragraph 264).

Hungary

"The Committee recommends increased attention to the protection of the Gypsies' civil, political, economic, social and cultural rights. The efforts to implement measures of affirmative action in that respect should be strengthened. Adequate indicators and other means of monitoring the economic and social conditions of this group should be developed... provide statistical data on the minorities in different districts, on their representation in the local authorities, as well as recent data on their situation in the fields of education, culture, the media and employment." (A/51/18, paragraphs 126-27).

Iraq

"The Committee requests the State party to provide economic and social data on the situation of ethnic minorities." (A/52/18, paragraph 270).

Israel

"Any statistics should show whether governmental expenditure and service provision are proportionate to the size of the different ethnic groups." (A/53/18, paragraph 88).

Italy

"The Committee recommends that the State party include in its next report statistical data on the ethnic composition of the country." (A/54/18, paragraph 131).

Latvia

"The Committee recommends the State party to reconsider the requirement to record ethnic origin in passports." (A/54/18, paragraph 407).

Lebanon

"The Committee recommends that the State party include information on the demographic composition of the Lebanese population in its next periodic report." (A/53/18, paragraph 179).

Lesotho

"The State party is invited to provide further information about the ethnic composition of the population" (A/55/18, paragraph 115).

Libyan Arab Jamahiriya

"The Committee recommends that the State party provide in its next report detailed information on the demographic composition of its population..." (A/53/18, paragraph 248).

Luxembourg

"...Provide further information in its next report on the breakdown of the population, particularly with regard to persons who are not nationals of States members of the European Union... further information on the number of complaints of racial discrimination, the outcome of the prosecution in cases of racial discrimination and the redress, if any, provided to persons suffering from such discrimination." (A/49/18, paragraphs 437 and 440).

Mauritania

"[T]he Committee recommends that the State party supply more detailed information concerning the ethnic composition of the population and socio-economic indicators." (A/54/18, paragraph 330).

Mauritius

"The lack of statistical data on the ethnic and racial composition of the population, and on the representation of ethnic and racial communities at all levels of the economic, social and political spheres, is regretted. In this regard, the statement in paragraph 4 of the report that censuses in Mauritius do not indicate the breakdown of the population on an ethnic or racial basis, 'in line with the government policy to promote a Mauritian identity amongst its people' is accepted by the Committee as long as it is not aimed at forced assimilation of people with different origins." (A/51/18, paragraph 552).

"... the Committee notes that it has still not been provided with statistical data on the composition of Mauritian society." (A/55/18, paragraph 231).

Mexico

"The Committee draws the attention of the State party to the necessity of adopting indicators to evaluate the policies and programmes aimed at the protection and promotion of the rights of indigenous peoples." (A/50/18, paragraph 389).

"... the need to devise 'indicators' to evaluate policies and programmes for protecting and promoting the rights of vulnerable populations." (A/52/18, paragraph 317).

Mongolia

"Although the Committee notes that the State party's report includes information on the demographic composition of Mongolia, it regrets the lack of information on the socio-economic situation of the different ethnic minority groups." (A/54/18, paragraph 241).

Morocco

"... Provide information on the ethnic composition of the Moroccan population." (A/49/18, paragraph 228).

Namibia

"Concern is expressed at the lack of information in the report relating to the implementation in law and practice of article 5 of the Convention, as well as on the situation of vulnerable groups, particularly the San/Bushmen." (A/51/18, paragraph 499).

Nepal

"...Provide fuller information on the demographic composition of the population..." (A/53/18, paragraph 433).

"The Committee expresses concern about the absence from the report of dis-aggregated data of the population, such as by age, sex, nationality, ethnic origin, religion, including caste, and language." (A/55/18, paragraph 297).

Norway

"…Provide information on the ethnic composition of the Norwegian population." (A/49/18, paragraph 260).

Pakistan

"The report does not respond to paragraph 8 of the Committee's general guidelines about the supply of information on ethnic or racial origin. The lack of such information makes it difficult to assess the situation of the various ethnic groups in Pakistan and to evaluate the practical impact and the effectiveness of the legislative and other measures adopted by the authorities to implement the provisions of the Convention." (A/52/18, paragraph 169).

Panama

"…Include in its next report disaggregated data, including information and socio-economic indicators, on the demographic composition of its population." (A/52/18, paragraph 353).

Peru

"…The Government failed to provide the Committee in its written report with accurate demographic data on Peru." (A/50/18, paragraph 198).

"The State party should provide information… on the ethnic make up of the population, in so far as such information is available." (A/54/18, paragraph 164).

Philippines

"The Committee recommends that information on the ethnic composition of the population and the standard of living of each group, as well as other educational and social indicators… be provided… with particular emphasis on indigenous ethnic communities and tribes." (A/52/18, paragraph 431).

Russian Federation

"...Provide further information on the breakdown by percentage of all ethnic groups of the population." (A/51/18, paragraph 155).

Rwanda

"The Committee also notes the efforts made by the State party to remove all references to ethnic distinctions from official texts and speeches, as well as from identity cards." (A/55/18, paragraph 141).

Slovakia

"The Committee notes the absence in the report of disaggregated data on the population, giving details of ethnic composition." (A/55/18, paragraph 258).

Spain

"Insufficient information was provided in the report about the demographic composition of the Spanish population... information is requested on the demographic and ethnic composition of the Spanish population... [and on] complaints of racial discrimination brought before the courts and on remedies made available to victims..." (A/49/18, paragraphs 500, 506, 509).

"It is regretted that no precise information was provided with regard to the socio-economic situation of the Gypsy community." (A/51/18, paragraph 206).

"...Provide further information... on... the ethnic composition of the population and the principal socio-economic situation of each group." (A/55/18, paragraph 170).

Sweden

"While the Committee notes that the official statistics of the State party do not contain data which distinguishes people based on their ethnic origin, it recommends that the State party provide, in its next periodic report, more comprehensive and updated statistical information along the lines of paragraphs 8 and 9 of the Committee's Guidelines." (A/55/18, paragraph 343).

Tunisia

"The next report should include information and statistical data about measures taken to implement the rights enshrined in the Convention and to guarantee effective remedies to possible victims of racial discrimination." (A/49/18,
paragraph 178).

United Kingdom of Great Britain and Northern Ireland

"The Committee looks forward to receive, in the next periodic report of the
State party, disaggregated data, giving details of the ethnic composition of the
population, the principal socio-economic situation and gender composition of
each group." (A/55/18, paragraph 368).

Zaire

"The lack of statistical data on the composition of the population and on the
representation of the various communities at all economic, social and political
levels and in the public service, including the police and the armed forces, is
regretted." (A/51/18, paragraph 521).

Zimbabwe

"Concern is expressed about the lack of information on the educational
attainments of ethnic groups at the primary, secondary and university levels.
More information is also needed on land distribution by ethnicity, and the registration of complaints and court cases related to racial discrimination."
(A/51/18, paragraph 94).

Some generalizations

This review shows how important paragraph 8 of the reporting guidelines is
to the Committee's work. Personal identification documents in Rwanda no
longer record ethnic origin because during the genocide in that country many
people lost their lives because of the way they were identified, though it should
also be remembered that in neighboring Burundi, where ethnic identity was not
recorded in this way, there have been comparable killings. There are other forms
of record-keeping which can be of concern to the Committee. For example, in

the case of Ghana in 2000 Committee members were told by a national NGO that, when attending hospital, persons with Muslim names, or women wearing a *hijab*, were liable to find that their records were marked so as to indicate that they were not of Ghanaian national origin and that they thereafter received less favorable treatment. If true, this is contrary to the Convention.

Paragraph 8 was drafted so as to take account of the sensitivity in black African countries of the recording of ethnic origin in the national census. Experience has shown that competition for resources between the residents of ethnically distinctive areas can result in the falsification of returns and that ethnic consciousness can hamper attempts to foster the sense of national unity.

The first entry in the review of recommendations to states, relating to Algeria, summarizes the Committee's rationale for requesting demographic data. It explains "Such information is essential for the Government itself to detect possible patterns of discrimination and for the Committee to monitor effectively the implementation of the Convention." The best example of governmental use of such data is provided by the United Kingdom[7], about which the Committee observed in 2000:

"The Committee welcomes the use of ethnic monitoring to ascertain the numbers of persons of particular ethnic and national origin in various kinds of employment and the setting of targets to increase the employment of persons of minority origins in fields where they are under-represented, as well as the use of ethnic monitoring in the criminal justice system, including the prison population, in order to identify points at which discrimination occurs and to develop means of rectifying it."

"The Committee welcomes the Home Secretary's employment targets for the ethnic minorities to be employed in different grades in the Home Office, the police, prison service, fire service and the probation service by 2002, 2004 and 2009 and for the armed service to reach 5 per cent by 2001/2002." (A/55/18, paragraphs 353-54).

Arguments for the keeping of records of ethnic origin with respect to the allocation of municipally-owned housing were first officially advanced in the United Kingdom in 1968. Over a period of thirty years the practice was gradually extended so that now it covers almost all employment in the public sector and much of the private sector. It has become an important tool enabling man-

---

7. See Michael Banton "Ethnic Monitoring in Britain" in this volume.

agers to see whether the composition of their workforce reflects the ethnic make-up of the population from which employees are recruited. The managing director of a retail organization employing 30,000 persons has been quoted in favour of the collection of such data, saying "If you can't measure it, you can't manage it."

Categories

CERD has not attempted to advise states on the categories they should employ for recording the ethnic origins of persons, other than to recommend that it should "be based upon self-identification by the individual concerned." However, when answering a question on its fifteenth report the United Kingdom circulated a paper showing that in the 2001 census persons would be asked "What is your ethnic group?" and invited to choose one of the following by ticking the appropriate box "to indicate your cultural background":

(a) *White*   British
            Irish
            Any other White background
            please write in below
            ....

(b) *Mixed*   White and Black Caribbean
            White and Black African
            White and Asian
            Any other mixed background
            please write in below
            ....

(c) *Asian or Asian British*
            Indian
            Pakistani
            Bangladeshi
            Any other Asian background
            please write in below
            ....

(d)   *Black or Black British*
        Caribbean
        African
        Any other Black background
        please write in below
        ....

(e)   *Chinese or Other ethnic group*
        Chinese
        Any other
        please write in below
        ....

A person who wished to indicate membership in the Roma ethnic group would presumably write this in the last section. It has been estimated that thirty percent of the Gypsies/Roma/Travelers live in caravans on the roadside, [8] but there is no way of obtaining a more accurate figure from official statistics. Roma living a sedentary life may be indistinguishable from the general population.

Conclusion

The UN Committee on the Elimination of Racial Discrimination has main-tained that if states' parties to the International Convention on the Elimination of All Forms of Racial Discrimination are to demonstrate that they are fulfilling their contractual obligations, they will usually need to supply demographic data in their reports. They may also need to monitor changes in such data to ascer-tain whether the measures they have adopted are effective. The Committee's views on this subject have not been challenged and therefore have a place in the developing international law for the prevention of racial discrimination.

Governments usually accept the invitation to send a delegation to present their reports to the Committee, but their obligation is to implement the provi-sions of the Convention, not to answer questions. If one state does not fulfil its obligations, it is other states' parties, which have cause for complaint, and it is they who can act against the defaulter. In practice they never do. On the inter-national level, the main pressure for implementation of the Convention derives from states' desire for a good reputation.

8. *Joint submission by NGOs to the UN CERD on the UK, Fifteenth Periodic Review.* (2000) London. Liberty. pp.20.

The Committee cannot press one state, or one region, to observe higher reporting standards than another. Nevertheless it will be apparent from this survey that the problems vary. African states have good reasons for avoiding any action that draws attention to ethnic differences, especially if it would compli-cate struggles over the allocation of state resources. European states do not have this difficulty; they have been ready to supply the Committee with such infor-mation as they have collected for their own purposes. Sometimes national law inhibits the collection of data on ethnic origins. In France the constitution of the Republic is interpreted as preventing official recognition of ethnic minori-ties, yet the government has never chosen to draw attention to this in its reports under the Convention. It is a question for French people to decide, not for-eigners.

The main Roma populations are in European states, so discrimination against them is perceived to be a regional problem. International bodies like CERD can set certain standards for data collection and can encourage states to monitor the effectiveness of their policies for the prevention of racial discrim-ination and the protection of minorities. Governments may take these consid-erations into account, but they are also subject to pressures from their officials and from the members of the general public whose votes they will be soliciting at election time. When, as in this instance, the regional dimension is impor-tant, international action requires support from action at regional and nation-al levels, including members of the public and non-governmental organiza-tions. Regional and national standards should not be lower than international ones. The Organization for Security and Co-operation in Europe, the Framework Convention for the Protection of National Minorities and the European Commission Against Racism and Intolerance (both of the Council of Europe) and the European Union (with its Community Action Plan to Combat Discrimination 2001-2006) can make distinctive and complementary contributions but they do not always liaise properly with action under the ICERD. The improvement of methods of data collection for the purposes of policy monitoring should be of interest to all of them. Better co-ordination is now a priority.

Acknowledgements

Christiano Condagnone and Rolf Nygren kindly helped me with information on specific points concerning personal data.

Annex

*References to Roma in CERD's concluding observations
on selected recent state party reports*

Bulgaria Twelfth/Fourteenth reports considered 1997 (A/52/18:275-295). "Concern is expressed that the economic crisis has affected people from ethnic minorities disproportionately. In this respect, the persistent marginalization of the large Roma population, in spite of continuing efforts by the Government, is a matter of concern. It is noted that the Roma face de facto discrimination in the enjoyment of their economic, social and cultural rights, which increases their vulnerability in a context of economic crisis. Concern is expressed about dis-crimination against minorities in the workplace, especially for Roma, most of whom have relatively little training and education. Concern is also expressed that Roma encounter difficulties in applying for social benefits and that rural Roma are discouraged from claiming land to which they are entitled under the law dis-banding agricultural collectives." (paragraph. 282). Also paragraph 284 regard-ing violence against Roma and paragraph 291 regarding de facto segregation.

Croatia Initial/Third reports considered in 1998 (A/53/18:306-329). No specific reference to Roma.

Czech Republic Initial/Second reports considered 1998 (A/53/18:111-138). Recommended to improve the protection against violence of Roma and persons belonging to minority groups, to pay more attention to persons and groups pro-moting racism, to the protection of Article 5 rights, and to the improvement of recourse measures for victims. Later in 1998 in Decision 2(53), CERD request-ed further information on reports that in certain municipalities measures were contemplated for the physical segregation of some residential units housing Roma families (see A/53/18 page 18) and expressed its concerns in dialogue with a State delegation (see CERD/C/SR. 1320 paragraphs 39-75 and CERD/C/SR. 1321 paragraphs 1-16) but CERD did not mention this in its report to the General Assembly. The third periodic report was considered in 2000, when CERD expressed its continuing concern over discrimination against Roma in housing, education and employment and de facto segregation in housing and education. (A/55/18:280-81).

Germany Thirteenth/Fourteenth reports considered in 1997 (A/52/18:152-75). No specific reference to Roma.

Hungary Eleventh/Thirteenth reports considered 1996 (A/51/18:106-131) when CERD expressed concern over racial violence, especially towards Gypsies, Jews and people of African or Asian origin and apparent harassment and use of excessive force by the police against Gypsies and foreigners. The Government was recommended to take more active steps to counter racial violence, to comply fully with Article 4, to supply information on allegations of discrimination and prosecutions, and pay increased attention to the protection of the human rights of Gypsies.

Latvia Initial/Third reports considered in 1999 (A/54/18:384-414). No specific reference to Roma.

Romania Twelfth/Fifteenth reports considered in 1999, when CERD stated "The situation of Roma is a subject of particular concern since no improvements have been noted in the high unemployment rates and the low educational level traditionally predominant among members of this minority; this contributes to the continuing unacceptable prevalence of the negative and stereotyped image of the minority in the rest of society. Given its disadvantaged situation in society, particular concern is caused by the absence of economic and social measures of the kind envisaged in Article 2(2) of the Convention in favour of this minority, Romania's current difficult economic situation notwithstanding." (paragraph 282). "... means should be found to ensure that the media constitutes an instrument that helps to combat racial prejudice, particularly against Roma." (paragraph 285). CERD requested the State party to attend to its general recommendation XIX concerning segregation (A/54/18:272-290).

Slovakia Initial/Third reports considered in August 2000. "The Committee is concerned about settlement patterns with respect to the Roma minority... The Committee recommends the State party to review legislation regulating local residence permits... to monitor trends which give rise to racial segregation and indicate its findings in subsequent reports" (paragraph 260). It expressed concerns about violence against Roma and that "a disproportionately large number of Roma children are not enrolled in schools, have high drop-out rates, do not complete higher education or are segregated and placed in schools for mentally disabled children" (paragraph 262). Roma were hardest hit by unemployment: "a disproportionately large number of Roma suffer higher mortality rates, have poorer nutrition levels, and a low level of awareness of maternal and child health... poor access to clean drinking water, adequate sanitation, and high exposure to environmental pollution." (A/55/18, paragraph 265).

Spain Thirteenth report considered in 1996 (A/51/18:197-218). Recommended to adopt more effective measures to punish racist actions and fully implement Article 4, to ensure enjoyment of Article 5 rights, particularly by members of the Gypsy community, and to supply information on the results of these measures. Fourteenth/fifteenth reports were considered in March 2000, when CERD expressed concern "over the high drop-out rates and registered absences of Roma children in primary schools, as well as the low number of Roma completing higher education." The State party is requested to provide information about measures undertaken and planned to ensure equal education opportunities for the Roma minority. (A/55/18, paragraph 168).

III.

Practice in Countries of Europe

Ethnic Statistics and Data Protection: The Case of Bulgaria

Krassimir Kanev and Alexander Kashumov[1]

I. Legal Framework

Legal Framework of Personal Data Collection, Processing and Protection in Bulgaria

There is no provision in the Bulgarian Constitution guaranteeing the protection of personal data and ensuring the rights to informational self-determination. The applicable constitutional provision is the one ensuring the right to inviolability of private life, Article 32 of the Constitution. Its paragraph 2 provides that no one shall be followed, photographed, filmed, recorded or subjected to any other similar activity without his/her knowledge or despite his/her express disapproval, except when such actions are permitted by law. This provision applies also to cases of collection of data related to one's ethnic and religious identity.

The Law for the Special Intelligence Devices[2] allows for the use of special intelligence devices for collection of personal data through surveillance, tapping, following, penetration, marking and inspection of the correspondence and computerized information applied in using technical devices. According to this law personal data may be collected by police and security services for two purposes: for the prevention and disclosure of severe crimes and "regarding activities related to the protection of the national security"[3]. In both cases the use must be authorized by a judge but in cases of immediate danger of perpetration of severe premeditated crime or threat to the national security the special intelligence devices can be used without the permission of the judge for 24 hours during which a judicial warrant is to be obtained. The procedure as established by law, however, is by and large violated. According to an investigation conducted by the Chief Prosecutor's Office in January 2001, for the past two years (1999 and 2000) the courts have issued 10,020 permissions for use of special intelligence devices.

---

1. Alexander Kashumov's work has been supported by the joint effort of the team of the Access to Information Program: Gergana Jouleva, Svetlana Ganevska and Ivailo Kolev.
2. State Gazette No. 95, 21/10/1997; last amended in State Gazette No. 49, 16/06/2000.
3. Article 4.

Of them only 100 were effectively used in the criminal procedure, i.e. were turned into evidence before the courts. The investigation found more than 2000 serious violations of the law at different stages of the procedure. One of the hypotheses of the Chief Prosecutor's Office was that the data obtained could have been used for "personal or group interests".[4]

"National security" is defined in a broad way in the Bulgarian legal system. According to Article 44 of the Law on the Ministry of Interior[5] it includes, among other things, also "unity of the nation." National Security Service is empowered to protect it through counterintelligence and information-collection. According to the routine practice of this service, this includes collecting data on ethnic and religious affiliations of some minorities (e.g. Bulgarian citizens of Macedonian identity and those belonging to unpopular religious groups branded as "sects"). The most recent evidence of such activity was the submission of the Ministry of Interior on the Constitutional Court case that led to the prohibition in February 2000 of UMO "Ilinden" — PIRIN, a political party that had its membership among the Bulgarian citizens of Macedonian ethnic identity.

There is no law for the protection of personal data in Bulgaria. The Council of Ministers prepared a Personal Data Protection Bill and introduced it to the Parliament on the 7th of December 2000. However it is not clear when it will be voted on by the Parliament. The bill regulates the right of natural persons to the protection of their personal data. The scope of this right includes data collection and processing by both public authorities and private entities and the right of the individuals to know about this process. Under the bill, personal data could be processed by public authorities just for purposes prescribed by law and only to an extent that satisfies that purpose. Such personal data processing is permissible only 1) on the basis of law; 2) with the consent of the data subject; 3) for the fulfillment of contractual obligations; 4) if it is necessary to protect the data subject's substantial interests; 5) for the protection of lawful interests of the data controller or third parties, in case that the right of personal data protection of the subject is not affected. The same rules apply to any data controller regardless of whether it is a public authority or private entity.

Currently personal data processing is regulated by different statutes, though the legal regime is far from the international standards set forth in the EU Directive 95/46[6] and the Council of Europe's Convention on Personal Data

---

4. Interview with Tsoni Tsonev, Deputy Chief Prosecutor, *Democracia*, 30 January 2001.
5. State Gazette No. 122, 19/12/1997; last amended in State Gazette No. 28, 23/03/2001.
6. Directive 95/46/EC of the European Parliament and of the Council of 24 October 1995 on the protection of individuals with regard to the processing of personal data and on the free movement of such data.

Protection[7]. These are the Statistics Act[8], the 2001 Census of Population, Housing and Agricultural Funds Act[9], the Citizens' Registration Act[10], the Bulgarian Identification Documents Act[11], the Tax Procedure Code[12], the State Archive Fund Act[13], the Access to Former State Security Service Documents Act[14], among others. Personal data processing in the private sector is regulated by the Banks Act[15], the Insurance Act[16], the Barristers Act[17], the Health Insurance Act[18] and the Notaries Act[19] among others.

Processing of data for statistical purposes is regulated by the Statistics Act. There is no legal prohibition for matching of personal data collected for statistical purposes and for non-statistical purposes. Personal data collected for statistical purposes, however, cannot be transmitted to any other institution whether public or not. The legal regime of the Register of Population, which is the most important nationwide register in Bulgaria, is provided by the Citizens' Registration Act. This act provides for a nationwide electronic register, which contains some categories of personal data, strictly determined by law.

Bulgarian legislation does not set forth own standards for personal data processing. The Bulgarian Identification Documents Act refers[20] to the standards set by the European Convention for Protection of the Persons in Automatic Processing of Personal Data as obligatory for the purposes of the protection of data kept in the informational funds for the Bulgarian identification documents. There are also several prohibitions against communicating personal data. These, however, do not apply to the public sector where in most of the cases exchange of data between public authorities is not prohibited.

According to the Statistics Act[21] the National Institute of Statistics (NIS) maintains a database on crime prevention. NIS develops the methodology of data collection on crime prevention; the Ministry of Justice, the Chief

7. Council of Europe's Convention for the Protection of Individuals with regard to Automatic Processing of Personal Data. ETS No. 108.
8. State Gazette No. 57, 25/06/1999; last amended in State Gazette No. 42, 27/04/2001.
9. State Gazette No. 16, 25/02/2000.
10. State Gazette No. 67, 27/07/1999; last amendment in State Gazette No. 37, 13/04/2001.
11. State Gazette No. 93, 11/08/1998; last amendment in State Gazette No. 42, 27/04/2001.
12. State Gazette No. 103, 30/11/1999; last amendment in No. 63, 1/08/2000.
13. State Gazette No. 54, 12/07/1974; last amendment in State Gazette No. 12, 8/02/1993.
14. State Gazette No. 63, 6/08/1997 with substantial amendments from 13/03/2001, in State Gazette No. 24.
15. State Gazette No. 52, 1/07/1997; last amendment in State Gazette No. 1, 2/01/2001.
16. State Gazette No. 86, 11/10/1996; last amendment in State Gazette No. 1, 1/02/2001.
17. State Gazette No. 80, 27/09/1991; last amendment in State Gazette No. 61, 25/07/2000.
18. State Gazette No. 70, 19/06/1998; last amendment in State Gazette No. 41, 24/04/2001.
19. State Gazette No. 104, 06/12/1996; last amendment in State Gazette No. 69, 03/08/1999.
20. Article 72.
21. Article 46-51.

Prosecutor's Office, the Supreme Court of Cassation and the Supreme Administrative Court are obliged, under the Judiciary Act[22], to comply in submitting the required information. On this legal basis NIS developed Statistical Form 1-CC, which is case-specific and is filled in on a case-by-case basis at all stages of the criminal procedure by police, investigation authorities and the courts. It contains, among other things, data on the ethnicity of the perpetrator of a crime. Although the authorities claim that data on ethnicity in this process is collected only with the consent of the defendant and according to his/her self-determination[23], in fact there is sufficient evidence to conclude that ultimately it is the law enforcement officer who determines ethnicity — the form has no option "undecided" at the entry "ethnic group" and the guidelines for filling in the form explicitly direct that the part with the personal data are filled in "by the person who conducted the preliminary investigation" or by the court (in cases of crimes prosecuted on the basis of private complaints). This is corroborated by interviews with investigators conducted by the Bulgarian Helsinki Committee in September and October, 2000.

Sensitive data, including race and ethnic data, are regulated by a separate provision of the Personal Data Protection Bill and are to be processed under more strict conditions than other personal data. The consent of the data subject should be in a written form. There are some exemptions from this principle, however. Written consent is not required when: 1) data processing is a legal obligation of the data controller; 2) data processing is necessary for the protection of substantial interests of the data subject or another person and the former is not able to give consent; 3) data are publicly announced by the data subject; 4) it is necessary for the exercise or protection of the data subject's rights; 5) data processing is for medical treatment; 6) data processing is conducted by law enforcement authority in connection with criminal and administrative offenses and torts; 7) data processing is necessary for the defense of national security.

Race and ethnic data collection is regulated by the Statistics Act and by the 2001 Population Census Act. Unlike the other data obtained through the census, giving such data to the census taker is left to the will of the data subject. Databases containing personal race and ethnic data cannot be merged with other databases or transmitted to any other authority.

In Bulgaria there are no specific legal requirements about personal data processing in academic research.

There are no specified legal differences between data collection by state authorities and by private actors in Bulgaria. Some distinctions could be drawn

22. Gazette No. 59, 22/07/1994; last amendment in State Gazette No. 25, 16/03/2001. Article 189.
23. Letter of the Director of the National Institute of Statistics to the BHC from 13 September 2000.

from the theoretical legal principle that public authorities only have the powers expressively given by law and are not permitted to overstep those. As laws for - mulate precisely what kind of personal data are to be collected for the purposes of the law, it is clear that collection of other categories of data is prohibited. Such laws are the Citizen's Registration Act and the Bulgarian Identification Documents Act. Practically, the relevant public bodies are not allowed to collect data, which are not listed in these laws. Data collection is less guaranteed when the categories are determined by the executive. The purposes of statistical data collection are determined every year by the National Program for Statistical Research adopted by the Council of Ministers. According to the Statistics Act the National Statistical Council, a body composed of public officials from dif - ferent ministries, introduces every year for approval to the Council of Ministers a national program for statistical research. The Council determines the type and the scope of data to be observed and analyzed, which might differ from year to year. Thus, the lack of legislation determining precisely the categories of data to be collected and the purpose of their collection opens the door for arbitrariness. This is especially the case with data collected by the Ministry of Interior and the judicial authorities. The latter includes, among other things, data collection on ethnicity.

In any case, collection of data within the private sector is less guaranteed nowadays as there are absolutely no rules for data collection, but just for disclo - sure of the collected personal data. Legal obligations on private sector actors to keep personal data secret exist for banks, insurance companies, barristers, physi - cians and notaries.

The Personal Data Protection Bill does not set forth different requirements for data processing in the public and private sectors. The only difference is that government authorities are permitted to process personal data only when pro - vided by law. Although this limitation is not relevant to data controllers in the pri - vate sector, they are bound by the general requirement that personal data pro - cessing is legal only if its collection and processing follows the rules defined by the law.

Rights of Access to Information

The Bulgarian Constitution provides for the right of everyone to hold and express opinion — either orally or in writing, through sounds, pictures or any other way[24], the freedom of media[25] and the right of everyone to seek, receive

24. Article 39.
25. Article 40.

and impart information and to obtain information held by the government authorities[26]. The Constitutional Court regards these rights as the group of so-called communication rights[27]. Since July 2000 the general right of all persons to access public information is regulated by the Access to Public Information Act (APIA) [28]. This Act requires that central and local government agencies should provide upon request any information connected with public life in Bulgaria, thus enabling the seeker to form his/her own opinion concerning the activities of public authorities, regardless of the type of recording. Public authorities are not required to provide information in cases in which that is protected by law. Generally personal data are excluded from the scope of the act, but in some cases personal data might be present in some documents. This, however, is not taken into account in the act.

The right of access to information is also provided for by the Environmental Protection Act[29], the Access to Former State Security Service Documents Act[30] and the Information about Unpaid Loans Act[31]. AFSSSDA gives citizens a limited access — only to documents containing their own data or data of their close relatives (spouse, parents and children) after their decease. The Information about Unpaid Loans Act states that all the personal information concerning unpaid bank loans, including the debtors' name, the amount of the loan, the debtors' ability to pay etc. shall not be confidential under the Banks' Act anymore.

Rights of Individuals Connected to the Protection of their Personal Data, Including Personal Data on Ethnicity

Under the Personal Data Protection Bill *the right of the data subject to access his/her personal data* is part of his/her right to personal data protection. If such access contains a possibility for disclosure of another subject's personal data, the data controller should provide limited access. Denials to provide entire or partial access and prolongation of the terms in which access should be given, can be appealed either before the Commission for Personal Data Protection or before the Court. If the Commission decides against the applicant, its decision is subject to judicial review by the relevant administrative court upon appeal.

Currently the data subjects can access their personal data registered in the local registers under the Citizens' Registration Act. Everyone who is concerned

26. Article 41.
27. Decision No. 7 from 1996.
28. State Gazette No. 55, 07/07/2000.
29. State Gazette No. 86, 18/10/1991; last amendment in State Gazette No. 26, 20/03/2000.
30. AFSSSDA, see footnote 14 above.
31. State Gazette No. 95, 21/10/1997.

is entitled to access to the nationwide register of the population under the same Act. Access denials can be challenged under the Administrative Procedure Act[32]. Bulgarian and foreign citizens who have Bulgarian identification documents issued are entitled to access their personal data contained in the nationwide electronic register under the Act. Denials can be appealed under the Administrative Procedure Act. Bulgarian citizens can access their data registered by the former national security service under AFNSSSDA. Other registers, like the taxpayers' one, are not accessible under the law.

Personal data about ethnicity are not contained in the above mentioned centralized registers but only in the statistical and census databases. The Statistics Act states that personal data collected for statistical purposes cannot be communicated to "other persons." It is not quite clear, however, whether this entails the right to access to one's own data. The law does not explicitly prohibit defendants to access data from the database of the NIS on crime prevention. In practice, however, it does not establish a procedure and does not provide for obligations of the officials in that regard. In the case of the secret services, collecting data on people's ethnic belonging, these databases are protected by law and are not available to people on whom they are collected.

Under the Access to Former State Security Service Documents Act, every Bulgarian citizen has the right to see any information collected on him/her by the former (Communist) State Security. When the information is given, all the names of other people present in the document are deleted.

Currently people and legal entities can access personal data of other people in four cases: 1) when data are held in public registers; 2) under the Access to Public Information Act; 3) after a court permission; 4) when a person is data controller.

The local and the national registers, as well as the database of the NIS, are not public. Before the adoption of the Citizen's Registration Act, some data from the population register were deemed public (birth, family status, death). Now natural persons can access others' personal data in the nationwide register of the population when they have a legal interest. Legal entities either Bulgarian or foreign can access personal data in the above registers just on the basis of law or court order. Personal data can be accessed by others if they are recorded in documents falling under the scope of the Access to Public Information Act.

Under the Access to Former State Security Service Documents Act, if the person is deceased his/her spouse, parents and children have the right to see the information collected on him/her under the general conditions of confidentiality.

---

32. State Gazette No. 90, 13/11/1979; last amendment in State Gazette No. 95, 2/11/1999.

The Personal Data Protection Bill provides for the protection of personal data against access by others provided by different laws in different spheres. The Personal Data Protection Bill prohibits such access except in cases when: 1) the data subject consented; 2) data are kept in public registers; 3) it is necessary for the protection of the data subject's life and health and she/he is not able to con - sent; 4) it is necessary to the judiciary and executive power; 5) it is necessary for the protection of fair competition under the law; 6) it is necessary for academic research or statistical purposes and anonymity is guaranteed; 7) the information is designed for the purposes of labor law control or control under the state administration regulations. Permission of the Commission for Personal Data Protection is needed in any case.

When the data controller is a private entity, the same requirements are applicable as in the public sector under the Personal Data Protection Bill. Currently such controllers should provide access to personal data by others just on the basis of lawful obligation or court order.

Under the above-mentioned Access to Public Information Act, everyone can access and inspect files held by public authorities including the ones containing information on communities and other groups. The Council of Ministers' draft of the Personal Data Protection Act initially had provisions on groups' rights to data protection. This was applicable for groups, which are not legal persons. Legal persons were also entitled to personal data protection. Due to the public pressure and criticism of NGOs, especially Access to Information Program[33], the proposal was abandoned.

As far as *the right to request altering or deleting personal data*, including data on ethnicity, is concerned, currently the Citizens' Registration Act and the Bulgarian Identification Documents Act are the only ones providing for data rectification procedures. Data registered in the population register can be altered either by administrative or court decision upon a request. An administrative decision is issued when the altering does not concern substantial facts. Such a procedure is not applicable, however, in cases of altering the name, sex, date of birth, marriage or death. Only courts can decide on such questions. The court proceedings could take a long time, often few months. The court decision is sent to the relevant local authority, either by courts *ex officio* (in cases of birth or divorce) or by the applicant (in cases of name change), depending on the cate - gory of the data altered. The change is reflected firstly in the act of civil status of the person concerned and secondly in the population register.

---

33. The NGO was established with the purpose of promoting everyone's right to access to public information and the right to personal data protection. It was involved in the public debate on the laws relevant to those issues.

The Personal Data Protection Bill provides that data subjects are entitled to request actualization or rectification of data. If data are processed in breach of law or are not necessary to satisfy the purposes of the processing, the data sub - ject has the right to request their deletion, or their being turned into anonymous data or blocking the processing. The data controller is obliged to react within a 30-day period. Any violation of these rights or refusal to satisfy such a request of the data subject can be challenged before the Commission for Personal Data Protection or courts.

Data collected under the Citizens' Registration Act and the Bulgarian Identification Documents Act do not contain information on ethnic belonging. All the other data is alterable under the conditions specified above. The Personal Data Protection Bill does not distinguish between data with respect to the right of the data subject to their altering or deleting. The Bill uses the term "rectification" instead of "altering."

Individuals can access their personal data contained in centralized registers under Article 106[34] of the Citizens' Registration Act and Article 70[35] of the Bulgarian Identification Documents Act. The latter states that access should be limited when the relevant data concern third parties. Other laws regulating per - sonal data processing, storage and registers do not expressively provide for the right of access. This is due to the time when these older regulations were passed. Criminal defendants and persons who have been sentenced for crimes can access their files where the statistical Form 1 — CC is kept.

The state archives store all files (personal or non-personal) which are no longer needed by the public authorities and are designed for storage. The inspection of these files is not limited to the concerned person's data by law. Bulgarian citizens can apply for access to the head of the relevant archive. They should define the purpose of use and the scope of interest. The head of the archive has the discretion to provide access. When foreigners would like to inspect archival files they should address their request to the General Archives Management body. The law is rather old and must be changed to provide for the right to access one's own personal data and the right to archival personal data protection.

According to the Data Protection Bill, everyone will have the right to access their own personal data stored by a data controller. The respective data con - troller is the one obliged to provide access to the personal data within its stor - age. The Personal Data Protection Commission shall publish regularly a list of the purposes for processing, categories of data subjects and other details about

34. Subarticle 1 paragraph 1.
35. Subarticle 1 paragraph 1.

each data controller's personal data registers. This information will not contain personal data. The same refers to the public register of data controllers to be kept by the Commission.

Legal Regulation on Transmission of Data

Currently the Citizen's Registration Act and the Bulgarian Identification Documents Act permit personal data transmission to public authorities in accordance with their legal powers and to private entities on the basis of law or court order. Data transmission beyond the borders of Bulgaria is permissible under international bilateral and multilateral treaties and is administered by the Ministry of External Affairs. The Statistics Act does not permit personal data transmission unless that data is contained in public registers.

Information from the database of the former (Communist) State Security can be transferred to political parties and coalitions on their demand in order to offer them information in the pre-election period about the affiliation with the former State Security of their prospective candidates for MP positions. Names of former State Security workers and collaborators are announced in a permanent report prepared and published by a special permanent commission on the internet.

Under the Personal Data Protection Bill, there are specific conditions in which personal data can be transmitted. They apply to cases in which data is transmitted to other Bulgarian controllers, as well as to cases in which they are transmitted beyond the boundaries. Data can be transmitted under the preconditions applicable for access to data, as described. They cannot be transmitted, however, before the data subject is notified of the purpose and means for their processing, the possible data receivers, the right to access the collected personal data and the name and address of the controller. If data are to be deleted, or the period for processing and keeping has expired, as well as if significant public interest requires so, personal data cannot be transmitted.

Transmission to third countries is permissible under the above requirements and after permission of the Commission. This is applicable only if the country provides the same level of personal data protection or better.

Legal Sanctions for Abusive Storage,
Transmission and Use of Information. Independent Supervisory Bodies

The Bulgarian Penal Code envisages criminal responsibility for use of information gathered through special intelligence devices for purposes other than criminal prosecution or defense of national security[36]. It also envisages criminal responsibility for intentional falsification of information gathered through special intelligence devices but only with intent to deceive judicial authorities[37]. Abusive storage of personal data is not an offense. According to the Statistics Act, disclosure of personal information by officials of the national and regional statistical offices is an administrative offense and is punishable by a fine imposed by the Director of the National Institute of Statistics. Disclosure of some categories of data (e.g. the disclosure of a personal secret; the disclosure of the adoption and the disclosure of data illegally acquired from the Archive of the Ministry of Interior) is a criminal offense. Court actions are also possible for damages caused by illegal disclosure.

Under the Bill for Personal Data Protection, the Commission for Personal Data Protection investigates upon complaints or *ex officio* whether data protection requirements were respected. If breaches are found the Commission gives mandatory instructions. If they are not complied with, the President of the Commission sanctions the violator with a fine. In cases when the Commission finds that rights of data subjects are infringed, it addresses the court.

There is no authority in Bulgaria, either independent or not, which monitors personal data processing both in the public and private sector. No authority exists in Bulgaria for human rights protection in general, such as ombudsman institutions. There are several proposals to establish an Ombudsman office. The Framework Program for Equal Integration of Roma in Bulgarian Society envisages establishment of a special body to deal with racial or ethnic discrimination with effective authority to investigate cases and impose sanctions. No action was taken to this effect, however, since the adoption of the program in April 1999.

The control over data controllers' activities is within the competence of the authorities, which exercise overall control for legality in the respective field, both in the public and private sector. Courts' actions are available in any case when rights and legal interests are concerned, but that takes time and money.

The Personal Data Protection Bill provides for an independent authority named Personal Data Protection Commission. Its independence from the executive is guaranteed since it is appointed by the Parliament and has a five year mandate, which is one year more than that of the Parliament. The Commission will be supposed to monitor the work of the data controllers' activities in light of the legal requirements and will be empowered to impose sanctions through the Head of the Commission. Its orders and decisions will be subject to judicial review.

36. Article 145a.
37. Article 287a.

There are no decisions or recommendations of judicial or administrative bodies in Bulgaria regarding the availability and/or use of ethnic statistics. This is
due partly to the fact that there is no general Personal Data Protection Act and
supervisory authority, and partly because laws do not provide guarantees for personal data processing. The fact that people are frequently not so sensitive to such
problems can be explained both by attitude and lack of legislation.

Regulation of Census and Central Population Registers

In Bulgaria the population register is centralized. All inhabitants (Bulgarian
and foreign citizens and stateless persons) are obliged to register with the local
authority of their residence. Data are recorded with the local authority, but they
are sent also to the centralized register, which is nationwide. The register relies
on a unique identifier for each inhabitant. Bulgarian citizens' identifier consists
of 10 numbers: 6 of them designate the date of birth; the others designate the
place of birth and the sex. In this respect the Bulgarian model is close to the
Scandinavian system. The categories of personal data recorded in the local registers are: 1) data identifying the personality; 2) data reflecting family status and
relationships; 3) permanent and current address; 4) education; 5) legal disabili-
ties. Data falling under these five categories are 22 and are collected in the local
register of every town or village in the country. They do not include data on ethnic or religious affiliations of Bulgarian citizens.

Another nation-wide, centralized register covering all the inhabitants in
Bulgaria is the electronic register under the Bulgarian Identification Documents
Act. The above identifier is also among the data collected in this register. This
register is permanently linked to the population register. Any data from the two
registers can be transmitted to other public authorities, in accordance with their
powers. The two laws state that the conditions and procedures of such transmission of data shall be determined by a decree of the Council of Ministers, but
no such decree has been brought so far.

Reportedly the population register is linked with the Ministry of Interior
(which has a register reflecting the same data), the National Institute for
Statistics, and the National Social Insurance Institute (because of pensions). Tax
registers are also linked with the population register.

In Bulgaria there are a number of centralized databases maintained for
specific purposes (e.g. unemployment benefits, pensions, taxpayers, criminal
offenses, telephone and mobile telephone users etc.). Some of these are linked
together on a permanent basis. In other cases data are transmitted upon a written request after the approval of the head of the respective authority. The local

unemployment bureaus, for example, regularly receive data from the local population registers and regularly transmit data to the post offices (where benefits
are paid), social assistance authorities and the National Social Insurance
Institute. Data are transmitted to the courts or police upon request.

Nowadays some municipalities start building permanent electronic linkage
between local registers and nationwide registers, such as the register of the
Ministry of Interior and the population register. Questions asked by Access to
Information Program staff reveal that personal data protection is not taken into
account in these cases.

The Statistics Act regulates all forms of collections of official statistics,
whereas the census is regulated by the 2001 Census of Population, Housing and
Agricultural Funds Act. Personal data collected for statistical purposes cannot be
used for other purposes (including any administrative purposes). The purposes
of the statistics are determined annually by the Program approved by the
Council of Ministers.

The 2001 Census of Population, Housing and Agricultural Funds Act provides the rules for the March 2001 census. Census data are collected primarily
from the data subjects except in extraordinary cases (for example when the data
subject is abroad or in the army.) Data about ethnicity, religion and mother
tongue are among the census data. The census embraces not only data about persons, but also about houses and farms. Under Article 28 of the Act, the statistical information collected from the census cards should be used only for statistical purposes. Personal data collected shall not be used as evidence before the
executive and judicial powers. The law differs from the regulations of the census
from 1992, when data on ethnicity, religion and mother tongue was also collected on a compulsory basis. In 1992 those who refused to declare their ethnicity,
religion and mother tongue were liable to an administrative fine. This regulation, however, has not been enforced although there were people who refused to
provide this information about themselves.

According to the Statistics Act individual data are kept separately. They are
made anonymous in the course of the statistics-making process. The relevant
authorities have to take all necessary measures to ensure this. They are obliged
by law to admit to work with such data only persons who have signed a declaration concerning respect for the protection of data they process. Only the statistical results are made public. There are no special privacy enhancing technologies used to specially protect ethnic data.

The Ministry of Interior and the judicial authorities maintain a uniform database on crime prevention, as required by the Statistics Act, in which data on the
ethnicity of the perpetrators of a crime is collected, stored and reported. In addi-

tion Security Services collect data on some ethnic and religious groups, whose activities are considered to be a threat to the national security.

Rights and Freedoms of Ethnic Minorities

There are several provisions in the Bulgarian Constitution relating to minor-ity rights. One of them prohibits creating political parties on ethnic, racial or religious basis[38]. Article 36[39] provides that citizens whose mother tongue is not Bulgarian can study and use their language alongside the compulsory study of Bulgarian language. Article 54 provides for the right to "everyone" to develop his/her own culture "in accordance with his/her ethnic identity." In fact there are a number of political parties in Bulgaria, whose members and voters belong to different minorities. One of them is the Movement for Rights and Freedoms, which is predominantly Turkish. There are several de facto Roma parties. Until February 2000 there was a Macedonian party, UMO "Ilinden" — PIRIN but it was prohibited by the Constitutional Court as a "threat to national security." None of these parties claim in their statutes that they are ethnically based. This, according to several decisions of the Constitutional Court since 1992, is enough to ensure their constitutionality.

The Radio and Television Act[40] permits radio and television programs in lan-guages different from Bulgarian. Since October 2000 there is a news program in Turkish on the national TV. The Law on National Education[41], as well as several decrees and ordinances regulate the study of mother tongue in municipal schools. At present this is organized on a "compulsory-selectable" basis, i.e. the students or their parents are provided an opportunity to select studying their mother tongue from among several other subjects of a similar "compulsory-selectable" kind. Once they have selected to study their mother tongue, they have to attend classes and the grade goes into their school record. There are several acts providing for a com-pulsory use of Bulgarian language in a number of spheres of social life (political process, army, prison system etc.). Bulgarian is obligatory also in judicial proceed-ings except for cases where the law-enforcement agencies and courts allow for the use of a different language and appoint an interpreter. There is no special anti-dis-crimination law in Bulgaria. However there are anti-discrimination provisions in a number of acts, which are enforceable through court action or through discipli-nary proceedings instituted by the agencies enforcing the respective laws.

---

38. Article 11, paragraph 4.
39. Paragraph 2.
40. 1998. Article 12, paragraph 2.
41. State Gazette No. 86, 18/10/1991; last amendment in State Gazette No. 68, 30/07/1999.

There is a state agency dealing with minorities in Bulgaria, the National Council on Ethnic and Demographic Issues. In the lack of effective ethnic and minority rights legislation, the power of this council, however, is only consulta-tive. One of the obligations of the Council is to enforce the Framework Program for Equal Integration of Roma in Bulgarian Society. The program was accepted by the Council of Ministers in April 1999. No measures have been taken to implement it so far.[42]

One clear contradiction between minority rights and data protection is the power of the police and judicial authorities to collect data on the ethnicity of the perpetrator of a crime without asking him/her, and without giving the opportu-nity to self-determine his/her ethnicity[43].

A clear abuse is the power of secret services to collect data on ethnicity and religion when working to defend the "unity of the nation," a term which is not defined by law. Actions against the "unity of the nation" are interpreted to include de-Bulgarizing Bulgarians, as well as spreading religious faiths other than the Eastern Orthodox religion.

There are legal provisions in Bulgaria that are discriminatory on their face, as well as laws of general application that have discriminatory effects. An exam-ple of the former is the provision of the Constitution[44], which prohibits political parties formed along ethnic or religious lines. Another example is the Citizenship Act, which provides for an alleviated procedure for acquiring of cit-izenship for "persons of Bulgarian origin."

Among the laws of general application that have a discriminatory effect, the laws that provide for the obligatory use of Bulgarian language (more than 100 in number) can be cited. They hamper effective participation of Turks and Roma who cannot speak Bulgarian at all or speak it poorly in a number of social rela-tionships in the sphere of education, employment, criminal and civil justice etc. Another law of general application that has a discriminatory effect is the provi-sion of the Regulations for the Application of the Social Assistance Act from November 1998, which limits the duration of payment of social welfare benefits for the working-age unemployed to a maximum of three years, thus denying social assistance to a relatively large share of Roma who are long-term unem-ployed.

Two laws in Bulgaria provide for collection of race and ethnic statistics. These are the Statistics Act and the 2001 Census of Population, Housing and

42. See more on the minority related national legislation in Bulgaria at:
www.riga.lv/minelres/NationalLegislation/Bulgaria/bulgaria.htm.
43. Article 3 of the Council of Europe's Framework Convention.
44. Article 11, paragraph 4.

Agricultural Funds Act. Article 21[45] of the Statistics Act provides that "physical persons cannot be compelled to provide data regarding their race, nationality, ethnic belonging, religion, health status, personal life, political belonging, offences committed, philosophical and political beliefs to the statistical agencies." Article 5 of the 2001 Census of Population, Housing and Agricultural Funds Act specifies the categories of data to be gathered during the March 2001 Census. Among them are ethnic group, religion and mother tongue. Sensitive data, including ethnic data, gathered under the Statistics Act during the census are kept in storage only for statistical purposes. They are made anonymous and processed under prohibition of disclosure. Disclosure of data is subject to sanctions for the perpetrator. This means that data cannot be transmitted to other public authorities and used for other purposes including administrative ones. However, there is no requirement for the deletion of data.

Statistical Form 1-CC is a guideline of the National Institute of Statistics. It requires collection of data on the ethnicity of the perpetrators of crimes at all stages of the criminal procedure. This data is collected by police and the judiciary (investigators, prosecutors and judges) on the basis of their own judgment of one's ethnicity. Data gathered through Statistical Form 1-CC is available for those who have access to the files. These include all law enforcement and judicial officers working on the case, as well as all private lawyers after the case goes to the archive. Processing of such data, however, is subject to the restrictions of the Statistics Act in accordance with the general regime for statistical data.

International Obligations

As a member of the United Nations Bulgaria has ratified most of the major human rights treaties, including the International Covenant on Civil and Political Rights with its two optional protocols, the International Covenant on Social, Economic and Cultural Rights and the International Convention on the Elimination of all Forms of Racial Discrimination. As a member of the International Labor Organization Bulgaria has ratified ILO Discrimination (Employment and Occupation) Convention 111. As a member of the Council of Europe from 1992, Bulgaria has ratified the European Convention on Human Rights (1992) and its protocols with the exception of Protocol 12. Bulgaria has not ratified the Council of Europe Convention for the Protection of Individuals with regard to Automatic Processing of Personal Data thus far, because it does not have the necessary domestic instruments to secure its

45. Paragraph 2.

enforcement (i.e. a Personal Data Protection Act). The Framework Convention for the Protection of National Minorities was ratified and entered into force in 1998. Since Bulgaria is not a member of the European Union, it is not party to the European Data Protection Directive 95/46/EC, but both the Directive and the Council of Europe Convention for the Protection of Individuals with regard to Automatic Processing of Personal Data were complied with in the Personal Data Protection Bill adopted by the Council of Ministers and introduced to the Parliament.

The above international instruments are part of the Bulgarian legislation and under Article 5[46] of the Constitution take precedence over domestic legislation that contradicts them. Consequently, they are directly applicable before the national courts. The obligations of Bulgaria under the European Convention on Human Rights are subject to the supervision by the European Court of Human Rights. There are no personal data protection challenges versus Bulgaria before the European Court of Human Rights by now. There haven't been any race dis - crimination cases in Bulgaria which have used race and ethnic statistics as a proof.

In April 1997 the Committee on the Elimination of Racial Discrimination released its concluding observations upon the submission of Bulgaria's 12th, 13th and 14th periodic reports under the International Convention on the Elimination of all Forms of Racial Discrimination. Among the numerous sug - gestions and recommendations that the CERD made to Bulgaria was one to develop "adequate indicators and other means of monitoring the economic and social living conditions of this [Roma] group." The Committee also required that the state provide, in the next report, "such statistical data and information as are available on the situation of all minorities on the matters covered under article 5 of the Convention." [47]

Future Prospects and Possibilities for Legal Reform in the Field

An important input to the Bulgarian data protection regime will be the expected adoption of the Personal Data Protection Act, which will provide the necessary guarantees for personal data processing and access. The Act will reg - ulate the data controllers' responsibilities and will provide for an independent body to supervise compliance with the law. The existence of this new law will require a process of harmonization of other legislation, to meet democratic stan - dards. Once the Act is in force, Bulgaria is expected to ratify the Council of

46. Paragraph 4.
47. CERD/C/304/Add.29, 23 April 1997, paragraph 14.

Europe Convention for the Protection of Individuals with regard to Automatic Processing of Personal Data.

Fulfilling its obligation under the Framework Convention and under paragraph 2 of Article 4 in particular, Bulgaria as a state should collect ethnic data in more fields of administration and in particular in the fields of unemployment, education and other sectors of the economical, social, political and cultural life in order to secure equal development of ethnic groups and minorities. The same responsibilities derive from the Constitution. Such collection of ethnic data is permissible only after the necessary guarantees for personal data protection are provided.

II. Practice of Data Collection
on Minority Groups and their Members

Overview of Registration of Data on Minorities

Data about minorities are collected during censuses. They are also collected regularly in the system of the Police and Ministry of Justice. The data are transmitted to the National Institute of Statistics where data are stored and processed. These data are compulsorily collected. The Ministry of Justice collects ethnic data about the suspects and defendants in every criminal case. As mentioned, there is a Statistical Form 1-CC filled in when the case starts. There are four options concerning ethnicity in the card: 1) Bulgarian 2) Turkish 3) Roma 4) others. The card is filled in and signed by the relevant authority (police or judicial). The card accompanies the case file during the case. It ought to be sent to the National Institute of Statistics.

Data registered by the police are filled in by a police officer, not the data subject. They are collected on a non-voluntary basis. Police officers also register people who were arrested when there is not enough evidence that they have committed a crime. In these cases they do not collect statistical information, including data on ethnicity. The information is processed by statistical authorities and by the Council of Criminological Studies at the Chief Prosecutor's Office. It can be purchased by third parties from the National Institute of Statistics. There is no individualized information in these files, however.

Other registries do not contain ethnic data. Most churches and religious communities, as well as ethnically based associations collect data on their members or on the participants in some of their rituals. Some of them process it for their internal purposes. Churches and religious communities (with the exception of the Jewish community) do not collect data on the ethnicity of their members. This is not a practice even for the ethnically based organizations and political parties.

There is no general prohibition or preconditions in Bulgaria to store information about persons; therefore illegal registers do not exist.

Processing and transmission of individualized data outside the national statistics system is possible only with the consent of the person to whom these data refer. This consent, according to Article 25, paragraph 3 of the Statistics Act can be withdrawn at any time. Data collected by the police and the judiciary is available for use of all who have access to the criminal files — law enforcement and judicial authorities, as well as the lawyers and the civil parties. Data collected by churches, religious communities and ethnically based groups is not public and is not transmitted to public authorities and to third parties.

The kind and scope of statistics produced is determined by the National Program for Statistical Research, adopted by the Council of Ministries under the proposal of the chief of the National Institute for Statistics. On the basis of census data, statistics were produced on unemployment, housing, disability, agglomeration etc. by ethnicity, religion and mother tongue. Criminal justice statistics produce regular reports on registered crime by ethnicity. No statistics have been produced on the basis of data collected by security services.

There is no doubt that collecting data on ethnicity, religion and mother tongue in the census has a positive effect in Bulgaria. It proves the existence of ethnic and religious minorities, something that Bulgarian authorities have denied repeatedly in the past. Their recognition even at present is uncertain. Organizations of ethnic and religious minorities have lobbied for the introduction of the respective questions in the census forms.

It is not, however, clear what is the positive effect in the collection of data in the criminal procedure. Theoretically, this data could be used for a variety of purposes related to prevention of discrimination and protection of minorities. In fact, however, this does not happen. On the contrary, this data is sometimes used to support racist claims that minorities are more susceptible to committing crimes and to invoke policies of harsher measures against them.

Collection of data on minorities by the security services can only have a harmful effect. Its very purpose is to attain entire groups of people and to use the state machinery to change their identity or to instigate other people against them.

An evident abuse of data about minorities is connected to the criminal justice register. In pending criminal cases the public prosecutor is apparently influenced by the data of this register, especially on ethnicity, which reflects negatively in the indictment. Evidently the court sees the defendant personally and sometimes can guess his ethnicity anyway, but it is questionable whether the principle of impartiality is complied with.

The collection of data on people's ethnic and religious belonging by the secu-rity services with no rules and for purely discriminatory purposes is also a clear abuse.

Another form of abuse, which is hidden, is the lack of ethnic data collected by a number of agencies such as the National Unemployment Service, National Health Fund etc. Since people's ethnicity and race are not registered, they do not exist before the public authorities and public at large with the specific problems this information raises. This prevents taking measures in these as well as in relat-ed spheres to combat discrimination, to alleviate poverty and to take other pos-itive measures.

Data Collected in Census

In February 2000 the Bulgarian Parliament passed the Law for Taking the Census of the Population, the Housing Fund and the Farms in the Republic of Bulgaria in 2001 (2001 Census Act). Under this Act the subjects of census are: 1) Bulgarian citizens, living in Bulgaria; 2) Bulgarian citizens, who went abroad after 29th of February 2000; 3) Bulgarian citizens who are abroad as agents of the Republic of Bulgaria; 4) foreigners constantly living in Bulgaria and having such status; 5) foreigners having refugee status; 6) Bulgarians living abroad who are in Bulgaria during the time of the census; 7) foreigners having permission to stay in Bulgaria; 8) foreigners who are subject to the procedures for getting refugee status; 9) housing fund in Bulgaria; and 10) agricultural fund in Bulgaria. The census was conducted from 1 to 14 March 2001.

The following important data were collected from the persons subject to cen-sus under article 5 of the act: name, ID number, age, address, citizenship, place of birth, family status, education, *ethnic group, religion, mother language*, employ-ment, profession, migration. The questions on the ethnic group, religion and mother tongue are the only optional ones. The interviewers were asked to instruct the respondents that they are not required to answer these questions. All the other questions had to be answered and the refusal to answer was punishable by a fine of 60 Leva (60 DM).

There are different census cards for collecting information about: 1) persons; 2) houses; 3) agricultural fund. The system of data collection during the census is compound. 1) There are "yes" or "no" answers to some questions; 2) A check-list is available to some questions; 3) The questions of ethnicity, religion and mother tongue had several options. "Ethnic group" had five possible answers: "Bulgarian," "Turkish," "Roma," "Other" and "not declared." The question on religion had seven options: "Eastern Orthodox," "Catholic," "Protestant," "Sunni Muslim," "Shi'a Muslim," "Other," and "not declared." The question on mother tongue had five options: "Bulgarian," "Turkish," "Romanes," "Other" and "not declared."

Although the law does not prohibit marking more than one ethnicity, accord-ing to the officials of the National Institute of Statistics the interviewers were instructed to mark only one option to the three questions under consideration. The authorities report persons who listed more than one ethnicity using the first one.

There are no other officially recognized ethnic groups under the Bulgarian system, than those that have decisions of the courts registering their organiza-tions. One such group in Bulgaria, the Macedonians, have met resistance by a number of courts in their attempts to register whatever organization. Nonetheless, Macedonians were able to register as such in the census under the option "other" to the questions of ethnic group and mother tongue. An official announcement of their current number is expected.

In 1993 the Parliament declared that the results of the 1992 census in the District of Blagoevgrad "does not reflect the demographic structure of the pop-ulation." The reason for this decision was the registration of more than 60 000 Bulgarian-speaking Muslims as "Turks" in the census with "Turkish" as their mother tongue. This had provoked protests from local Bulgarian nationalistic circles. No such event has followed the March 2001 census.

Official and Unofficial Data Collection
on Ethnicity Through Other Procedures

Information on ethnicity under crime prevention provisions is collected by law enforcement officials and the judicial bodies and is kept by the National Institute of Statistics. Data on ethnicity collected by the security services is col-lected and kept in their own databases. Data collected by the police and the judi-ciary are kept with a centralized register, which is maintained by the National Institute of Statistics. Data collected by security services is also stored and used centrally.

Authorities (police and the prosecutor's office) use non-census statistics on ethnicity in their regular reports on crime and crime prevention. Surveys of crime and sentenced people by ethnicity are conducted every year by the National Institute of Statistics and are published in a general publication on crime and sentenced people[48]Surveys, including data on ethnic, religious and linguistic groups are conducted by the NIS on the basis of the census data and are published in a number of publications, both general and by different profile (unemployment, disability etc.).[49]

There have been a number of publications of surveys, based on ethnic data, conducted by private research institutions dealing with economic status, interethnic and inter-religious relations, value orientations, voting behavior etc. by ethnicity and religion.[50]

Private entrepreneurs can use statistical data from the publications of the National Institute of Statistics. They can also purchase this information before publication. Under Article 26 of the Statistics Act, its transmission should not be individualized, however, and no violation of this provision is known to have taken place.

A number of non-state research institutions have done surveys on interethnic attitudes, on social conditions of some ethnic minorities, on religious practices etc. They have come up with statistical data collected in the course of their research. At least one dozen such institutions are known to have done this in the course of the last ten years. This data is usually based on representative samples of ethnic or religious minority population as well as on representative samples of the entire Bulgarian population. These research institutions are professional groups, their work is up to the universally accepted professional standards and, therefore, there is no doubt as to the representative character and the quality of the statistical data they have collected and published.

The code that is most widely used for data processing in Bulgaria by state authorities is the identifier number. Census data, however, is collected and kept by using both the identifier number and terminology describing the identity of the person who gave data on his/her ethnicity. Although there is no precise data,

48. See *Crime and Sentenced People*, annual publication of NIS (in Bulgarian).
49. The first comprehensive publication of NIS of the 1992 census data by ethnicity, religion and mother tongue was: NIS, *Results from the Population Census: Demographic Characteristics*, vol. 1 (in Bulgarian), Sofia; 1994.
50.See the English-language publications of some of them: Ilona Tomova, *Gypsies in the Period of Transition*, Sofia, IMIR, 1995; *Relations of Compatibility and incompatibility between the Christians and the Muslims in Bulgaria*, Sofia, IMIR, 1994; Krassimir Kanev, "Ethnic Identity, Interethnic Attitudes and Religiosity [of the Bulgarian Jews]" in: Baruh, Emmy (ed.), *Jews on the Bulgarian Lands*: Sofia: IMIR, 2001; Krassimir Kanev, "Changing Attitudes towards the ethnic minorities in Bulgaria and the Balkans 1992-97" in: *Ethnicity and Nationalism in East Central Europe and the Balkans*, Thanasis Sfikas and Christopher Williams (eds.), Ashgate: Aldershot etc., 1999; Krassimir Kanev, "Dynamics of Inter-ethnic tensions in Bulgaria and the Balkans" in: *Balkan Forum*, Vol.4, No.2 (15), June 1996; *Social integration of the Roma population in Bulgaria*, Report of the Anti Poverty Information Center, Sofia: UNDESA/UNDP, October 2000.

security services are also suspected of keeping data by using descriptive termi-nology. Private research institutions usually keep coded data.

In cases in which authorities keep data on ethnicity, they usually do so by using both proper nouns and qualifiers. Research institutions use as a rule only a qualifier.

When the Census Act was proposed, a number of organizations of ethnic minorities suggested filling in information on ethnic group, religion and moth-er tongue on a compulsory basis. The argument was that people from ethnic and religious minorities usually avoid stating their ethnicity and religion because of the social stigma and that, therefore, their number in the official census results will be less than the real one. Another argument targeted the uncertain recogni-tion of the Bulgarian state of ethnic diversity. Publication of the census results will thus prove the existence of ethnic and religious minorities in Bulgaria.

According to Article 17 of the Statistics Act, the census in Bulgaria is taken by the National Institute of Statistics. The provision does not require the involvement of the organizations of ethnic minorities. Development of the methodology is a task of the staff of the institute, which usually consults with other government agencies and possibly also with organizations of some ethnic minorities. Organizations of ethnic minorities are usually not consulted. The 2001 Census Act provides for the establishment of a temporary National Census Committee to implement the act. It is appointed by the Director of the National Institute of Statistics and usually consists of institute employees. There is no provision that ethnic minorities are recruited as members of the Census Committee. Ethnic minorities can take part in the census as interviewers. They are selected by the regional statistical offices. There usually is some, although very limited, number of people from ethnic minorities working as interviewers. There is no involvement of ethnic minorities in the process of storage and use of data after the census. Ethnic minorities are not involved in the other instances of ethnic data collection either (collection of ethnic data by the judiciary, the police, or the security services).

III. Methods and Means Used for Collecting and Processing Data Relating to Minorities

The census is primarily conducted by collecting data from the subjects. In exceptional cases data are collected from the families. These cases are precisely enumerated by law: when data subjects are not present for some time, minors' data, data of prisoners and army soldiers, etc. The interviewer knows the identity of the respondent and the circumstances of such exceptional cases are indicated in the statistical card.

The police and the judiciary officers collect ethnic data on crime prevention through filling in the Statistical Form 1-CC. It is filled in by the law enforcement or the judicial officer obligatory, with or without consultation of the defendant.

Security services collect ethnic data by all possible means — both direct and indirect. It is not clear whether they have access to personal data from existing databases (in any event, it would be illegal).

Private research/civil society groups collect ethnic data in a variety of ways — through direct interviews, through observation of secondary sources — case files, government documents etc. Some non-governmental organizations use personal data from persons other than the data subject. Both research institutions and civil society groups use available statistical data, data derived or aggregated from other available data, as well as data based on estimations.

Potential data subjects are reached in different ways in the different instances of data collection. The census is taken in Bulgaria on the basis of households. According to Article 25 of the 2001 Census of Population Act, the census taker must visit all inhabited buildings in his/her census region. He/she obtains data on the buildings from the municipal authorities, which are required to cooperate in the census. The interviewer is not supposed to have the names of the inhabitants of the buildings in advance.

Ethnic data for crime prevention purposes is taken directly from the criminal defendant at the place of his/her detention or at the court where he/she appears.

Ethnic data by security services is taken in a variety of ways, including direct interviews, from intermediaries, documents and other indirect means.

Research institutions usually buy samples of population from the National Institute of Statistics. These samples contain names and addresses but no other statistical data. Transmitting names and addresses is apparently not considered to be a violation of Articles 25 and 26 of the Statistics Act. On the other hand, the act itself allows the NIS to sell its products. There are several methods by which research institutions reach people from ethnic and/or religious minorities. The first one is through a general sample of population, big enough to ensure that sufficient numbers of members of at least the bigger ethnic/religious minorities will be included to make their sub-sample representative. Members of these minorities are determined in the course of the interview through self-identification. The second method is to make a booster-sample of the general sample in the regions with mixed (Bulgarian-Turkish) population. The method of determination of the members of ethnic minorities is the same as the above. The third method used is the quota sample. It is made in the work with Roma and some other minorities and includes selection of certain numbers of Roma on the basis of regional and demographic characteristics typical for this minority, which are not the subject of the study. In this case ethnicity could be determined either by the interviewer or by the interviewee. A fourth method that has been used includes the use of databases of some minority organizations. In the case of the Bulgarian Jews, their organization has a database that pretends to include every Jewish person in Bulgaria. On the basis of this initial information a sample is made and the research conducted.

Information privacy/data protection in the course of research by private insti-tutions is ensured through the fact that information is usually not individualized. There is, however, no law forbidding individualizing information in the course of such research.

Ensuring Data Quality and Compatibility

Data on ethnic identity coming from the censuses in Bulgaria has never been reliable as to general numbers, regional distributions and shares. The main rea-son is the fact that some ethnic minorities (for the most part Roma) indicate other preferred identity when asked to voluntarily declare their identity because of the social stigma and discrimination associated with their minority group membership. In addition, the NIS changed the methodology during the last (March 2001) census, which made recent data incomparable with that from the 1992 census with regard to general numbers. Statistics in the criminal justice sys-tem are more reliable as they have been based on the same methodology over a long period of time.

Surveys on ethnic relations that are conducted periodically in Bulgaria use the same methodology when they are conducted by the same institutions. This is the main guarantee of their compatibility. Comparison of data obtained through the use of different methodologies is also possible if one uses the requisite amount of caution.

Ethnic Statistics and Data Protection:
The Czech Case

Barbora Bukovska (Kvocekova)

In the Czech Republic, the issue of collection of race and ethnic statistics and the issue of data protection has proved enormously controversial. Collection of information about, and identified with, individuals existed for decades during the communist regime. The fall of communism and the arising awareness regarding the rights of minorities, however, have brought with them concern about personal and social implications of the existence of such databases. Moreover, these databases being now in digital form can be rapidly searched, instantly distributed, and seamlessly combined with other data sources to generate ever more comprehensive records of individuals.

Czech Roma have been especially sensitive about the existence of ethnic statistics due to the negative repercussions they suffered during the Nazi regime during World War II or, more recently, when on the basis of available ethnic data their rights were abused. Till very recently[1] these concerns were especially present due to a lack of adequate legal norms that would protect individuals from abuse of their personal data. A number of high profile scandals involving abuse of personal information could be mentioned here. In 1992, for example, the Interior Ministry sold the addresses of all children under the age of two and all women between 15 and 35 — a total of two million people — to Procter & Gamble. The company used the information for a direct marketing campaign for Pampers diapers and Always brands. One official was charged with violating the law. In 1995, Prague City Police Chief Rudolf Bla_ek admitted that city police employees had access to information about criminal suspects that was legally available only to the Czech Republic Police.[2] In 1996, a black-market CD-ROM that listed all telephone numbers in the Czech Republic, including President Vaclav Havel's home number, appeared on the market. A poll conducted in January 1997 found that seventy-nine percent of Czechs cite undisturbed priva-

---

1. The Law on Protection of Personal Data in Information Systems No. 256/1992 Coll. that was the only data protection law in force till June 1, 2000 was highly ineffective. Although it established certain rules on data processing, it did not include any sanctions and thus, was unable to enforce compliance with the law.
2. Tomas Kellner "Information Protection Laws Must Be Passed Now" *The Prague Post* January 11, 1995.

cy as a top personal priority[3] while one released in October 1998 found that seventy-five percent believe that their personal data is misused and two thirds consider data protection a serious problem.[4]

The EU has been putting pressure on the Czech Republic to move more quickly in adopting new legislation in the field. In February 1998, the European Commission set as a "medium term goal" for the Czech Republic, as part of its accession to the Union, the establishment of an independent body for supervision of data protection[5]. In November 1998, the Commission was critical of the slow pace of adopting a new data protection law[6] and in April 1999, the European Parliament issued a resolution urging the Czech Republic to put more effort into adopting a new law on data protection. Legislative developments during the last year resulted in comprehensive legislation on data protection, but despite the improvement of the legislative framework violations of personal data remain a concern. The law has provided for significant exceptions to a number of public agencies, law enforcement and intelligence agencies, leaving thus significant gaps in the overall protection of personal data. Finally, without adequate oversight and enforcement, the mere existence of a law may not be sufficient to provide individuals with adequate protection.

At the same time, due to constitutional restrictions the Czech Republic is lacking accurate and objective data on the size of various minority populations. This fact is often used by governmental officials as an excuse not to deal with problems that ethnic minorities are facing. On the other hand international organizations, such as the Council of Europe, the Organization for Security and Cooperation in Europe or the European Commission, require the Czech government to provide information concerning Roma and the abuse of their human rights.

This paper provides an overview of the issue of ethnic statistics in the Czech Republic. When discussing the concerns about ethnic statistics, it deals almost solely with data connected to the Roma minority, a minority that is practically the only visible ethnic minority in the country. Under Czech law, Roma are considered a national minority. This paper however will use instead of the term "nationality" the term "ethnicity."

---

3. "Undisturbed Privacy Top Priority-Poll" *CTK National News Wire* January 23, 1997.
4. "Most People Believe that their Personal Data is Misused — Poll" *CTK National News Wire* October 6, 1998.
5. E.U. Enlargement "What the Accession Agreements Contain, Country by Country" *European Report*, February 11, 1998, pp. 2290.
6. Quentin Peel „E.U. Warns Applicants on Slow Preparations", *Financial Times*, November 5, 1998, pp. 3.

I. Legal Framework

Constitutional Protection

The provisions of the Czech Constitution[7], the Charter on Basic Rights and Fundamental Freedoms[8] and other documents on human rights have *formally* guaranteed the right to equal treatment, rights to privacy and protection of personal data and other relevant rights in the Czech Republic from early 1990s. Relevant constitutional provisions are:

– Article 1 of the Charter (which forms part of the Czech Constitution), guaranteeing the equality of all;
– Article 3 of the Charter, prohibiting the discrimination on any grounds and the right to choose one's nationality[9];
– Article 4 paragraph 3 of the Charter, securing equal treatment under the law [10];
– Article 7 paragraph 1 of the Charter, guaranteeing the protection of private life[11];
– Article 10 of the Charter declares the right to protection of one's good reputation and prohibits unauthorized collection and misuse of personal data [12];
– Article 17 of the Charter guarantees the right to free access to information[13];

---

7. The Law No. 1/1993 of the Coll., the Constitution of the Czech Republic.
8. The Law No.2/1993 of the Coll. Charter in the following.
9. Article 3 of the Charter reads:
"(1) Everyone is guaranteed the enjoyment of her fundamental rights and basic freedoms without regard to gender, race, color of skin, language, faith and religion, political or other conviction, national or social origin, membership in a national or ethnic minority, property, birth, or other status.
"(2) Everybody has the right freely to choose his nationality. It is prohibited to influence this choice in any way, just as is any form of pressure aimed at suppressing a person's national identity.
10. "(3) Any statutory limitation upon the fundamental rights and basic freedoms must apply in the same way to all cases that meet the specified conditions."
11. Article 7 paragraph 1 of the Charter reads: "The inviolability of the person and of her private life is guaranteed. They may be limited only in cases provided for by law."
12. Article 10 of the Charter reads:
"(1) Everyone has the right to demand that his human dignity, personal honor, and good reputation be respected, and that his name be protected.
"(2) Everyone has the right to be protected from any unauthorized intrusion into her private and family life.
"(3) Everyone has the right to be protected from the unauthorized gathering, public disclosure, or other misuse of his personal data."
13. Article 17 of the Charter reads:
"(1) The freedom of expression and the right to information are guaranteed.
"(2) Everyone has the right to express his views orally, in writing, in the press, in pictures, or in any other form, as well as freely to seek, receive, and disseminate ideas and information irrespective of the frontiers of the state.
"(3) Censorship is not permitted.

- Articles 24 and 25 of the Charter proclaim the protection of the rights of national and ethnic minorities[14];
- Article 36 of the Charter, stipulating the right of persons to pursue their rights before independent and impartial courts, the right to seek damages and the right to request legal review of the activity of public authorities[15];
- and Article 10 of the Czech Constitution[16] that provides for the direct applicability of international instruments to which the Czech Republic is a party and their precedence over national legislation.

Nevertheless, until recently there was no appropriate legal instrument to set the conditions and detailed procedures for the enforcement of these rights. Especially the protection of minorities from discrimination is still formulated inadequately by Czech statutory law; it lacks necessary sanctions and effective remedies to the victims of discrimination.[17]

"(4) The freedom of expression and the right to seek and disseminate information may be limited by law in the case of measures that are necessary in a democratic society for protecting the rights and freedoms of others, the security of the state, public security, public health, or morals."
"(5) State bodies and territorial self-governing bodies are obliged, in an appropriate manner, to pro-vide information with respect to their activities. Conditions therefor and the implementation there-of shall be provided for by law."
14. Article 24 of the Charter reads: "A person's affiliation with any national or ethnic minority group may not be to her detriment." And Article 25:
"(1) Citizens who constitute a national or ethnic minority are guaranteed all-round development, in particular, the right to develop, together with other members of the minority, their own culture, the right to disseminate and receive information in their native language, and the right to associate in national associations. Detailed provisions shall be set down by law.
"(2) Citizens belonging to national and ethnic minority groups are also guaranteed, under the con-ditions set down by law:
a) the right to education in their own language,
b) the right to use their own language when dealing with officials,
c) the right to participate in the resolution of affairs that concern national and ethnic minorities."
15. Article 36 of the Charter reads:
"(1) Everyone may assert, through the legally prescribed procedure, his rights before an independent and impartial court or, in specified cases, before another body.
"(2) Unless a law provides otherwise, a person who claims that her rights were curtailed by a deci-sion of a public administrative authority may turn to a court for review of the legality of that deci-sion. However, judicial review of decisions affecting the fundamental rights and basic freedoms list-ed in this Charter may not be removed from the jurisdiction of courts.
"(3) Everybody is entitled to compensation for damage caused him by an unlawful decision of a court, other state bodies, or public administrative authorities, or as the result of an incorrect official procedure.
"(4) Conditions therefor and detailed provisions shall be set by law."
16. Article 10 of the Constitution reads: "International treaties concerning human rights and funda-mental freedoms which have been duly ratified and promulgated and by which the Czech Republic is bound are directly applicable and take precedence over statutes."
17. ECRI Second Report on the Czech Republic mentions that the rights and freedoms guaranteed by the Charter apply equally "to all irrespective of sex, race, color of skin, language, faith, religion, political or other opinion, national or social origin" and "this principle can also be found in other statutes, including the Civil Code and the Penal Code" it concludes that" little legislation has been adopted so far to implement these constitutional provisions." (*ECRI Second Report on the Czech Republic*, paragraph 2).

The specific legislation regulating the protection of personal data is repre-sented by Law No. 101 from April 4, 2000 on Protection of Personal Data and on Amendments to Some Related Laws[18] that entered into force on June 1, 2000.[19] The Act regulates the protection of personal data of natural persons[20] and applies to all personal data, regardless of whether it is processed automatically or in another way.[21] It covers the processing and handling of data by both public and private entities unless provided for differently by the Data Protection Law or other law.[22]

The exceptions under the Data Protection Law are defined on material basis and on the basis of entities handling the data. On *material basis*, the Data Protection law excludes:

- data processing which is executed by a natural person exclusively for his or her needs[23];
- random personal data collection, provided that such data is not further processed[24];
- processing of the personal data for statistical and archival purposes[25] that are regulated by specific laws.[26]

On the *basis of entities handling the data*, the Data Protection Law does not apply in specific provisions[27] to the processing of personal data by[28]:

- the intelligence services[29];
- the Police of the Czech Republic, including the National Center of Interpol of the Police of the Czech Republic while detecting criminal acts[30];

18. Data Protection Law in the following.
19. Except Articles 16, 17 and 35 which entered into force on December 1, 2000.
20. See Article 1 of the Data Protection Law.
21. See Article 3 paragraph 2 of the Data Protection Law.
22. Ibid. at paragraph 1.
23. Ibid. at paragraph 3.
24. Ibid. at paragraph 4.
25. Ibid. at paragraph 5.
26. The Law No. 89/1995 Coll., on the State Statistical Service; the Law No. 158/1999 Coll., on Census of Citizens, Houses and Flats in 2001; the Law No. 97/1974 Coll., on Archives, as amended by the Law No. 343/1992 Coll.
27. In obligations under Articles 5, 9, 11, 16 and 27 of the Data Protection Laws. These provisions relate in general to the obligations of the data controller in processing personal data, including sen-sitive data, obligation to inform the data subject concerning the processing of data connected to him and obligation to register.
28. See Article 3 paragraph 6 of the Data Protection Law.
29. The Law No. 153/1994 Coll., on Intelligence Service of the Czech Republic, as amended by the Law No. 118/1995 Coll.
30. The Law No. 283/1991 Coll., on the Police of the Czech Republic, as subsequently amended.

- the Ministry of Finance within the framework of the financial and analytical activity according to a specific law[31];
- the National Security Office when executing a security screening according to a specific law[32];
- the Ministry of Interior upon issuing certificates under a specific law, upon issuing covert documents and in the activity of the Inspection Division of the Ministry of Interior.[33]

As for the level of protection, the Data Protection Law recognizes two types of data:

- personal data with general protection and
- sensitive data to which it guarantees greater levels of protection.

According to Article 4(a) data is considered *personal data* if relating to an identified or identifiable data subject. A data subject is considered to be identified or identifiable if his or her identity may be directly or indirectly ascertained on the basis of one or more items of the personal data. If a disproportionate quantity of time, effort or material resources are required to determine the identity of the data subject, data is not considered to be personal data anymore.

The condition for the lawful handling and processing of personal data is the consent of the data subject. Without such consent, data might be processed only:

- for statistical or scientific purposes. In these cases, the data must be made anonymous as soon as possible and the protection against abuse of the data has to be ensured[34];
- if the controller is processing the data based on a specific law or if the controller is required to comply with the duties set by a specific law[35];
- if it is essential in order for the data subject to enter into negotiations over a contractual relationship or in order that the data subject can comply

31. The Law No. 61/1996 Coll., on Certain Measures against Legalization of Proceeds from Criminal Activity and on Amendments and Changes of Some Related Laws, as amended by the Law No. 15/1998 Coll.
32. The Law No. 148/1998 Coll., on Protection of Classified Information and on Amendments of Some Related Laws, as subsequently amended.
33. Law No. 451/1991 Coll. Specifying Some Additional Prerequisites for the Performance of Certain Positions in State Authorities and Organizations of the Czech and Slovak Federal Republic, the Czech Republic and the Slovak Republic as subsequently amended. Law No. 279/1992 Coll. on Some Additional Prerequisites for the Performance of Certain Positions Filled in on the Basis of Assignment or Appointment of Officers of the Police of the Czech Republic and of the Correctional Service Corps of the Czech Republic, as subsequently amended.
34. See the Article 5 paragraph 4 of the Data Protection Law.
35. E.g. Act No. 111/1998 Coll., on Universities and on Changes and Amendments of other Acts (the Universities Act); Act No. 564/1990 Coll., on the State Administration and Self-administration in Education, as Subsequently Amended; Act No. 153/1994 Coll., as Amended by Act No. 118/1995 Coll. and Act No. 61/1996 Coll., as Amended by Act No. 15/1998 Coll.

with the arrangements arising from agreements concluded with the controller;
- if it is essential, *inter alia*, for the protection of important interests of the
data subject. In such a case consent of the data subject must be obtained
without undue delay and if he or she does not consent, the controller must
terminate the processing and destroy the data;
- in cases when the personal data has been justifiably published pursuant to a
specific Act.[36] Even is this case the right to the protection of private and personal life of the data subject should be respected;
- if it is essential for the protection of the rights of the controller; however,
such personal data processing may not be in contradiction with the data
subject's right to protect his or her private and personal life.

The legislation is giving stricter protection to a specific category of personal
data, namely to *sensitive data*. Sensitive data is personal data referring to nationality, racial and/or ethnic origin, political attitudes, membership in political parties and/or movements, or trade union or employee organizations, religious or
other convictions, criminal activity, health condition, and sexual orientation of
the data subject.[37] The law sets a general prohibition to process sensitive data
unless one of the below conditions is met[38]:

- the data subject has granted explicit consent to such processing. The consent must be granted in writing, signed by the data subject and must clearly specify the data with respect of which the consent is being granted. It
must also specify to which controller, for what purpose and what period of
time the consent is being granted, and by whom it is being granted. The
consent may be revoked at any time
- it is unavoidable in order to preserve the life or health of the data subject
or of another person or to ward off an immediate danger threatening to
their property. If the consent cannot be obtained, especially due to lack of
physical, mental or legal capacity of data subject, or if he is missing or in
other similar cases. The controller is obligated to terminate the data processing as soon as the mentioned reasons cease to exist and has to destroy
the data, unless the data subject grants his or her consent for further processing;
- in the case of providing health care[39] or another examination of the health

36. Act No. 81/1966 Coll., on the Periodical Press and Other Media of Mass Information, as subsequently amended.
37. See Article 4 (b) of the Data Protection Law.
38. See Article 9 of the Data Protection Law.
39. Act No. 20/1966 Coll., on the Care of the People's Health, as subsequently amended.

condition of the data subject pursuant to a specific Act, especially for social security purposes[40] or if a specific law[41] provides for it.

The Data Protection Law generally provides the conditions for the handling of data by both public and private entities. At the same time, the law provides significant exemptions only for the public institutions that are not subjected to the same obligations as other — mostly private — institutions.

Handling of data by public administration is also governed by a special law, the Law on Information Systems in Public Administration.[42] The law does not cover the information systems of certain entities that are governed by special laws.[43] Those entities are authorized to establish the rules by their internal norms.

Right to Free Access to Information

The Czech legislation contains provisions allowing free access to public information. However, the Law on Free Access to Information[44] does not apply to the protection of personal data.

Protection of Privacy

The Civil Code[45] stipulates the protection of personality in its Article 11 when guaranteeing a natural person's right to protection of her personality, particularly the protection of her life and health, civic honor and human dignity and privacy, her name and manifestation of personal nature.

The Criminal Code[46] covers the infringement of the right to privacy in the definitions of criminal acts of infringement of the home[47], slander[48], infringe-

---

40. E.g. Law No. 582/1991 Coll., on Organization and Implementation of the Social Security, as subsequently amended.
41. E.g. Law No. 48/1997 Coll., on Public Health Insurance and on Changes and Amendments of Some Related Acts, as subsequently amended; Law No. 280/1992 Coll., on Ministry, Branch, Undertaking and Other Health Insurance Companies, as subsequently amended; Law No. 551/1992 Coll., on the General Health Insurance Company of the Czech Republic, as subsequently amended; and Law No. 158/1999 Coll.
42. Act 65/2000 from September 14, 2000.
43. Those are: information services, Police of the Czech Republic, Ministry of Finance, National Office for Security and the Ministry of Defense.
44. The Law No. 106/1999 of the Coll., the Law on Free Access to Information, as Subsequently Amended.
45. The Law No. 40/1964 of the Coll., the Civil Code as subsequently amended.
46. The Law 140/1961 of the Coll., the Criminal Code as subsequently amended.
47. See Article 238 of the Criminal Code.
48. See Article 206 of the Criminal Code.

ment of the confidentiality of mail[49] and unauthorized processing of personal data.[50] Wiretapping is regulated under the criminal process law.[51] Police must obtain permission from a judge to conduct wiretapping. The judge can approve an initial order for up to six months. There are special rules for intelligence services.

Special Laws

There is a number of sectoral acts in the Czech Republic concerning statistics, medical personal data, banking data, data on taxpayers, social security and police data.[52]

Rights to Access to Data

In the Czech legislation, the right of access to personal data can be derived from the provisions of Article 12.2 of the Data Protection Law. The Article imposes the obligation of the controller to provide the data subject, upon written request, with information on the personal data being processed about the data subject. Such information should be provided free of charge only once in a calendar year, otherwise any time for a reasonable compensation not exceeding the cost incurred for the provision of the information. The controller is not obliged to proceed in this way if the Data Protection Law or other law stipulate so.[53]

49. See Article 239 of the Criminal Code.
50. See Article 178 of the Criminal Code.
51. Law No. 141/1961 of the Coll., the Criminal Procedure Law, Article 88.
52. For example: Law No. 89/1995 Coll., Law on State Statistical Service; Law No. 97/1974 Coll., Law on Archives; Law No. 148/1998 Coll. on Protection of Secret Circumstances and on the Amendment of Some Laws, as subsequently amended; Law No. 451/1991 of the Coll. on Establishing Some Other Requirements for Execution of Function in State Authorities of the Czech and Slovak Federal Republic, as subsequently amended; Law No. 279/1992 Coll. on Establishing Some Other Requirements for Execution of Functions Appointed as Members of Police Forces of the Czech Republic, as subsequently amended; Law No. 111/1998 of the Coll., the Law on Universities, as subsequently amended; Law No. 81/1966 of the Coll. on Periodical Press and Other Media, as subsequently amended; Law on Public Health reference needed; Law No. 582/1991 of the Coll. on Organization and Administration of Social Security; Law No. 48/1997 of the Coll. on Public Health Insurance, as subsequently amended; Law No. 551/1991 of the Coll. on General Public Insurance of the Czech Republic; Law No. 21/1992 of the Coll. on Banks; Law No. 513/1991 of the Coll., the Commercial Code, as subsequently amended; Law No. 552/1991 of Coll. on State Control; Law No. 337/1992 of Coll. on Administration of Taxes and Fees; and others.
53. Exceptions apply for example according to the Law No. 153/1994 from July 7, 1994 on Reporting Services of the Czech Republic, Law No. 61/1996 Coll., on Certain Measures against Legalization of Procedures from Criminal Activity and on the Amendments and Changes of Some Related Laws, as amended by Law No. 15/1998 Coll.; Law No. 283/1991 Coll. from June 21, 1991 on Police Forces of the Czech Republic; or the Law No. 154/1994 Coll. from July 7, 1994 on Security Information Service.

Moreover, according to the Article 11.1 of the Data Protection law the controller is obliged to notify the data subject in a timely and duly manner of the fact
that data is being collected about her, the scope of the data and the purpose of
the data collection and handling, who will be further processing the data and for
what purpose, to whom the data may be disclosed, or for whom the data are designated. The seat of the data controller's office or if appropriate the seat of the
processor's office[54] shall also be included in such notifications. At the same time,
the controller must notify the data subject concerning the right to access to the
personal data as well as on other rights stipulated in Article 21 of the Data
Protection Law.[55] These obligations do not apply to cases of processing the data
exclusively for statistical, scientific or archival purposes, or if the controller is
processing the data based on stipulation of the law or if a special law stipulates
that the controller is not obliged to provide the personal data.[56]

As far as access to other persons' data, including the right of access to information about communities or other groups, is concerned in general, the Data
Protection Law does not recognize the right of access to the data kept on other
persons. The controller and processor of the personal data must ensure that the
data subject's rights will not be breached, in particular the right to preserve human
dignity; and must ensure that the data subject's private and personal life are protected from unjustifiable intervention.[57] At the same time, they are obliged to
adopt measures that will prevent any unauthorized or accidental access to the personal data; alteration, destruction or loss, unauthorized transmissions, unauthorized processing, or other abuse of the personal data. This obligation extends even
for the period after termination of the processing of the personal data.[58]

However, access to certain personal data is permitted under special laws, for
example the Law on Register of Inhabitants[59] and the Law on Criminal
Register.[60]

Under the Law on the Register of Inhabitants, ministries, district offices and
municipalities are providing data from their systems to an extent required by the
special law and to the extent necessary for the fulfillment of their tasks.
Moreover, data are provided if the activity of a state institution or the institution
delegated by the state requires them.[61] Recipients of such data from information

54. Article 11 paragraph 1 of the Data Protection Law.
55. Article 11 paragraph 3 of the Data Protection Law.
56. Article 11 paragraph 5 of the Data Protection Law.
57. Article 10 of the Data Protection Law.
58. See Article 13 of the Data Protection Law.
59. Law No. 133/2000 of Coll. on Register of Inhabitants and on Birth Numbers and concerning the
Amendment of Certain Laws (the Law on Register of Inhabitants).
60. Law No. 269/1994 of the Coll.on Criminal Register.
61. Article 8 paragraph 1 of the Law on Register of Inhabitants.

systems, according to special law, are not allowed to gather, transfer and use data outside of the scope of such a special law[62] and are obliged to secure the data from accidental access, illegitimate access or processing.[63]

Information from the criminal register can be provided only to the subject of data on his/her request and upon an identity check.[64] The information can be otherwise provided only upon request of the court for purposes of other criminal procedures, for procedures other than criminal and to another state administration institution in a procedure on misdemeanors. For other reasons, the criminal register transcript can be provided only if a special law allows so.[65]

Right to Correction or Cancellation of Personal Data

Individuals have a right to the correction and cancellation of data kept on them in case the controller or processor of data breached its obligations of processing the data.[66] The law does not set any differences in this respect with regard to the type of the data. The individual can not only request the correction or completion of data in order to make it authentic and accurate or the blocking or destruction of the personal data; but may also seek financial compensation if her right to human dignity, personal honor, good reputation or the right to protect her name was violated.[67] This right applies *mutatis mutandis* to cases when the data was collected without authorization.[68]

The data must always be destroyed after the expiry of the time period that is necessary for the purpose of its processing. After expiry of this period, the personal data may be kept solely for statistical, scientific and archival purposes; even for these purposes, it is necessary to protect from unauthorized infringement the right to private and personal life of the data subject.

However, the right to demand blocking[69] or destruction[70] of personal data cannot be sought in cases when the controller is obliged to process the personal data pursuant to a specific law or if failing to process could result in a detriment to the rights of third parties.[71] Moreover, in cases where the right to demand the

---

62. See Article 8 paragraph 1(a) of the Law on Register of Inhabitants.
63. See Article 8 paragraph 1(b) of the Law on Register of Inhabitants.
64. Article 11 paragraph 1 of the Law on Criminal Register.
65. Compare Article 12 of the Law on Criminal Register.
66. Article 21 paragraph 1 of the Data Protection Law.
67. Article 21 paragraph 2 of the Data Protection Law.
68. Article 26 of the Data Protection Law.
69. According to Article 4 (h), blocking personal data means establishing that condition upon which the personal data shall be inaccessible for a certain period of time and may not be otherwise processed.
70. According to Article 4 (i), destruction of personal data means the physical destruction of the data, physical deletion of the data or permanent exclusion of the data from further processing.
71. Article 22 of the Data Protection Law.

correction or cancellation of data applies, the law is lacking the deadlines in which such measures should be conducted.

Data Transfer and Transmission of Data to Other Countries

Data transmission is in detail regulated only for the transmission of data between the institutions of public administration. The public administration bodies can transfer the data kept in a system administered by them only to anoth - er public administration authority, and only for justified reasons and to the extent necessary. They are obliged to transfer the data exclusively via reference margins.[72]

As for transmission to other countries, personal data may be transferred only if the national legislation of the country where the personal data is to be processed correspond to the requirements stipulated by the Czech Data Protection Law. Otherwise, the transmission of the personal data can be carried out only:

- with the consent of, or on the basis of an instruction of, the data subjects [73];
- in case it is essential for the protection of the data subject's rights or inter - ests[74];
- in cases when the personal data are part of public registers or registers accessible to everyone who proves a legal interest; nevertheless, this shall apply only to the individually determined data or pieces of the data [75];
- if the transfer ensues from an international treaty which is binding for the Czech Republic[76];
- if the transfer is necessary for the conclusion or performance of a contract between the data subject and the controller or of a contract which is being concluded in the interest of the data subject[77];
- if it is essential for protecting the life of or providing health care to the data subject[78];
- in other cases, if it is done for the benefit of the data subject and if it is accompanied by a bilateral contract between the controller and the recipi - ent that the recipient shall secure the required personal data protection. [79]

---

72. See Article 5 paragraph 2(g) of Law No. 365/2000 of the Coll.
73. See Article 27 paragraph 2 (a) of the Data Protection Law.
74. Ibid. letter (b).
75. Ibid. letter (c).
76. Ibid. letter (d).
77. Ibid. letter (e).
78. Ibid. letter (f).
79. See Article 27 paragraph 3 of the Data Protection Law.

The controller is obliged to apply to the Data Protection Office for single or multiple authorizations for transferring personal data to other countries. The Office shall decide on the application without delay, within 7 calendar days at the latest. If the Office fails to make a decision within this period, it is presumed that the Office gave consent to the transfer of the personal data for the period stated in the application. If there is danger in the delay of the transfer, the Office should issue its ruling immediately. Appeals against the ruling do not have suspending effect.

Independent Supervision Over Data Protection

In the Czech Republic, there is no special supervisory body for protection of data on minorities as such. There is no body with executive power responsible for the protection of national minorities either.

A supervisory body for the protection of personal data, the Office of Data Protection[80] was established by the Data Protection Law and started its activities on July 1, 2000 (with the exception of the registration of controllers that started on December 1, 2000). The Office had to face several difficulties at the begin - ning of its activity. In a very short time, it was supposed to hire a qualified staff with the relatively low salaries characteristic of state administration in general. Another problematic task was to start the registration of controllers and to assure that corrections are pursued in illegally kept data systems.

The Office is an independent state agency[81], interference with its activity is only possible on the basis of the law. The institution is covered by a special chap - ter of the state budget of the Czech Republic.[82] The Office is managed by a chairman who is appointed for a period of five years and recalled by the President of the Czech Republic based on a proposal of the Senate of the Parliament of the Czech Republic.[83]

The Office's main tasks are[84]:

- to supervise the fulfillment of obligations stipulated by the Data Protection Law in the course of personal data handling;
- to register data controllers under the Data Protection Law. A registration or a revocation must be published in the Office Bulletin no later than with - in 2 months, unless a specific law requires that the registration or the revo - cation shall not be officially published. A notification on registration or

80. The Office in the following.
81. See Article 28 paragraph 1 of the Data Protection Law.
82. Ibid paragraph 2 and 3.
83. See Article 32 paragraph 1 of the Data Protection Law.
84. See Article 29 paragraph 1 of the Data Protection Law.

revocation may also be published by the Office in other suitable manners[85];
- to investigate citizens' complaints with regards to breaches of the Data Protection Law;
- to prepare annual reports of its activity and make it available to the public;
- to exercise other tasks mandated to it by law;
- to investigate misdemeanors and other administrative offenses and impose penalties pursuant to the Data Protection Law;
- to secure fulfillment of requirements ensuing from relevant international treaties which are binding for the Czech Republic;
- to provide consultations in the field of personal data protection;
- to co-operate with similar supervisory authorities in other countries.

The Office is publishing the Office Bulletin and its employees are obliged to keep confidentiality concerning the information they have access to throughout the execution of their tasks.

Another somewhat similar body in the Czech Republic is the Office for Public Information Systems established by the Law on the Information Systems of Public Administration[86] in order to supervise the activities and services of public administration authorities in the realm. The task of this office is to supervise certain rules on how data are handled in state institutions. These are mostly technical requirements and forms prescribed for the processing of data.

Public Register of Personal Data Controllers

There is no centralized register where individuals could review the data kept on them by various institutions. There is only a register of authorized data controllers kept by the Data Protection Office. Under the Data Protection Law, whoever intends to handle personal data is required to register with the Office in writing, prior to commencing the collection of personal data. The registration obligation does not cover[87] those who maintain publicly accessible registers and those who process data based on obligations imposed on them by special laws.[88]

The controller is also obliged to notify the Office if intending to change the personal data processing.[89] These requests are all recorded in the Register.

---

85. See Article 35 paragraph 2 of the Data Protection Law.
86. Law No. 365/2000.
87. See Article 18 of the Data Protection Law.
88. See for example Law No. 153/1994 Coll.; Law No. 61/1996 Coll., as Subsequently Amended; Law No. 283/1991 Coll., as subsequently amended; and Law No. 158/1999 Coll.
89. See Article 16 paragraph 1 of the Data Protection Law.

The register is publicly accessible, with the exception of information on the manner of processing data and the information on measures taken for required protection of personal data.[90]

Sanctions

Sanctions for abuses in processing of personal data are established in criminal and administrative law.

Criminal Law: the amendment to Criminal Code on 10 November 1993 introduced a new crime, that of unauthorized handling of personal data, under Article 178. Its crucial part reads: "Whoever shall, be it through negligence, unjustifiably disclose, make accessible, otherwise process or appropriate personal data on another person, data collected for purposes of public administration, shall be punished by imprisonment of up to three years or by injunction or by a financial penalty." Similarly, sanctions are established for those who reveal or make public personal data obtained in execution of their employment, work or function, and who break the obligation of confidentiality established by the law.[91] A prison sentence of up to two years or prohibition of activity or a fine will be given to those who cause by such an act serious harm; or if the act is committed through press, film, broadcasting or television or other similar manner or if he breaches his functions within the employment.[92]

Article 178 provides sanctions for abuses committed in both the public and the private sphere.

Public officials will also be sanctioned in case of abuse of power by a public official.[93]

Administrative Law sanctions are established by the Data Protection Law. Three types of sanctions are established for data controllers and processors: sanctions for committing a misdemeanor, disciplinary sanctions and fines.

If *misdemeanor* is committed:
   a) by a person who is in employment or a similar relationship with the data controller or the processor, or who carries out activities on behalf of the data controller or the processor on the basis of an agreement, or a person who, as a part of fulfilling legally mandated competencies and obligations, comes into contact with the controller or processor if he breaches the obligation to maintain confidentiality stipulated by the Data Protection

---

90. The Data Protection Law in its Article 16 set the requirements for the registration.
91. See Article 178 paragraph 2 of the Criminal Code.
92. Ibid. in paragraph 3
93. Regulated by the provisions of Article 158 and 159 of the Criminal Law.

Law, the sanction is a fine up to 50,000 CZK[94];

b) by a person mentioned above when breaching another obligation stipulated by the Data Protection Law, the sanction is a fine up to 25,000 CZK.[95]

Hearings on misdemeanors are governed by the Law on Misdemeanors.[96] The authority competent to process the hearings is the Data Protection Office.

Disciplinary penalty may be imposed, even repeatedly, on a person who does not conform to the Data Protection Office's supervisory activity. The penalty consists of a fine of up to 25,000 CZK.[97]

Sanctions to data controllers and processors can also take the form of fines ranging:

a) 10,000,000 CZK to a controller and/or a processor who breaches the obligations stipulated by the Data Protection Law[98];

b) 20,000,000 CZK to a controller and/or a processor who repeatedly breaches the obligation stipulated by the Data Protection Law within one year from the day when the first decision of imposing a penalty came into force[99];

c) 1,000,000 CZK to a controller and/or a processor who obstructs the supervision executed by the Data Protection Office.[100]

The fine may be imposed within one year from the day when the respective authority ascertained the breach of the obligation, nevertheless, within 3 years from the day when the breach actually occurred. The Data Protection Office has the task to collect the fine, and also administers the procedure of imposing it. When imposing a fine the Office must consider, in particular, the character, seriousness, and manner of activity, degree of offense, duration and consequences of the unlawful activity. The penalty is levied by the competent local financial office and its revenues constitute part of the income to the State budget of the Czech Republic.[101]

No particular sanctions are applicable in case of abuse of sensitive personal data. Sensitive data are due higher protection with respect to the circumstances under which they can be processed. This means that if they are processed as per-

---

94. See Article 44 paragraph 1of the Data Protection Law. (50,000 CZK is approximately 1,316 USD).
95. Ibid. in paragraph 2. (25,000 CZK is approximately 658 USD).
96. Law No. 200/1990 of the Coll.
97. See Article 45 of the Data Protection Law. (25,000 CZK is approximately 658 USD).
98. See Article 46 paragraph 1 of the Data Protection Law. (10,000,000 CZK is approximately 263,158 USD).
99. Ibid. in paragraph 2. (20,000,000 CZK is approximately 526,316 USD).
100. Ibid. in paragraph 3. (1,000,000 CZK is approximately 26,316 USD).
101. See Article 46 paragraphs 3 — 8 of the Data Protection Law.

sonal data and not like sensitive data, that constitutes a violation under the law, and as such is to be sanctioned.

Special Regulations Governing Registration of Personal Data, Including Census and Registration of Inhabitants

Czech law requires obligatory registration for data controllers. The data can be collected only in an open manner; collecting data with a purpose or activity different than the one stated is prohibited, unless a specific law stipulates other - wise. The registered controllers are obliged to specify the purpose for which they handle personal data and to specify the means and manners of the personal data processing. The application for registration must contain the exact name of the controller, the address of their registered office and the identification num - ber if it has been assigned; the categories of the data subjects and the personal data which relate to these subjects, the sources of the personal data, the descrip - tion of the method of processing the personal data; the location of processing the data if that differs from the address of the controller's registered office; the recip - ient or a category of recipients to whom the personal data may be accessible, transferred or disclosed; possible transfers of personal data to other countries; description of measures taken for securing the required personal data protection and the links to other controllers or processors.

The controllers must then collect the personal data corresponding exclusive - ly to the specified purpose and to the extent necessary for the fulfillment of the specified purpose. The personal data must be processed in conformity with the purpose for which the data was collected, unless a specific law provides differ - ently. The personal data may be processed for a purpose that differs from the originally stated one only if the data subject has given her consent.

The census is conducted once every ten years and must be ordered by a law adopted by the Parliament of the Czech Republic. The last census in the Czech Republic was ordered and regulated by Law No. 158/1999, the Law on Census of Residents, Houses and Flats in 2001. The census describes the situation as of midnight February 28 to March 1, 2001. Providing correct data for the census was obligatory in accordance with the law. Data for the census is gathered by census commissioners. The commissioners are obliged to keep the rules of confidentiality with respect to the personal data they had access to during the census. This obligation extends to everybody who has access to the data through its handling or through the administration of the census. [102]

---

102. See Article 13 of Law No. 158/1999 of the Coll., the Law on Census.

The data on names and surnames obtained in the census can be used only for future development of the census database and for preventing the duplication of census interviews. These data cannot be kept in electronic systems nor stored in computer databases. The census forms must be destroyed after processing. The state is reliable for abuse or misuse of the data obtained in the census.

Special rules apply for the collection of data for basic registers such as:

• *the register of residents*. The central register of residents is kept by the Ministry of Interior of the Czech Republic and includes addresses of per-manent residents. The Ministry of Labor and Social Affairs administers and updates the register of buildings and addresses.

• *the register of economic subjects*,

• *the register of realty*,

• *the register of territorial identification*.

None of the registries kept in the Czech Republic contain ethnic data.

International Law

According to Article 10 of the Czech Constitution, the international treaties on human rights and fundamental freedoms which have been duly ratified and promulgated and by which the Czech Republic is bound are directly applicable in the Czech Republic and take precedence over domestic law. Of the relevant human rights treaties, the Czech Republic is signatory to the Universal Declaration of Human Rights, the International Covenant on Civil and Political Rights[103], the Convention for the Elimination of All Forms of Racial Discrimination and the European Convention on Human Rights.[104] The Czech Republic signed Protocol 12 to the European Convention on Human Rights on November 4, 2000 but so far has not ratified it.[105]

The Czech Republic has also signed but not ratified the Convention for the Protection of Individuals with Regard to Automatic Processing of Personal Data of the Council of Europe.[106] In the course of preparation for accession to the European Union, the Czech Republic implemented Directive No. 46 from 1995 of the European Commission on data protection through the Data Protection Law.

103. By the Decree of the Ministry of Foreign Affairs from May 10, 1976, Decree No. 120/1976 of the Coll.
104. Decree of the Ministry of Foreign Affairs No. 209/1992 of the Coll.
105. See the Treaty Office of the ECHR: *conventions.coe.int/treaty/EN/cadreprincipal.htm*
106. ETS No. 108.Signed by the Czech Republic on September 8, 2000.

There are no laws or regulations that would openly discriminate on the grounds of racial and ethnic origin in the Czech Republic. However, there are laws that indirectly discriminate against the Roma minority. The Czech Republic has been criticized for its discriminatory law on Citizenship[107] for its effect on Roma population. Local municipalities all around the country adopt decrees and other measures[108] that *de facto* discriminate against Roma and against individuals with low income with respect to their access to municipal housing. These decrees usually condition the allocation of municipal flats on various criteria, for example absence of criminal record, certain length of permanent residence within the municipality, good morals or the interest of the municipality in the applicants' dwellings in the town. The applicants for municipal flats must submit a written application to Municipal Housing Boards that review and store the application.

In light of the importance of the data protection issue, the condition of submitting the data on criminal records proved controversial. Such data is considered to be sensitive according to the Data Protection Law, and as such can only be processed under specific conditions, one of which is the explicit consent of the data subject. Nevertheless, the consent must also satisfy the conditions set by the Data Protection Law. Namely, it must clearly specify the data with respect to which the consent is being granted; as well as to which controller, for what purpose and what period of time the consent is being granted, and by whom it is being granted. The data subject may revoke the consent at any time. The controller has the obligation to instruct the data subject about her rights in advance. The controller is obliged to keep the consent for the entire period of the data processing for which the consent has been granted.[109] These conditions are not met by the municipalities when collecting the applications for flats. The Data Protection Office has so far failed to issue a statement regarding the situation.[110]

There is no case law either on the constitutional level or on the level of regular courts in connection to ethnic statistics. There is an extensive case law on general data protection, though.

Outlooks for the Future, Proposals for Changes in the Legal System

106. ETS No. 108. Signed by the Czech Republic on September 8, 2000.
107. Law No. 40/1993 of the Coll. on Acquisition and Loss of Czech Citizenship from December 29, 1992, which entered into force on January 1, 1993.
108. Decrees in the following.
109. See Article 9 (a) of the Data Protection Law.
110. Project „Taking Discrimination Seriously" of the Counseling Center for Citizenship, Civil and Human Rights based in Prague. The Project has registered 75 municipal decrees concerning the issue.

In the Czech Republic the issue of data protection is regulated by the recently adopted Data Protection Law, which assures high standards of data protection. Its implementation revealed several problems almost immediately after its enactment. A number of controllers of personal data have a very low awareness of the registration duty they have. This is especially shown, according to the information of the Data Protection Office, by the number of questions coming from employers that are not obliged to register given that their data collection does not exceed a certain level. [111] It is not clear whether the law covers the sphere of medical documentation by state hospitals. The obligation to keep medical documentation is not set by any law that governs state medical institutions. The Office issued a statement, which stated that the obligation to keep medical documentation arises from other laws. As a result medical institutions have no obligation to register with the Office. [112] At the same time, there are problems with establishing the time when processing of personal data commences and when the Office can subject the data controller to review.

The collection of race and ethnic statistics is still officially considered as prohibited.

The above-mentioned concerns of data protection need to be clarified. It can be assumed that the Office will issue a statement sooner or later. The need to adopt a comprehensive system of legal review of municipal decrees should be raised.

With regard to implementation of the Race Directive of EC[113], which is part of the Czech Republic's accession agenda to the EU, the issue of collection of ethnic statistics will probably be part of the Directive's implementation process.

111. See *Newsletter of the Data Protection Office* No. 1/2001, chapter: Launching of Registration
112. See *Information of the Data Protection Office* from January 18, 2001.
113. Council Directive 2000/43/EC of 29 June 2000 published in the *Official Monitor of the European Communities* on 19.7.2000. L 180/22.

II. Data on Individuals Belonging to Minority Groups and on Minority Groups and Application of Such Data and Statistics in Practice

Overview of Official Records Containing Data on Minorities

The Czech Charter on Human Rights and Fundamental Freedoms[114] states that everybody has the right to choose freely his or her nationality. Any form of influence on an individual's choice of nationality is prohibited, as is any form of pressure aimed at suppressing a person's national identity. A strict interpretation of this principle does not permit official registration of minorities, since state authorities are prohibited from inquiring about one's nationality/ethnicity, except anonymously, during the census. Therefore, there are no exact official data available about the total number of minorities, especially the Roma minority, in the Czech Republic.

The Data Protection Law has stricter provisions on ethnicity. It states that information revealing nationality, racial or ethnic origin is sensitive data and is subjected to the provisions of the Law. It means that recording such data must comply with the Data Protection Law. There is also the problem of identifying what the nationality/ethnicity of an individual is.

Despite these restrictions, a number of institutions keep race and ethnic statistics and the Czech government is aware of and officially recognizes the situation.[115] The majority of these institutions register ethnic data based on the subjective assessment of those who recorded the data. Those are especially:

- The *Ministry of Interior* is collecting data on the ethnicity of the suspects. The data are gathered based on "Forms No. 17: Form on Known Perpetrators of Crimes." Point 11 of the form asks the official to make an entry on whether the perpetrator is from "a statistically significant group," and lists a code for when the perpetrator is Roma.
- The *Ministry of Education*: there is lack of recent statistics on Roma in Czech educational institutions. The last time the Institute of Education of the Ministry published records on the number of minority children in the education system was in the Yearbook of 1997. This data was based on declarations made upon registration to the schools.[116] Individual schools, how-

---

114. Article 3 paragraph 2.
115. *Report on the Situation of the Roma Community in the Czech Republic and Governmental Measures Assisting Its Implementation in Society from 1997.* In an introduction chapter it states: "In practice authorities sometimes keep an official register of the Roma population."
116. See *Special Remedy, Roma and Schools for Mentally Handicapped in the Czech Republic,* ERRC Report No. 8 from June 1999.

ever, deny recording such data on their pupils. Universities are inquiring about the nationality of applicants in the registration for entrance examinations.

- *Employment Offices.* According to the provisions of the Law on Employment[117], employment offices are obliged to provide services that pay special attention to several groups of citizens, among others, to "citizens having difficulties in social adaptation." In order to provide them with adequate services and keep track of them, it seems logical there would be registers on the clients. Roma are very often considered as incapable of social adaptation.[118]
- *Social Security Services.* Social Security Services have a similar obligation as employment offices established by the Law on Social Security.[119]
- *Municipalities.* Extremely detailed figures concerning housing of Roma were presented by some municipalities at the Congress of Local and Regional Authorities of Europe in October 1997.
- *Roma Assistants* at District Offices. Roma Assistants to District Offices were established based on the governmental decree No. 686/1997 in order to assist the offices in dealing with problems related to Roma population. In reports on their activities to the Ministry of Interior, they are stating rather precise numbers on the Roma population in their constituencies.[120]

These records are not publicly accessible and do not result in published statistics. The cases of misuse of databases as such are not recorded. The only case was in October 1999 when employees of Czech Airlines stated that British immigration officers had requested information on the ethnicity of Czech citizens travelling to Britain on Czech Airlines flights and they had been providing it, marking lists with "G" for "Gypsy."[121] Otherwise, abuses of the databases containing ethnic data come to attention on an individual basis. There have been several cases when data on certain individuals were abusively used by employment offices for the purposes of not recommending Roma for jobs.[122]

There are several NGOs known for collecting ethnic statistics for the implementation of their projects attempting to address discrimination against Roma. For example:

---

117. Law No. 1/1991 of the Coll. on Employment from December 4, 1991, as subsequently amended. Article 9.
118. E.g. Housing Policy Concept of the Ministry of Regional Development based on Government Resolution of October 18, 1999. pp. 23.
119. Law No. 100/1988 of the Coll. on Social Security, as subsequently amended, Article 91.
120. See e.g. the letter of the Chief of the District Office in _esk_ Krumlov from March 17, 2000.
121. See Claude Kahn „Liars", *ERRC Newsletter* 4/2000. pp. 4.
122. Last time Olomouc Employment Office in May 2000.

- Tolerance Foundation and the Counseling Centre for Citizenship in its projects on the disparate impact of the Citizenship law on the Roma minority;
- European Roma Rights Centre in order to tackle discriminatory treatment of Roma children in special schools;
- First Step Project of NGO Tolerance and Civil Society in order to estimate the disparate treatment of Roma offenders by criminal justice authorities.

Census

All natural persons present on the territory of the Czech Republic during the time of census (not only those with a permanent or long-term residence) are subject to the census. Individuals are obliged to provide the identification data and other required data including: citizenship, nationality, mother tongue, religious belief, etc.

So far, all the Czech (Czechoslovak) censuses have been successfully processed.[123] The last officially recorded figures are those from the 1991 Czechoslovak census. Out of a total population of 10,302,210 inhabitants, only 33,489 people declared their Romany ethnicity. It is clear that this figure, much lower than previous ones, grossly underestimated the number of Roma in the Czech Republic. The previous census, from 1980, counted 88,587 Roma, while annual records kept regionally by the National Committees counted 107,274 Roma individuals in 1980, rising to 145,711 by 1989. The 1997 Council for Nationalities' Report accepts "unofficial estimates" of 200,000 Roma; in fact, most unofficial estimates show a Romany population of between 250,000 and 300,000, meaning 2.5 — 3.0 percent of the total population of the country.

With regard to nationality, the census forms in the 2001 census listed a blank space with no options for selections[124], leaving the respondents free to list any nationality. Nationality depends on the personal identification of the subject. The explanatory note to the 2001 census form in the point 7 states that data subjects can list more than one nationality.

As far as mother tongue is concerned, the 2001 census treated it separately as a special category independent from ethnicity. The census form listed the following options: Czech, Slovak, Romany, Polish, German and other with a blank space for specification. Instructions for this category requested selecting the lan-

123. In the last census only 639 citizens officially informed census commissioners they were refusing to provide their personal data for census purposes, and thus violated the Law on Census, see: *www.czso.cz/cz/sldb/index.htm*
124. See the Census Form for the Census in 2001, point 6: Nationality („Narodnost").

guage spoken with one's mother or other persons who raised the respondent during childhood.

The authority responsible for organization, management and coordination of the census is the Czech Statistical Office. The Statistical Office is preparing and conducting the census in cooperation with the Ministry for Regional Development, Ministry of Defense, Ministry of Justice, Ministry of Interior, Ministry for Foreign Affairs, the Czech Office for Land Registry, the district offices and the municipal offices.[125] The Census is conducted in census constituencies that were established by the Statistical Office in cooperation with municipalities.[126]

The collection of data in individual constituencies is administered by census commissioners and census inspectors appointed by the Statistical Office based on suggestions of municipalities. The municipality shall suggest persons for commissioners and inspectors at least 60 days before the census date. If the municipality does not submit any proposal, the Statistical Office can appoint persons from their own lists.[127]

The data are collected based on information provided by respondents to the census forms. The forms are issued based on the decree of the Statistical Office.[128] There are three types of forms:

a) form of census on persons,

b) form of census on flats,

c) form of census on houses.

The form on residents in the 2001 census contained 25 categories. One of the categories (listed under number 6) was the question on nationality. Respondents had the opportunity to choose any nationality; there were no categories listed.

Census subjects were obliged to provide the requested information for the census, with a fine of up to 10,000 CZK[129] for refusal.

Data obtained in the census can be used solely for statistical purposes. The Czech Statistical Office shall not provide information on individual data subjects to anybody, neither to state institutions, public administration nor to private entities. For the first time in the Czech census history, personal data identification obtained in the 2001 census will be destroyed after being processed.

---

125. See Law No. 158/1999 of the Coll. on Census of Persons, Flats and Houses in the year 2001 (further only Census Law), Article 16.
126. Ibid. Article 8.
127. Ibid. Article 9.
128. For the 2001 census ordered by the Decree of the Czech Statistical Office No. 354/2000 of the Coll. from October 2, 2000.
129. Ibid. Article 15.

The names of data subjects in the census are processed electronically. The birth numbers are deleted from the computer memory after conducting all con-trol. All personal identification data are deleted and thus data files remain anony-mous. Electronic processing of data is conducted in secured and protected premises of the Czech Statistical Office. Computers, on which the processing is conducted, do not have any item that allows copying; everything is processed on an internal computer network. All employees of the Office are monitored by a network of cameras all the time. None of the employees are informed ahead of time which partial amount of data they will process.

Ethnic Statistics and Data Protection: The German Experience

Dr. Alexander Dix

I. Legal framework

Personal Data Protection

Since the German State parliament of Hessen passed the first Data Protection Act in 1970[1], the use of personal information has been regulated in the Federal Republic both on the state as well as on the federal level. All German states adopted data protection legislation governing the public sector (state administration) and the Federal Parliament passed the first Federal Data Protection Act in 1977.[2] Due to the federal structure and the constitutional distribution of legislative powers, this Federal Act governs the processing of personal data by the Federal Government (public sector) as well as by the entire private sector.

In 1983 the Federal Constitutional Court in its landmark decision on the Census Act held that the Basic Law in its guarantees of human dignity and individual self-determination contained the right to informational self-determination.[3] "A society," the Court stressed, " and an underlying legal system in which the individual cannot know, who knows what, when and under which circumstances about him, would be unconstitutional." [4] Later the Court explicitly spoke of the fundamental right to data protection. According to the consistent jurisprudence of the Court, personal data may only be collected by the state either on a clear and unambiguous legal basis or with the informed consent of the individual. Data collected for one purpose may in principle not be used for other purposes. This applies particularly to data collected for statistical purposes. One of the main legal reasons for which the Census Act was declared unconstitutional was the fact that it allowed for the matching of personal data collected for statis-

1. *Hessisches Datenschutzgesetz* (Hessen Data Protection Law) , *Hessisches Gesetz- und Verordnungsblatt* 1970, pp.625.
2. *Bundesdatenschutzgesetz* (Federal Data Protection Act), *Bundesgesetzblatt* (Official Journal) 1977 I, pp. 201.
3. BVerfGE 65, 1ff.
4. BVerfGE loc.cit., 43.

tical purposes with the inhabitants' registers which exist in Germany on a local level. Previously these registers had been updated on the basis of the census data. The Constitutional Court called for a strict informational (and physical) separation of powers between the official statistics and all other government departments. The rationale for this is that the citizens may only be obliged to answer detailed personal census questions (and can be expected to cooperate) if they can trust that these data are kept secret. Although the secrecy of statistics had previously been laid down in the statistics legislation, the Court held that personal data which are collected for statistical purposes may only be used for statistical purposes, not for any administrative measures against the individual (e.g. updating the inhabitants' register which may lead to penalties for not registering as an inhabitant). The fundamental right to information self-determination has since been explicitly incorporated in a number of state constitutions of the German Länder. In view of the jurisprudence of the Constitutional Court it was not felt necessary to include it in the text of the Basic Law. The Draft Charter of Fundamental Rights of the European Union — which was proclaimed recently by the European Council at Nice — also contains this right. [5]

At present there are no specific data protection provisions in force concerning sensitive data such as race or ethnic origin. This will have to change according to Article 8 of the European Data Protection Directive. [6] The Federal Data Protection Bill contains a provision transforming Article 8 of the European Directive. [7] There are, however, special regulations in force concerning the secrecy of official statistics (microdata), the professional privileges of doctors and solicitors (secrecy of patients' or clients' data) and the secrecy of data relating to taxation and social (e.g. unemployment) benefits.

There is no legal possibility to link statistical databases on an individual basis to non-statistical databases due to the jurisprudence of the Constitutional Court. Statistical databases may under certain circumstances be linked to other statistical databases. There are other provisions outside the statistics field allowing for linking and matching of certain databases.

The German Data Protection legislation contains specific provisions on academic research. Personal data may only be collected for research purposes on the

---

5. Article 8. Interestingly enough it is part of the citizen's right to good government, see: *http://db.consilium.eu.int/df/docs/en/CharteEN.pdf*
6. Directive 95/46/EC of the European Parliament and of the Council of 24 October 1995 on the protection of individuals with regard to the processing of personal data and on the free movement of such data.
7. Article 3 (9) The Bill has been enacted in the meantime as *Bundesdatenschutzgesetz* (Federal Data Protection Act) 2001, *Bundesgesetzblatt* 2001 I, p.904; in the following text and footnotes reference is still being made to the Federal Data Protection Bill.

basis of an informed consent of the data subject. There is no legal requirement for citizens to participate in scientific projects or surveys. The German Basic Law guarantees freedom of science and research (Article 5 (3)); but this fundamental right does not include the right of access to any data in government files or archives. However, under the Data Protection Acts independent scientific research is privileged in several respects (e.g. the requirement of consent in written form is eased in this context; data which have been collected for research purposes may only be used for these purposes and they have to be anonymized as soon as the research purpose allows for it; in the meantime the identifying data have to be stored separately from the data which are the subject of the research project).[8] This privilege stems from the Constitutional Court ruling in the Census case of 1983 where the Court held that academic researchers are not interested in individual persons as such but only as holders of certain characteristics.[9]

According to the Federal Data Protection Bill[10], sensitive data may be collected for research purposes under less strict conditions than otherwise permitted.[11] But the principle remains unchanged that they may only be collected with informed consent of the data subject; if, however, there is an overriding public interest in the research project and this could not be carried out or could only be carried out with disproportionate costs, sensitive data may be collected without the consent of the persons concerned.

In general, data protection laws (Federal and State Data Protection Acts) regulating state authorities contain stricter rules on the use of personal data than those regulating the private sector (Federal Data Protection Act). This lower level of protection in the private sector has historical reasons since the Federal Parliament when passing the present Federal Data Protection Act was reluctant to apply the same strict rules as in the public sector. Also the right to informational self-determination was originally (as most fundamental rights) seen as being directed against state authorities rather than against private companies.

However, two factors will lead to a narrowing of the gap and to raising the level of protection in the private sector: one factor is the increasing tendency in public administration to outsource tasks such as the processing the data to private enterprise; the other — legal — factor is the European Data Protection Directive. This Directive requires harmonization of the data protection laws of Member States largely without distinguishing between the public and the pri-

8. Article 40 BDSG.
9. BVerfGE 65, 69.
10. Cf. footnote 8 supra.
11. Articles 13 (2) No.8.

vate sector. The underlying rationale is that privacy of citizens deserves equal protection in relation to public and private data controllers.

The *right of access and to review one's own personal data* is part of the fundamental right to informational self-determination according to the jurisprudence of the German Federal Constitutional Court.[12] It has been explicitly laid down in a number of state constitutions such as the Constitution of the State of Brandenburg of 1992.[13]

Furthermore the right of access has been included in the Data Protection Acts of the Federal Republic as well as of all 16 states. It covers the public sector as well as — with some restrictions e.g. with regard to costs — the private sector. The right of access is often referred to in Germany as the "Magna Charta" of data protection. The Draft Charter of Fundamental Rights of the European Union contains this right as well.[14]

Personal data are generally protected against *access by others* under German data protection law. There are some exceptions to this rule in accordance with the Federal Data Protection Act.[15] Personal data may be disclosed by public data controllers to private persons if this is necessary to fulfill one of the tasks within the jurisdiction of the data controller or if the private recipient has a legitimate interest to receive the data. At present there are no special provisions in effect regarding the access to personal data about ethnicity. However, the European Directive on the protection of individuals with regard to the processing of personal data and on the free movement of such data[16] provides for the processing of special categories of data (including data revealing racial or ethnic origin) only under certain circumstances.[17] Germany still has to transform this Directive into national law and the Bill to amend the present Federal Data Protection Act[18] contains special provisions on these categories of data[19] and on the disclosure of such data to private persons. The disclosure will only be permitted under even stricter conditions as compared with non-sensitive data. The private recipient will either have to show that he has legal (not only a legitimate) interest to receive these data (e.g. that he plans to institute legal proceedings) or a scientific interest or if other exceptions apply in accordance with Article 8 paragraph 2 of the Directive.[20]

12. *Bundesverfassungsgericht* (German Federal Constitutional Court).
13. Article 11.
14. Article 41 (2).
15. Articles 16, 28 *Bundesdatenschutzgesetz* (Federal Data Protection Act).
16. Data Protection Directive 95/46/EC of 24 October 1995.
17. Article 8 of the Directive.
18. Cf. footnote 8 supra.
19. Article 3 paragraph 9.
20. Article 16 paragraph 1(2) Federal Data Protection Bill 2000.

Similar rules will apply to the private sector.[21] There is a special provision in the Bill, which allows private organizations with a political, philosophical, religious, or trade union character to process sensitive data (including data about racial or ethnic origin).[22] These organizations may only process such data if they concern members of the organization or persons, which have regular contacts with the organization. Such data may only be transmitted to other persons or agencies with the informed consent of the data subjects.

In addition there are Access to Information Acts in force in three German states (*Länder*), i.e. in Brandenburg (1998), in Berlin (1999) and in Schleswig-Holstein (2000). In Brandenburg there is even a fundamental right enshrined in the State Constitution, which gives every person the right to access to files held by public bodies. This new legislation only applies to public agencies in the three states. The Federal Government has declared its intention to prepare a Bill, which would extend a general right of access to the federal level in the near future. Under the new legislation personal data is in principle protected against disclosure to the general public. But there are exceptional provisions, which allow for disclosure of specific personal data against the will of the data subjects if there is an overriding public interest to know. Under the Federal Act on Access to Environmental Information, [23] personal data may only be disclosed to third persons if this would not encroach upon legitimate interests of the data subjects.[24]

On the basis of the above-mentioned general Access to Information legislation, individuals may apply for access to and inspection of files held by public bodies, which contain information on communities and other groups. There is also a right of access for those participating in administrative proceedings under the Administrative Procedure Act (identical on the federal and the state level).

Under the German data protection laws everyone has a *right against public bodies to have his or her data altered if they are incorrect*. If the correctness is disputed by the data subject and the public agency controlling his or her data cannot prove their correctness, then the data have to be blocked. Blocking personal data means that the data remain stored but they may no longer be used without the data subject's consent. The data subject has a right to have his or her data deleted under certain conditions, especially if they have been collected illegally or if they are no longer necessary for the lawful purpose for which they were origi-

---

21. Article 28 paragraph 6 Federal Data Protection Bill 2000.
22. Article 28 paragraph 9 Federal Data Protection Bill 2000.
23. *Umweltinformationsgesetz* (Federal Act on Access to Environmental Information), *Bundesgesetzblatt* III 2129-4.
24. Article 8 paragraph 1(1) *Umweltinformationsgesetz* (Federal Act on Access to Environmental Information).

nally collected. There are certain limitations referring to what data can be altered or deleted but these do not refer to specific categories of sensitive data such as ethnicity.

All German data protection laws contain specific *conditions on which personal information may be transmitted*. These conditions are different in relation to public or private entities as recipients. Public agencies may transmit personal data to other public agencies — generally speaking — if the transmission is necessary for the fulfillment of legitimate tasks of the transmitting or receiving agency. Private entities may process (which includes the transmission of) personal data in a wider range of circumstances, the most important being the fulfillment of contractual or other legal obligations; in addition, a legitimate interest of the transmitting company will suffice to justify the disclosure if there is no legitimate interest of the data subject to prevent it. [25]

The export of personal information in Germany as in all Member States of the European Union has to comply with the provisions of Directive 95/45/EC. Under the Directive all Member States are deemed to have an adequate level of data protection. Therefore the transborder flow of personal data within the Union may not be prevented by any Member State on the grounds of data protection.

On the other hand, stricter rules apply to the export of personal information into third countries outside the European Union. Personal data may only be transmitted into third countries, which provide an adequate level of protection compared to the level provided for in the Union. Adequate protection in the receiving country may be provided for primarily by laws but also by codes of practice and — especially in the private sector — by contractual agreements between the companies transmitting and receiving personal information.

Whether a third country receiving personal data provides for an adequate level of protection has to be determined by the supervisory authority in the exporting EU Member State. The European Commission — after consultation with the Working Party under Article 29 of the Directive — has stated generally that in certain third countries such as the United States, Hungary and Switzerland the level of protection is adequate. The cases of Hungary and Switzerland were rather clear-cut since these countries have general legislation on the protection of personal data in the public and the private sector. The case of the United States has only been settled on a provisional basis (so-called "Safe Harbor Principles") since the U.S. has no omnibus data protection laws governing the private sector. The question of adequacy in the U.S. will therefore be

---

25. Article 28 paragraph 1 Federal Data Protection Act.

revisited after three years by the European Commission to evaluate whether the Safe Harbor Principles have yielded satisfactory results. On the other hand, there are certain indications that the U.S. Congress may pass legislation on data protection in the private sector within this time-span.

As far as legal sanctions and remedies available in this field are concerned, individuals can enforce their rights before the courts, which takes time (generally due to a huge amount of cases pending) and may be costly. Alternatively a complaint may be lodged with the supervisory authorities in charge of data protection. This may lead to a quicker solution of the conflict and is cost-free. However, the supervisory authorities in Germany can only try to mediate state violations of the law and make them public; unlike the courts they have no formal powers of enforcement.

There is no independent supervisory authority for the protection of minority rights in Germany in general. However, there are Ombudspersons in charge of problems raised by foreign nationals (*Ausländerbeauftragte*) on the Federal and State levels, sometimes even on the local authority level. They have no formal authority but they can receive and take up complaints of foreigners.

There are independent supervisory authorities (Data Protection Commissioners /*Datenschutzbeauftragte*) in the data protection field on the Federal and State level for the public sector. An increasing number of German States (Nordrhein-Westfalen, Niedersachsen, Schleswig-Holstein and the three City States of Hamburg, Bremen and Berlin) have handed jurisdiction also over the private sector to the Data Protection Commissioners. So in these six States there is a uniform independent supervisory authority in place dealing with all issues of data protection. In the remaining ten States there is a split jurisdiction since the independent Data Protection Commissioners are only overseeing the public sector (the administrative agencies of their respective State or of the Federal Government) whereas the supervision of private data controllers lies in the hands of ministerial departments (very often the State Department of the Interior) which cannot be considered to act "with complete independence" within the meaning of Article 28 of Directive 95/46/EC.

As described above, under German Data Protection Law any individual can inspect and demand information about his or her personal data that are processed by the state. He or she has to address the respective data controller. There is no central registry or archive storing all personal data about any citizen.

There are of course the general archives storing all files (personal or non-personal) which are no longer needed by government agencies and which the archives themselves consider to be of historical importance. They may be inspected by the data subjects (limited to their own data) even before the time limits laid down in the Archive Laws[26] have expired. These time limits apply only to inspection by third parties (not the persons concerned).

Registers are being kept by supervisory authorities in charge of data protection in the private sector only with regard to specific companies, which process personal data on a regular and commercial basis for others (e.g. credit reference information). But these registers do not contain any personal information themselves; they only describe the types of information that are being processed in abstract terms. Previously most Data Protection Acts used to provide for equivalent registers (*Datenregister*) at the offices of the Data Protection Commissioners, describing the automated personal data files held by all public agencies. These registers have now mostly been decentralized so that only the public agency in question is obliged to keep a register of personal data files and descriptions of hard- and software used.

Registries and Statistical Data

In Germany all inhabitants (regardless of nationality or ethnic origin) are obliged to register with their local authority wherever they take up residence. There is, however, no nationwide (or even statewide on the basis of the *Länder*) inhabitants' register.

In the former GDR there existed a national inhabitants' register[27], which had links to and was used also by the Ministry for State Security.[28] This register relied on a unique identifier for each inhabitant.[29] It was dismantled after unification and the data were transferred to the local authorities concerned (only to the extent that their continuous storage was permitted by the law of the united Federal Republic). Under the German Basic Law centralized inhabitants' registers, as well as unique identifiers, have always been considered unconstitutional in view of the specific German historical experience. In this respect the German legal situation and tradition differs from other European (especially Scandinavian) countries.

There is, however, an increasing number of centralized databases in Germany for specific purposes (e.g. unemployment benefit; old age pensions for employees; cancer research; taxation of interest payments; traffic offenses; public grants for students; foreign nationals; asylum seekers; radio listeners and TV viewers for the purpose of fee collection). These databases are under the responsibility

---

26. E.g. *Bundesarchivgesetz* (Federal Archive Laws), *Bundesgesetzblatt* III 224-8.
27. *Zentrales Einwohnerregister* — ZER (National Inhabitants Register).
28. *Ministerium für Staatssicherheit* — Stasi (Ministry for State Security).
29. *Personenkennzeichen* — PKZ (personal identifier).

146

of separate controllers and may only be linked or matched under specific legal conditions.

There is detailed legislation in effect governing censuses and official statistics in Germany. The Federal Statistics Act[30] regulates all forms of official statistics whereas specific laws regulate the general census (*Volkszählung*), as well as the sample census (*Mikrozensus*). The German Statistics Acts are strongly influenced by the judgement of the Federal Constitutional Court on the general census of 1983.[31] Information collected for statistical purposes may not be used for any administrative purposes. The Court emphasized the legal requirements of purpose specification and informational separation of powers. Statistical information is collected primarily from the data subject (except the occasional secondary statistics where data are collected from third parties, e.g. universities concerning students); this personal information has to be anonymized as soon as possible by separating the statistical data from name and address of the data subject. But even the remaining set of anonymized data is still "personal data" within the meaning of the data protection laws, the reason being that in certain instances the data may still be linked to the data subject even without name and address due to the singularity of the data set.

The official census in Germany contains no ethnic questions. The only questions in this field refer to nationality (e.g. Turkish, but not Kurdish). The questions relating to nationality do not always ask for precise nationality but form sometimes groups of nationalities (e.g. East Asia except Japan, Korea, Philippines). There is a separate category for "stateless" people.

As already mentioned, in 1983 the Federal Constitutional Court in its Census ruling held invalid parts of the Census Act.[32] This was arguably also a result of considerable civil unrest and imminent non-participation in the census process in former West Germany. However, the Court did not have to pronounce on any question relating to racial or ethnic origin since such questions were not part of the census form. The form did contain a question relating to religious belief, but this was held to be constitutional, despite the fact that especially citizens of Jewish belief had strongly opposed this question in view of the historic experience. However, the Constitutional Court held that the negative freedom of religious belief could be restricted by the state asking for this information if certain rights and duties depended on it or if there was a legal basis for such statistical registration.[33] The churches (including the Jewish Community)

---

30. *Bundesstatistikgesetz* (Federal Statistics Act), *Bundesgesetzblatt* III 29-22.
31. BVerfGE 65, 1.
32. BVerfGE 65, 1.
33. BVerfGE 65, 1, 39.

did not oppose that question, and thus it was included in the later census of 1987, as well.

Discrimination

There are no laws or regulations in force in the Federal Republic which openly discriminate on the grounds of race or ethnic origin. Any such law or reg - ulation would be unconstitutional.[34] German courts after 1945 have declared null and void legal measures by the Nazi-regime, such as the expatriation of Jewish emigrés and the confiscation of their assets[35], on the grounds that they violated fundamental principles of law such as the non-discrimination principle.

There are no legal regulations in effect in Germany which obviously have an indirect discriminatory effect on ethnic minorities. The Federal Constitutional Court in interpreting Article 3 paragraph 3 of the Basic Law has stated that any reg - ulation which differentiates based on one of the criteria of race or (with certain exceptions) sex, would be unconstitutional even if it did not aim at discriminat - ing against any particular race or sex.[36] In this respect, the German Federal Constitutional Court relies on the extensive jurisprudence of the European Court of Justice regarding the free movement of workers in the European Community[37] and the right to equal remuneration for equal work.[38]

There is a legal dispute going on at present (yet unresolved) as to whether the school authorities can order a Muslim teacher not to wear a headscarf during classes. Such an order — if upheld — could be considered as restriction on the exercise of one's religious belief, but not an issue of discrimination.

No Constitutional Court decisions, Ombudsman's recommendations, or concrete cases regarding the availability and/or use of race statistics are known in Germany. However, the Labor Courts as well as the Federal Constitutional Court have used the concept of "indirect discrimination" following the European Court of Justice in order to determine whether there has been an instance of discrimination on the grounds of sex (e.g. by treating differently part-time and full-time workers because the proportion of women working part-time is often higher than that of men).

German law does not allow for the official (obligatory) collection of statisti - cal data based on racial or ethnic origin. The reasons for this are historical as well as legal:

34. Contravening Article 3 (3) of the Basic Law.
35. BGHZ 16, 350; BVerfGE 23, 98, 106.
36. BVerfGE 97, 186, 197.
37. Article 39 Treaty of Amsterdam.
38. Article 141 Treaty of Amsterdam.

The Nazi Regime prepared for the deportation and mass murder of Jews and Sinti and Roma by launching registration campaigns under the pretext of official statistics. So-called researchers were participating in this and other criminal exercises at the "Institute of Racial Hygiene" (*Institut für Rassenhygiene*).

"Due to the racist fanaticism under the National Socialist (Nazi) tyranny, the Sinti and Roma in Germany and in the areas occupied by German armed forces were subjected to persecution and genocide with the aim of their extermination. Hundreds of thousands of Sinti and Roma were murdered, and their cultural heritage was, for the most part, destroyed. Of the 40,000 officially registered German and Austrian Sinti and Roma, more than 25,000 were murdered by May 1945. This persecution, aimed at systematic and definitive extermination, left its mark on the survivors and also has an impact on the members of the generation born after 1945. The memories of those persecuted will continue to decisively influence their consciousness and their identity.... The German Sinti and Roma (today) are estimated to number up to 70,000 persons." [39]

The Council of Europe Framework Convention for the Protection of National Minorities in Article 3 (1) forbids any public body in one of the Member States to determine who belongs to a national minority and who does not. It is the individual free choice of any person to make this determination for himself. "Thus it is everybody's individual personal decision — which is neither registered, reviewed or contested by the German State — whether he/she chooses to be considered a member of any of the groups protected under the Framework Convention." [40] This applies equally to other minorities besides the Sinti and Roma, e.g. the Sorbian people in the Land of Brandenburg. Furthermore, even if an individual identifies with a certain minority, she cannot be forced to disclose this information to state agencies or private persons. It is her free choice to disclose it or to keep it for herself. Under the German Constitution there is a right not to disclose one's religious belief [41]; equally there is a right not to make public one's (subjective) membership of a national minority.

As far as connections, overlaps and contradictions between the fields of minority rights and data protection are concerned, one apparent connection is the special protection afforded to personal information on race and ethnic origin by Article 8 of the Directive 95/46/EC. Such information is regarded as sensitive information, which may only be processed under specific conditions and safeguards. On the other hand it has to be remembered that data protection leg-

39. First Report submitted by the Federal Republic of Germany under Article 25(1) of the Council of Europe's Framework Convention for the Protection of National Minorities (1999), pp.10.
40. First Report of the Federal Republic, pp.19.
41. Negative freedom of religion or conscience, Article 4 Basic Law.

islation provides for individual rights for the data subject, not — so far — for group rights. From a political point of view (*de lege ferenda*), it is debatable whether modern data protection laws should also address the problem of the protection of information related to groups such as minorities. Article 8 of the European Directive is arguably a first step to afford protection against informa - tional discrimination on the grounds of racial or ethnic origin but it affords this protection only to individual data subjects.

However, no cases are known in which ethnic statistics have been used to prove indirect racial discrimination.

International Obligations

As a member of the United Nations, the Federal Republic has ratified all major international legal documents in this field such as the International Covenant on Civil and Political Rights, the International Covenant on Social and Cultural Rights and the International Convention on the Elimination of All Forms of Racial Discrimination. The Council of Europe Conventions on Human Rights and on Data Protection (No. 108) as well as the Framework Convention for the Protection of National Minorities have also become binding part of national German law (as all ratified international treaties). The Framework Convention for the Protection of National Minorities entered into force in Germany on February 1, 1998.[42]

An important distinction has to be made in legal terms between the UN International Convention on the Elimination of All Forms of Racial Discrimination on the one hand, and the Council of Europe Conventions on Human Rights and for the Protection of National Minorities on the other: whereas the UN Convention only contains obligations for the contracting "States' Parties" and does not give rights to the individual, the Conventions of the Council of Europe do give rights to the individual. The Framework Convention for the Protection of National Minorities guarantees at least the right of every person belonging to a national minority to choose his or her minority.[43] This provision has particular importance with regard to statistical surveys covering national minorities. The enforcement mechanism of the Council of Europe Framework Convention for the Protection of National Minorities is, however, weaker than the European Convention on Human Rights: under the Human Rights Convention any individual may bring an action against a Member State (Contracting Party) before the European Court of

---

42. *www.dhdirhr.coe.fr/Minorities/Eng/SiteMap.htm* .
43. Article 3 (1) of the Framework Convention.

Human Rights. The mere monitoring and reporting system under the Framework Convention for the Protection of National Minorities resembles more the monitoring procedure set up under the International Convention on the Elimination of All Forms of Racial Discrimination.

All Recommendations adopted by the Committee of Ministers of the Council of Europe can be relied upon in Germany (although they — in contrast to the conventions and treaties — do not have binding legal effect). This applies in par-ticular to the Recommendation R (97) 18 to Member States Concerning the Protection of Personal Data Collected and Processed for Statistical Purposes [44] which by and large corresponds to the German legislation on official statistics briefly analyzed above. However, unlike the German legislation the Recommendation R (97) 18 expressly refers to the collection of sensitive data [45], which include personal data revealing racial origin and other data, defined as sensitive by domestic law. It contains particular provisions on the lawfulness of collecting sensitive data for statistical purposes. [46]

When signing the Council of Europe Framework Convention for the Protection of National Minorities, the German Federal Government in 1994— with the agreement of the Länder— made the following declaration: "The Framework Convention contains no definition of the notion of national minori-ties. It is therefore up to the Contracting Parties to determine the groups to which it will apply after ratification. National minorities in the Federal Republic of Germany are the Danes of German citizenship and the members of the Sorbian people of German citizenship. The Framework Convention will also be applied to members of the ethnic groups traditionally resident in Germany: the Friesians of German citizenship and the Sinti and Roma of German citi-zenship."

The Government of the Federal Republic is also periodically reporting on the above-mentioned national minorities and ethnic groups to the UN Committee under the International Convention against All Forms of Racial Discrimination. The Sinti and Romany were mentioned for the first time in a German State Report under this Convention in the fourteenth report (UN doc. CERD/C/299/Add.5, paragraph 8).

---

44. Adopted by the Committee of Ministers on 30 September 1997.
45. Appendix to the Recommendation, paragraph 1.
46. Paragraph 4.3 and 4.8 — Paragraph 4.8 says: "If sensitive data are to be processed for statistical purposes, these data shall be collected in a form in which the data subjects are not identifiable. If the processing of sensitive data for specific legitimate purposes necessitates the identification of the data subjects domestic law shall provide appropriate safeguards including specific measures to separate identification data as from the stage of collection unless it is manifestly unreasonable or impractica-ble to do so."

As mentioned above, the European Directive 46/95/EG contains in Article 8 a first step to protect individuals against informational discrimination on the grounds of race or ethnic origin.

Future Prospects, Possibilities for Legal Reform in the Field

The Framework Convention expressly states that compensatory measures in favor of ethnic minorities do not constitute unlawful discrimination within the meaning of this Convention.[47]

In order to be able to adopt such compensatory ("positively discriminating") measures statistical data are needed. Such data may only be collected on an entirely voluntary basis. It is recommended that such data are exclusively collected by private organizations representing the national minorities in question. Thus there is no conflict between the legal ban on compulsory collection of ethnic personal data and the possible need to prove indirect discrimination on the grounds of ethnicity. There is, however, a problem of financial resources for victims of discrimination if the state refrains from collecting such data on an official (compulsory) basis.

It should be noted that under Council of Europe Recommendation R (2000) 4 on the education of Roma/Gypsy children in Europe, member states are called upon to take positive action in the school sector and to encourage innovative research/small-scale action projects as well as to monitor education policies for Roma/Gypsies.[48]

47. Article 3 (1) says: "Every person belonging to a national minority shall have the right freely to choose to be treated or not to be treated as such and no disadvantage shall result from this choice or from the exercise of the rights which are connected with that choice." Article 4 (2 and 3) says "(2) The Parties undertake to adopt, where necessary, adequate measures in order to promote, in all areas of economic, social, political and cultural life, full and effective equality between persons belonging to a national minority and those belonging to the majority. In this respect, they shall take due account of the specific conditions of the persons belonging to national minorities. (3) The measures adopted in accordance with paragraph 2 shall not be considered to be an act of discrimination."
48. Recommendation R (2000) 4 to Member States on the Education of Roma/Gypsy Children in Europe. (adopted by the Committee of Ministers of the Council of Europe on 3 February 2000) Paragraph 5 of the Appendix says: "Appropriate support structures should be set up in order to enable Roma/Gypsy children to benefit, in particular through positive action, from equal opportunities at school." Paragraph 19 says "The involvement of all parties concerned (ministry of education, school authorities, Roma families and organizations) in the design, implementation and monitoring of education policies for Roma/Gypsies should be promoted by the state."

II. Uses of Ethnic Data and Statistics in Practice

Registration of Data on Minorities

Recognized Churches in Germany such as the Protestant and Roman-Catholic Church, the Jewish Community and certain other religious organiza-tions have their registries of members. These churches are even privileged by constitutional law in that they receive regular data from the inhabitants' regis-ters as to who has moved into the local community or who has left, died etc. Equally trade unions and interest groups have their registries of membership. All these data are collected on a voluntary basis. There is no state-based register which contains information on the "racial origin" of a specific person of a group of persons (the only exception being the police in some German States, see below). There are, of course, official statistics based on sex describing the par-ticipation and discrimination of women in the various sectors of society.

Sinti and Roma have been registered for some time (and in Bavaria still are) by the police whenever they are accused of a crime. In the framework of the police statistics initially the term *"Zigeuner/Zigeunertyp"* was used and later replaced by other more "neutral" terms. Only in 1988, after public protests by the organiza-tion representing the Sinti and Roma in Germany[49], the Conference of Interior Ministers decided to drop any such description in the police statistics.[50] It is claimed by representatives of the Sinti and Roma that the practice still continues in certain German States. In Bavaria it has been confirmed that the term *"Sinti und Roma"* or *"Typ Sinti und Roma"* is still used by the police when registering or investigating criminal offenses. The organization representing the German Sinti and Roma in 1998 applied to the Bavarian State Constitutional Court to have this practice declared unconstitutional. The case is still pending. The Bavarian author-ities are defending their practice on the grounds that it does not rely on prejudices but on the "perceptions of average citizens."[51] The Bavarian Government has, however, on the demand of the Bavarian Data Protection Commissioner, discon-tinued the practice of collecting data on vagrants without cause in the database *"Information Landfahrerbewegung — ILAN"*[52] at the end of 1998.

The data in the police registers can only be used by the police and the courts. In a sense the above-mentioned collection of data on Sinti and Roma by the police

---

49. *Zentralrat der Sinti und Roma.*
50. Cf. *Staatsanzeiger Hessen* (Hessen Government Gazette) 1994, 1091.
51. For details see Rose, Romani "Public Law Agreement on the Protection and Promotion of German Sinti and Roma — Principles and Contents" in Zentralrat Deutscher Sinti und Roma (Ed.) *Public Law Agreements about the Minority-Protection for the German Sinti and Roma*, Heidelberg 1998. pp. 83.
52. Information on the movement of vagrants.

can be considered to be an abuse. The Federal Constitutional Court has consistently ruled that not only the later use but already the collection of personal data must take place on a constitutional legal basis and has to be necessary and proportionate to fulfill a legitimate task. No statistics have been produced or published based on the police registries. The information concerning ethnic origin in this particular case thus is stored in central databases (statewide, since police matters are the jurisdiction of the Länder). The police authorities initially used the term *"Zigeuner"* in their statistics which was later replaced by "coded" terms such as *"Landfahrer"* (migrant people), or abbreviations such as "HWAO" *(Häufig wechselnder Aufenthaltsort* — frequently changing place of residence). Later all police authorities except Bavaria's abandoned this practice; the Bavarian police continues to use the term *"Sinti und Roma"* or *"Personentyp Sinti und Roma."*

Apart from the Bavarian police example quoted above, no instances of authorities using non-census statistics on ethnicity have become public. Even the organization representing the German Sinti and Roma has stated that they are not collecting statistics based on ethnic origin.

As far as known, no one ever has been tried and convicted for crimes related to the gathering, storing or distributing data on ethnicity.

No provisions have been made in law or in practice, for the inclusion of minority groups for participation in decision making about the gathering, storage and use of data on ethnicity.

Foreign Nationals and Immigrants

The Federal Border Police in Germany and the Federal Criminal Office[53] only register the nationality of suspects and add the ethnic origin (if known; e.g. Kosovo-Albanians).

There is an ongoing debate on whether foreign nationals tend to become criminals in greater numbers than German nationals. The evidence shows that this is not the case.

There is no detailed statistical material available on immigrants such as second- or third-generation Turks. What has been said about the problems of collecting ethnic data on Sinti and Roma in Germany likewise applies, by and large, to Turks and other immigrants. Schools may only register the ethnic origin or nationality of their pupils with the consent of the parents.

However, there are laws in force in Germany specifically regulating the admission of foreign nationals, their need to apply for residence and work per-

---

53. *Bundeskriminalamt* (Federal Criminal Office).

mits, their registration in a central register *(Ausländerzentralregister)* and on the status of asylum seekers. These regulations differentiate (if not discriminate) on the grounds of nationality rather than on the grounds of race or ethnic origin. Therefore they are not analyzed in greater detail here. Under the Foreign Nationals Register Act[54] the Federal Office of Statistics receives data on foreigners who have stayed in the Federal Republic not only temporarily (and who have registered with the authorities) to generate annual statistics for planning purposes. To this end the Federal Register discloses *inter alia* the date of birth, sex, nationality, marital status, nationality of the spouse, date of death and file number to the Federal Statistics Office.

Methods and Means of Collecting and Processing Data Relating to Minorities

As far as methods and the type of primary data being used for collecting and processing minority data by researchers and civil organizations is concerned, no reliable answer can be given since no research studies on Sinti and Roma in Germany (at least to my knowledge) have been published. This may in part be attributed to the fact that there are no statistical data available which could form the basis of such research. There is research on the large Turkish community in Germany but they are not an "ethnic minority" within the meaning of this paper.

According to the legal framework analyzed above, any researcher could conduct surveys among ethnic minorities by directly addressing individual members of these minorities and collecting data with their informed consent. The problem is how to contact individual persons. Public registers — as was mentioned above — do not contain any information about the status as a member of an ethnic minority. Thus researchers would mainly have to use their personal knowledge and contacts unless community leaders would be prepared to act as an intermediary. This would be possible in accordance with data protection law by sending out questionnaires to data subjects giving them the choice to get in touch with the researchers.

In Germany no surveys, national or international, are known up till now, which used, collected, or processed data on ethnic minorities.

If research on ethnic minorities or statistical data collection would be carried out in the future, the Data Protection Commissioners and Supervisory Authorities in Germany would certainly require that these sensitive personal data be anonymized at the earliest possible date and that anonymous or pseudonymous techniques of data collection would have to be applied.

---

54. *Ausländerzentralregistergesetz* (Foreign National's Register Act), *Bundesgesetzblatt* III 26-8.

In Germany public funds are given to some disadvantaged ethnic communities (e.g. Sorben and Wenden) and these funds are administered by special commissioners (e.g. Sorben-Beauftragte at the local or regional level in Brandenburg). No statistical evidence is used beforehand but a certain documentation is required for auditing purposes (who received grants for what purpose). This is not considered to be a compulsory registration of ethnic data because applicants from these communities come forward and apply for grants; if they receive funds, then the administrators of these funds could be under a duty to show to Parliament and to the Auditor-General that the money has been spent in accordance with the Budget Law.

III. Conclusion

In Germany the protection of personal data has been part of the legal system for thirty years and was given the status of a fundamental right by the Federal Constitutional Court in 1983. Personal data on race or ethnic origin have been qualified as sensitive data by the European Directive 95/46 on Data Protection, and this has been incorporated in German law.

The Council of Europe Framework Convention for the Protection of National Minorities forbids any public body in one of the Member States of the Council of Europe to determine who belongs to a national minority and who does not. It is the individual free choice of any person to make this determination for him- or herself.

Therefore national data protection legislation and international obligations in the Federal Republic of Germany have the same legal effect: no public body is allowed to require individuals to disclose their race or ethnic origin on an obligatory basis. This is to be seen against the background of the German historical experience: the Nazi Regime prepared for the deportation and mass murder of Jews and Sinti and Roma by launching registration campaigns under the pretext of official statistics.

In order to be able to adopt compensatory ("positively discriminating") measures in favor of ethnic minorities, statistical data are needed. Such data may only be collected on an entirely voluntary and informed basis. It is recommended that such data are exclusively collected by private organizations representing the national minorities in question. Thus there is no conflict between the legal ban on compulsory collection of ethnic personal data and the possible need to prove indirect discrimination on the grounds of ethnicity.

Ethnic Monitoring and Data Protection:
The Case of Hungary

Andrea Krizsán

The issue of registration of ethnic data has been in the air in Hungary for the last few years. The need for registration raised three issues related to national and ethnic minorities. The first was the efficient enforcement of the right not to be discriminated against on grounds of national or ethnic origin. The second was the meaningful election of minority self-governments: the issue of efficient rep-resentation of minorities. The third issue raised concerning registration of eth-nic data was the efficient use of special minority rights and entitlements by mem-bers of minority groups: the way in which affirmative action programs, minori-ty education programs and other equal opportunity increasing programs can be tailored so as to reach the appropriate pool of people— the members of the con-cerned minority groups.

Two major arguments were formulated against registration of ethnic data in the Hungarian debate. According to the first one, the legal framework concern-ing the protection of personal data does not allow for any registration of ethnic data, thus making impossible both the efficient enforcement of the right to be free from discrimination, and the right to meaningful minority self-government. According to the second one, even if the legal context would be permissive, minorities have no confidence with this in respect to state institutions. Based on their historical experiences, they will never "surrender" their data to state authorities even if certain forms of registration of ethnic data or monitoring would serve the purposes of enforcement of their minority rights. Both of these arguments against ethnic monitoring deserve separate consideration and need to be addressed differently.

The aim of this paper is to address the former argument, the one coming from the criticism of the legal context. I shall argue throughout this chapter that the Hungarian legislation on data protection, if properly understood, allows for the registration and monitoring of ethnic data, within carefully designed condi-tions.

If this argument is successfully made, the major hindering factor standing against monitoring of ethnic data will be the mistrust and opposition of the con-cerned minority groups. Addressing that factor will require other means such as consciousness raising through campaigns, through informed public debates, through mediations. These strategies, however, shall be the concern of a different paper.

I. Legal Framework

According to Article 59 of the Hungarian Constitution[1], in Hungary everyone has the right to the good standing of her reputation, the privacy of her home and the protection of secrecy in private affairs and the protection of her personal data. Meanwhile Article 61 of the Constitution provides for everyone the right to freely express her opinion, and furthermore to receive and impart information of public interest. The Constitution also establishes the conditions for the state to enact laws on the protection of personal data and on the publicity of data of public interests: two-thirds majority of the votes of all Members of the Parliament is needed for passing such laws. This duality of protection for personal data and access to public data characterizes the entire Hungarian system of data protection. This paper will only be concerned, however, with the principles and provisions referring to the protection of personal data.

The Hungarian Constitutional Court in its decision 15/1991 interprets the right to protection of personal data not as a negative right, but as a positive, an active right, a right to informational self-determination. The Court argues that in general personal data can only be collected and processed with the permission of the individual to whom it belongs. Data processing has to be accessible and controllable. Everybody has the right to know who uses her personal data, and when, where and for what purpose it is used. This is the general rule; the law shall provide for exceptions from this rule, but its limitations in any case have to be in conformity with Article 8 of the Constitution, meaning that they "may not restrict the basic meaning and content of the fundamental right."

Collection and processing of personal data can be done along two constitutional principles: according to the first principle, personal data can only be processed in accordance with a well-defined and lawful purpose. The personal data has to be necessary and appropriate for the achievement of the above purpose; the data can only be processed to the extent and for the period necessary for the fulfillment of this purpose.[2] According to the second principle, personal data can only be collected, processed, transferred or made public if the concerned person has given her informed consent or the law authorizes it.

1. Act XX. of 1949.
2. Constitutional Court Decision 15/1991 (IV.13).

The Hungarian Act on the Protection of Personal Data and Freedom of Information[3] (Data Protection Act in the following) was passed in 1992. The Act codifies the above constitutional principles and provisions. The grounding principles that stand behind this law are, on the one hand, that everybody has the right to dispose over her personal data; on the other hand, that information of public interest shall be accessible to everybody. As such, the law differentiates between personal data and public data. The Act defines *personal data* as any data that can be connected to a natural person, and any conclusions that can be drawn from such data referring to that person. Such data remains personal until its connection to the data subject can be reestablished that is until identification of the data subject is possible on its basis.[4]

Data of public interest is data that is processed by a body or a person performing state or local government functions, or any other public function defined by the law except for personal data.[5]

The law also defines a special category of personal data: sensitive data. *Sensitive data* is all personal data that concerns racial, national or ethnic identity, political opinion or party membership, religious or other conviction, health, addiction, sexual life or criminal record.[6] Sensitive data requires special protection according to Hungarian law. The Data Protection Act provides the framework for all other laws as far as protection of personal data is concerned. This protection is also reflected, at least as far as ethnic data (data concerning racial, national or ethnic identity) is concerned, in the Minority Act.[7] Article 3.2 of the Minority Act says: the right to national or ethnic identity is a basic human right to which both individuals and communities are entitled. Later, under the heading of individual minority rights, Article 7 says: "identification with and expression of belonging to a national, ethnic minority is the exclusive and inalienable right of the individual. No one can be forced to declare his or her national or ethnic identity. The right to national or ethnic identity and recognition and expression of belonging to such a minority group does not exclude the possibility of double or multiple identity." Finally Article 13. (c) says: "the individuals belonging to a minority have the right to have protection of their personal data related to their belonging to a minority group as laid down by a separate Act."

Article 3 of the Data Protection Act provides the circumstances under which personal, and, within that, sensitive data, can be controlled and processed. Personal data, says the act, can only be processed in two cases:

3. Act LXIII. of 1992.
4. Article 2 (1).
5. Article 2 (3).
6. Article 2(2).
7. Act LXXVII. of 1993 on the rights of national and ethnic minorities.

– if the data subject gives her consent;

– or in the absence of such a consent if it is authorized by the law — or in cases provided for by the law — by local government decrees.

The conditions for handling sensitive data are somewhat stricter. Sensitive data can only be handled in two cases:

– if the data subject gives her written consent;

– in case of ethnic data, if international convention justifies it, or law authorizes it for the purpose of enforcement of a basic constitutional right, or promotion of national security, crime prevention or criminal investigation;

– in case of other sensitive data, if it is authorized by law.

Furthermore, all personal data (including sensitive data) can only be handled (meaning: collected, registered, stored, processed, used — including transfer and dissemination — deleted, altered) with specified purpose, for exercising rights or complying with obligations.[8] The personal data has to be necessary and appropriate for the achievement of the above purpose, and can only be used to the extent and for the time necessary for the achievement of that purpose.

Transfer of personal data (disclosing the data to a defined third party) is only lawful if the data subject gives her consent to it, or in the absence of consent if law authorizes it, and the transfer respects the principle according to which only transfer with a specified and legitimate purpose, and adequate, relevant and not excessive in relation to that purpose, is consistent with the right to informational self-determination. These conditions shall be respected even in case of transfer between or within state administration bodies, and also in case of connecting databases.

Personal data can be disseminated for reasons of public interest, upon authorization of the law or in any other case only upon the consent (written consent for sensitive data) of the data subject. In such cases the disclosed data set has to be defined explicitly. In the absence of clear indication, the refusal of the consent of the data subject has to be presumed.

Processed personal data has to fulfill at every stage of processing a set of conditions:

– has to be obtained and processed fairly and lawfully;

– has to be accurate, complete and kept up to date;

– has to be preserved in a form that is appropriate for allowing the identification of the data subject only for the time that is necessary for the purpose of the storing of data.

Databases can only be linked[9] with the consent of the data subjects or the

8. Article 5 (1).
9. Article 8 (1) of the Data Protection Act.

authorization of the law, if these conditions stand for each and every set of personal data.

Transborder transfer of data is only lawful if the data subject has consented to it, or if it is authorized by the law and the above conditions for data processing are satisfied by the foreign data controller with regard to each data set.[10]

The Hungarian Data Protection Act refers to private and state actors equally. Protection of the right to informational self-determination is a protection that extends to both the private and public sector in Hungary.

Rights to Access and Review Personal Data

According to article 11 of the Data Protection Act, the data subjects have the right to information on the processing of their personal data, may ask for corrections or updating of data, and for erasure of data with the exception of data that was obtained on grounds of legal requirement. Data controllers have the obligation to provide information, upon request, on the controlled data; on the data processed by the data processor; on the legitimate purpose of the data processing, the legal grounds for it, the name and address of the data processor, and the list of those who had access to the data, and the justification for it. The data controller has the duty to answer the claim within the shortest time possible from submission, but no later than within 30 days. The information provided has to be written in a clear and understandable form. Information is free of charge once a year. From the second request on a fee may be requested. Information may be refused for reasons of state security, state defense, national security, crime prevention and crime detection, for financial interests of the state or local government, and for the protection of rights of the concerned person or of other persons. Refusal has to be justified to the claimant and should be registered yearly with the data protection Commissioner.[11]

Data that is incorrect should be rectified. Personal data should be erased if its processing was unlawful, if the data subject requests it (with the exceptions provided in the law) or the legitimate purpose of controlling the data ceased to exist. The data subject and all those who received the data previously for processing have to be notified about corrections and erasure. Notification can only be neglected if the legitimate interests of the data subject are not violated.

According to the Data Protection Commissioner, the right to access to data, and rights to modification and erasure of data is to be respected also in the case

10. Article 9 of the Data Protection Act.
11. Article 13.

of scientific research referring to or containing questions referring to sensitive data.[12]

In general individuals cannot have access to others' personal data. Allowing access to others' personal data falls under the category of disclosure of personal data, and as such it is lawful only if the data subject has consented or law authorizes it (with the above mentioned restrictions referring specifically to sensitive data). This is clearly so in case of sensitive data on ethnic or national identity. But, for example, in case of personal data falling under Act CXIX. of 1995 on name and address data in the field of research and direct marketing and data falling under Act LXVI. of 1992 on the registration of identification and address data, access to these special subcategories of personal data is permitted under the circumstances provided for by the Acts. Name and address data is accessible to all persons, organizations with or without legal personality for the sake of implementation of a right or lawful interest, for purposes of scientific research, for construction of samples for research of markets and of public opinion and, finally, for construction of lists serving the purposes of direct marketing.[13]

Personal data connected to members of groups or communities is not accessible especially if appropriate for identification of data subjects. Depersonalized statistical data is available about groups from the Central Statistical Office and other state and non-state bodies that may conduct data collection for statistical purposes.

The Data Protection Act also establishes a data protection registry, the aim of which is to provide information for persons on all data registries where their data is stored and processed. All persons have the right to access to the data protection registry, can record the information obtained there and can ask for extracts on it, for which they may be charged. The Data Protection Registry[14] is managed by the Parliamentary Commissioner for Data Protection and Freedom of Information. All controllers of data have to register in the Registry: before processing data they have to declare the purpose of the data processing, the type of the data to be processed and the legal justification for it, the concerned data subjects, the source of the data; in case of transfer, the type of data, the destination and the legal grounds for the transfer, the deadline for erasure of data, the name and address of the data controller, and the location of actual data processing. All data controllers have a registration number that has to be used at every data transfer, disclosure, or access of the data subject to the database. Every data processing which has a new purpose or creates a new database, and every change

12. 655 /K/1998.
13. Article 19.
14. Provided for in articles 28-30 of the Data Protection Act.

to these, has to be registered separately in the Registry within 8 days from change. Omitting the registration is punished with criminal sanctions. The Data Protection Act defines ten exceptions to the requirement of registration. Data processing shall not be registered if it:

- covers the data of persons maintaining employment, membership, student or business relations with the data controller;
- is governed by internal rules of churches, religious denominations or religious communities;
- covers personal data relating to the sickness or health of persons receiving medical care, for purposes of medical treatment or preservation of health or claiming social insurance benefits;
- covers data for the purpose of granting financial or other social benefits to a person;
- covers personal data relative to the conduct of administrative, prosecutorial and judicial proceedings;
- covers personal data for the purpose of official statistics;
- covers data processed under the Press Law for their unique informative activity;
- serves the purpose of scientific research if relevant data remain unpublished;
- was transferred from the controllers to archives;
- serves the sole purpose of a natural person.

Under Act LXVI of 1992 on registration of personal identification data, the Central Population Registry has the obligation to maintain a separate registry containing all the information on provision of data. [15] The Registry has to contain information concerning: the registration number of the data controller, the date of providing data, the purpose and legal grounds for providing data, the name of the person or body that requested data, and the description of the cluster of provided data. Individuals have the right to receive information from this Registry, as well as information about the data transfers relating to their data. The information stored in the Registry shall be saved for 5 years. [16]

Sectoral Laws Regulating
the Right to Informational Self-Determination

The Data Protection Act defines the general circumstances and conditions for data controlling and processing. The particular fields where data protection concerns may occur are regulated separately.

15. Article 31.
16. Article 31(4).

A separate law, Act XLVII of 1997, refers to the protection of a subcategory of sensitive data, namely health data. Health data is meant to include under this act: data concerning the physical, mental and psychical condition of the data sub-ject, addiction, conditions of illness or death, data concerning any explanation of the cause of these, and any data that can be connected to the above, respectively may influence the above, and finally data on sexual orientation if connected to health care.

Act CXIX of 1995 refers to the special data protection conditions applicable in the field of research and direct marketing. This law, however, only refers to access to and processing of a subset of personal data, namely data concerning name and address. The law provides for special conditions under which scien-tific research, public opinion research, market research and direct marketing may use data concerning name and address unless the data subject has explicitly banned processing her data for such purposes. This data does not include ethnic data. Moreover, the law explicitly bans[17] the use of any criteria for the definition of a sample to be used for research, or for the list to be used for direct market-ing, which even indirectly would allude to sensitive data.

Act LXVI of 1995 on the Protection of Public Documents, Public and Private Archives regulates the functioning of archives in light of the above data protec-tion provisions. Its aim is to provide for the functioning of archives so that both the constitutional right to access to public data and right to freedom of scientific research and, on the other hand, the right to protection of personality and per-sonal data are respected. Article 24 of the Act provides for the conditions under which documents containing personal data can be researched. Such documents are available to everybody from 30 years after the death of the data subject; if that is not known, from 90 years after the birth of the data subject; if that is not known either, from 60 years after the creation of the document. Exceptions can be made: if the document can be anonymized at the expense of the researcher or if the research can be justified scientifically and it conforms to certain conditions (among others the researcher signs a written declaration saying that she will obey the conditions of data processing defined in the Data Protection Act).

Provisions concerning sensitive data can be found in the Act for Public Education[18] and the Act for Higher Education.[19] Both laws mention, among the data registered and processed by institutions falling under their jurisdiction, the category of data to be obtained and processed with the permission of the data

17. In article 3(2).
18. Act LXXIX of 1993. Appendix to article 40.
19. Act LXXX of 1993. Appendix on personal and sensitive data controlled by higher education insti-tutions

subject (under the heading of data connected to student status). The Public Education Act allows for the transfer of *all* controlled data to the following bodies: the maintainer of the institution, court, police, attorney's office, local government, administrative body, state security. Also the Act provides for the use of these data for statistical purposes, but only with the condition of making it inappropriate for the identification of data subjects. The Act on Higher Education also allows for transfer of data for statistical purposes, within similar circumstances. However, otherwise it only authorizes the transfer of data concerning name, place and date of birth and only to the Ministry of Education. It should be mentioned here that before the promulgation of Data Protection Act ethnicity (belonging to the Roma minority) was registered in schools and other educational institutions. Based on this registration ethnic statistics could be made. With the passing of the Data Protection Act, registration of ethnicity was stopped.

Special Regulations on Census and Central Population Registries

Constitutional Court decision 15/1991 established the unconstitutionality of all regulations concerning population registries available at that time. Meanwhile, it defined the new constitutional conditions in accordance with which population registries can be kept, conditions that respect the right to informational self-determination. It argued that two guarantees have to be respected: personal data can only be controlled and processed with a defined and legitimate purpose, and transfer and disclosure can only be done within certain well-defined conditions. The Court argued that the regulations concerning population registries failed to respect these conditions and as such were unconstitutional.

Act LXVI of 1992 provides the conditions for the lawfulness of the registration of a special subcategory of personal data, personal identification data and address data: the name, citizenship, sex, place and date of birth, mother's name, personal identification number, place and date of death, address, marital status, photo and signature. In Hungary all legal inhabitants are obliged to register at the local authority when they take up residence. The Act provides for the conditions of lawful functioning of registries from the local to the national level. It provides for the conditions of lawful use of personal identification numbers. The law is written with the purpose of finding an equilibrium between the right to informational self-determination, enforcement of other constitutional rights and the public interest for efficient state administration.

Other centralized registries are available for social security and for taxation purposes. Both of these provide identification numbers for all of their data subjects: a social security number and a separate taxation number. The three cen-tralized registries cannot be linked together.

The Act on Statistics (Act XLVI of 1993) regulates the collection, process-ing, storing, transfer, analysis, provision and disclosure of data by using statisti-cal methods. It refers to the activities of all institutions, organizations or persons that conduct statistical activities, and, as far as statistical use of their data is con-cerned, also the institutions and persons that collect data for other purposes. This Act regulates the functioning of the Central Statistical Office and the cen-sus. According to this act, personal data supply can only be made obligatory by means of law (Article 8.3).

Article 8 of the Minority Act provides for the right of all citizens belong-ing to national or ethnic minorities to declare their identity at the national census secretly and anonymously. In accordance with this provision and Article 8(4) of Act XLVI of 1993 on Statistics, sensitive data on race or belonging to a national or ethnic group can only be collected for statistical purposes on a voluntary basis— if the data subject has given her written con-sent to it, and if the data is inappropriate for personal identification, meaning that it is anonymous.

Act CVIII of 1999 provides for the January 31, 2001 census. It makes par-ticipation in the census obligatory for all persons living on the territory of Hungary (Hungarian citizens, non-Hungarian citizens: persons residing on the territory of Hungary for more than 3 months, stateless persons and refugees). Answering the questions concerning health condition, religion, mother tongue and nationality is voluntary. The data collected in the census can only be used for statistical purposes. Name and exact address are not registered in the cen-sus.

An interesting debate was going on before the census in Hungary. It con-cerned the census question referring to religious affiliation. It has been argued [20] that if following the principle of separation of church and state, data referring to the religious affiliation of the Hungarian population cannot be the concern of the state. The neutral state is not supposed to finance the "marketing" and "mar-ket assessment" of the churches. As such including the question on religion in the state-financed census is contrary to the basic principles of the Hungarian constitutional democracy. Part of the argument against this question concerned the inevitability of an outcome favorable to the so-called historic churches and disadvantageous for the smaller, newer denominations.

20. Sajó András „ Népszámlálás a sztkorona országában" (Census in the land of the holy crown) and Fazekas Csaba "A bevallás statisztikája" (The statistics of self-identification) in *Népszabadság* 22 January 2000

Legal Sanctions for the Violation of the Right
to Informational Self-Determination

According to Article 17 of the Data Protection Act, the concerned person can sue the data controller in case of violation of her rights to informational self-determination. The burden of proof for proving the legality of the data control-ling and processing procedures falls on the data controller. If the claim is found to be justified, the court can compel the data controller to provide the requested information, to correct the data, or delete the data, or oblige the Commissioner for Data Protection to enable inspection of the Data Protection Registry. If required for the purposes of data protection, and in the interest of the protection of informational self-determination rights of a larger number of people, the court may rule the inclusion of the judgment in the Data Protection Registry.

Article 18 of the Data Protection Act provides for compensation of damages caused by unlawful data processing or by the violation of the technical circum-stances of data protection. The data controller is liable for the damages caused to the data subject both by the data controller and the data processor.

According to Article 177/A of the Criminal Code, data controllers and data processors who:

a. process personal data without proper authorization or disregarding the purpose of its collection;

b. unlawfully surrender or make public personal data;

c. fail to fulfill reporting obligations relating to the controlling of personal data;

d. conceal personal data from a party entitled thereto;

e. falsify controlled personal data;

f. conceal or falsify public data;

commit a misdemeanor, and are liable to no more than one year of imprison-ment, to communal work or to a fine.

Meanwhile the Criminal Code sanctions separately and more heavily the abuse of sensitive personal data. Article 177/B says:

"(1.) a.) Making unlawfully public or

b.) unlawfully using or disclosing to unconcerned persons

the sensitive data obtained during data controlling that was in accordance with the law concerning the protection of personal data is a crime and shall be punished with no more than three years of imprisonment.

"(2.) Unlawfully obtaining sensitive data for own use or use by others is an offence and shall be punished with no more than two years imprisonment, com-munal work or a fine."

There have been no court proceedings connected to unlawful handling of ethnic data thus far. But citizens complaining about abuse, or the direct danger of such an abuse, of their right to informational self-determination may also turn to the Parliamentary Commissioner for Data Protection. The Data Protection Commissioner cases can be perceived as constituting some kind of case law. However, the Commissioner can only issue recommendations, has no enforce- ment power and has no power to issue sanctions.

Parliamentary Commissioners and the Use of Ethnic Data

In Hungary the Constitution[21] and the Parliamentary Commissioner Act[22] establish the independent, ombudsman-like parliamentary commissioner insti- tution. There are altogether four Parliamentary Commissioners in Hungary: a Parliamentary Commissioner for Civil Rights, the general deputy of the Civil Rights Commissioner[23], the Parliamentary Commissioners for the Rights of National and Ethnic Minorities (Minority Commissioner) and the Parliamentary Commissioner for Data Protection. The Commissioners are not subordinated to each other.

The Commissioner for Data Protection is provided for by the Data Protection Act in its fourth chapter. The Commissioner is an independent insti- tution with ombudsman-type jurisdiction. It is elected by the Parliament for the protection of the right to informational self-determination, meaning the pro- tection of personal data and also the right to access to public data. The tasks of the Commissioner are to review the enforcement of the Data Protection Act and other legislation relevant to this field, to investigate complaints coming to him concerning the abuse or direct danger of abuse of the right to informational self- determination, and to manage the data protection registry.

In case of data protection complaints concerning sensitive data related to race, nationality or ethnicity, the Minority Commissioner and the Data Protection Commissioner often consult each other. Several such complaints have occurred dur- ing the first six years of activity of the Commissioners. When speaking about the legal context concerning data protection and processing and use of sensitive data, the recommendations of the Parliamentary Commissioner for Data Protection cannot be disregarded. Let me look at the most important cases that occurred in this field.

One issue that came before the Data Protection Commissioner[24] concerned

21. Article 32/B.
22. Act LIX of 1993 on the Parliamentary Commissioner for Civil Rights.
23. This position is not currently filled.
24. 611/A/1996; 867/K/1997.

the requirement to declare ethnic identity in order to become entitled to certain benefits provided on grounds of preferential treatment for members of national or ethnic minorities. The Commissioner argued that the requirement is lawful in the case of participation in such programs; the data-subjects can be required to declare their identity before the body managing the program, but not publicly, if they want to be entitled to preferential treatment. However, the managing body is obliged to respect the rules applying to data processing and data security, has to declare that the obtained data will not be transferred or disclosed and, finally, has to inform the applicants about the purpose for which their data is collected. But the program has to be one that aims at the improvement of equality of opportunity of minorities, has to be a minority program and not a general one. Participation in such programs is voluntary, and this makes declaration of identity voluntary, as well.

Somewhat connected to this issue was the case concerning the taping of declarations made by Roma to the police.[25] The practice has shown that declarations of Roma made before the police were often misunderstood, wrongly interpreted and later turned against them. As a form of preferential treatment, the police decided on an experimental basis to introduce the possibility of taping the declarations of Roma. Given the fact that making declarations of national or ethnic identity compulsory is unlawful, and the right to declare one's identity is the exclusive and unalienable right of the data subject, the police failed to find a proper legal solution for implementing the project. According to the Commissioner, everybody should have been informed about the availability of the special opportunity of taping declarations for Roma, and making use of this opportunity should have been voluntary, and grounded on the voluntary written declaration of identity of the concerned for this purpose. The police chose to drop the project because of the technical impossibility for taping all declarations (of Roma and non-Roma) and the practical difficulties in implementing the project as some kind of preferential program.

Another reoccurring issue in the activity of the Commissioner concerned the disclosure of real or presumed ethnic identity in police reports. The Commissioner argued that disclosure of such sensitive data is capable of raising the prejudiced attitude of the population and as such cannot be disclosed. Later on the Commissioner accepted that there are exceptions to the general prohibition: namely when the disclosure is not unlawful (written consent of the data subject is obtained) and does not tend to raise prejudices against the respective ethnic group.

25. 362/A/1996.

Referring to registries of ethnic data maintained by state bodies, the Commissioner formulated recommendations in two cases. One concerned the compensation of Holocaust survivors and the possibility of creating registries containing data on ethnicity or religion based on the list of compensated persons. [26] The other concerned issuing certificates on ethnicity by Roma minority self-governments for the purpose of proving ethnicity before immigration authorities of other countries. [27] In both instances the recommendation said: state bodies cannot possess officially information about data concerning national or ethnic identity or religion unless they have the written consent of the data subject. State bodies may not even give the appearance that they possess such data. In the compensation case the data was in fact available, partly because of the list of compensated people, partly because of pre-1952 registries containing information on such data; the Commissioner's recommendation banned its unlawful processing and disclosure. In the latter case the recommendation argued that the data is not available and yet the certificate on ethnicity can make it appear that the state body possesses it. Finally he argued that certificates can only be issued concerning the voluntary declaration made by the data subject on her identity, saying "this or that person declared before us to be of Roma origin." Meanwhile the recommendations suggest that non-state bodies (minority parties, cultural associations, NGOs) may act differently; these may lawfully issue upon request certificates containing ethnic data.

Several cases in the activity of the Commissioner concerned collection of ethnic data for the purpose of writing reports on the social situation of Roma communities at local level with the aim of their development. In 1997 [28] a local Roma minority self-government complained about a social report of the local government, which contained data on the proportion of Roma in different social groups such as pregnant woman, school age children etc., data that seemed to suggest that the local government has registries concerning the Roma population. The complaint was especially concerned about certain prejudiced conclusions drawn from the data presented in the report. The notary declared that the local authority had no registries of data concerning ethnicity, that the report was based on estimations made by the different experts on the field. The Commissioner found the numerical representation of the Roma community in the report as contrary to the Data Protection Act. Later on, in 1999 the Commissioner contributed to the development of lawful data collection procedures in some similar cases [29] where the local or regional authority aimed to develop programs for the better

26. 441/A/1997.
27. 317/K/1998.
28. 308/A/1997.
29. 743/K/1999, 420/K/1999.

integration of the Roma population into society, and for this purpose needed to collect sensitive data. The Commissioner found lawful the collection of ethnic data for such purposes, with the condition that it strictly follows certain data pro-tection rules: publication of results should in no case be appropriate for the iden-tification of the data subjects; the data subjects should be properly informed about the purpose and utilization of the collected data; the registration and stor-ing of the data should be such that the data subjects can only be identified on its basis for the period absolutely necessary in relation to the purpose for which they are stored; data processing should be safe and inaccessible to unwarranted per-sons; creation of self-standing "Roma registries" shall be avoided. It should also be mentioned that the Commissioner at this point also found acceptable the esti-mation of proportion of Roma in certain groups, e.g. the head of school esti-mating the proportion of Roma pupils in the school. [30]

As far as collection of ethnic data within the framework of scientific research is concerned, the Commissioner's point of view can be reconstructed based on rec-ommendations made in several cases in which the Commissioner was mostly asked to review the questionnaires, the research plans, or the consent forms. [31] According to the Commissioner, collection of such data can only be done on a voluntary basis and after obtaining the written informed consent of the data subject (if the research refers to more than one set of sensitive data — i.e. ethnicity and health condition — written consent is needed for the collection of each set of data). Information to be provided when obtaining consent shall concern: information on the data con-troller and data processor, the purpose of the data collection, the length of pro-cessing the data, the voluntary nature of providing the data, the rights of data sub-jects concerning access to data and modification, erasure of data, the way in which the data will be utilized. The obtained data has to be controlled and processed at all times in accordance with the purpose for which they were collected, always respecting data protection rules. Throughout the processing the data subject's right to information, to access to data, to request erasure or modification of data has to be respected. The data preferably shall not be stored separately according to ethnicity, but there rather should be a registry containing all data, including sen-sitive data. In case of statistical data collection, the obtained data can only be used in a way that makes identification of data-subjects impossible.

Also connected to scientific research is the Yad Vashem case [32] of the Data Protection Commissioner. The petition concerned research on the Holocaust

30. 743/K/1999.
31. 655 /K/1998, 643/K/1999, 1/K/1999, 107/K/1999.
32. For the English language text of the report on the case and the recommendations made by the Commissioner see *www.osa.ceu.hu/bridge/access&protection/06.html.*

of Hungarian Jews and in particular on the issue of recording on microfilm documents containing sensitive personal data and passing them on to the Yad
Vashem Archives in Jerusalem. The case revolved around the conflict between
the right to informational self-determination and the right to reverence and
another constitutional right: freedom of science and scholarship including the
right to scientific and scholarly research. In this case the privileges of scientific
research, as defined in the Archives Act[33], were explicitly referred to. According
to the report "documents containing personal data may be researched even
before the general protection to which they are subject expires, on condition that
the researcher presents a statement of support by a scientific body and signs a
written declaration accepting the limitations on the use of the acquired personal data under the Data Protection Act." Meanwhile, the report goes on:
"access...does not automatically entail the possibility to transfer or publish material...these can only be disclosed without the consent of the data subject if this is
required in order to demonstrate the results of the historical research." In all
other cases the researcher qualifies as data controller handling personal or sensitive data and as such has to follow the rules set by the Data Protection Act in
that it needs the consent (written consent) of the data subjects for the data handling. In this particular case the Commissioner suggested as a solution for gathering the consent of the data subjects the opt out method, i.e. the right to protest
instead of the right to consent. In such a solution "the data subject must be
informed of the fact, purpose, and other circumstances of the data handling and
that he can prohibit the handling of his data any time and without providing a
reason, and what way he can do so." Also a data protection contract shall be
signed between the data controlling bodies (every document-issuing body in
Hungary and the recipient archive) which shall contain the terms of handling
documents containing personal data, the terms of research and disclosure.

Ethnic Data and the Protection of Minorities.
The Connections, Overlaps and Contradictions between the Enforcement of Minority
Rights and the Principles of Data Protection.

The institution of the Commissioner for the Rights of National and Ethnic
Minorities is established by the Constitution. It is the duty of the Commissioner
for the protection of national and ethnic minority rights, says the Constitution,
to investigate or to have investigated any abuse of national or ethnic minority
rights that has come to his attention, and to initiate general or particular mea-

33. Act LXVI. of 1995 on public records, public archives and the protection of private archives.

sures for redress.[34] The activity of the Commissioner is regulated by Parliamentary Commissioner Act which refers to all Parliamentary Commissioners, and by the Minority Act.[35] In accordance with the Minority Act, the Minority Commissioner is to "take measures in issues coming under the ruling of the present Act" [36] (meaning complaints connected to provisions of the Minority Act, all rights provided for in that act). Complaints filed by members of immigrant groups or other minorities, which are not part of the thirteen, recognized "historical minorities" of Hungary (defined in the Minority Act) are beyond the scope of action by the Commissioner.

One of the most fundamental minority rights defined by the Minority Act is the inalienable and exclusive right of all members of national and ethnic minorities to declare their national or ethnic identity. This right also includes the right to refuse to make such a declaration and the right to declare multiple identity. It is clear already from reading the Minority Act that the right to national or ethnic identity is a right which needs very careful protection. National or ethnic identity is part of individual self-determination, a sensitive part of it which deserves special protection at least partly because of its historically well known abuses. Meanwhile the formulation of this right also alludes to the absence of objective criteria in the definition of its subject — national or ethnic identity — to its entirely subjective, personal character and also to its shifting character (be that within the life time of one individual or longer). This subjectivity and changing character also leads to the necessity of enormous care in handling national or ethnic identity, especially by state actors.

The same national or ethnic identity forms the core of what the Data Protection Act defines as sensitive data. The rules defined in the Data Protection Act for the protection of sensitive data seem to materialize the care and caution argued for by the Minority Act. The protection of national or ethnic identity, while one of the basic minority rights, is also of concern for the right to informational self-determination; control over data concerning national and ethnic identity forms one of the very important aspects of this right. The inalienable and exclusive right to national or ethnic identity is thus the major connection between the fields of minority rights and data protection, if examined along this right the two fields seem to work together, to complement each other perfectly.

However, if reading the legislative material available in the two fields several contradictions arise, as well. The Minority Act provides for a set of special rights for members of national and ethnic minority groups in Hungary. Minorities

34. Aricle 32/B, paragraph 2.
35. Article 20 (2).
36. Article 20 (3).

have the right to establish from local to the national level minority self-governments, the members of which are to be elected. The Act also provides for minority education from kindergarten level up to higher education where needed.[37] In
case of a minimum of eight children belonging to the same minority, whose parents request minority education, a minority class or group shall be established.
In accordance with the Hungarian Constitution[38], the Act also prescribes the
possibility of providing special educational programs for Roma in order to
decrease the educational disadvantages of the group.[39] The state is supposed to
cover the additional expenses occurring from the special conditions of minority
education.[40] Given that these special rights and forms of support are specific for
minorities— they are strictly connected to membership in a national or ethnic
minority group— it seems rather contradictory to claim the necessity of ignorance of the state with regard to ethnic or national identity of its citizens.

Some of these rights and benefits are dependent on the self-identification of
persons belonging to national or ethnic minorities. In order to make use of the
advantages of minority education the parent has to declare the identity of her
child, and the minority education has to be requested. However, from the
moment when this declaration is made, the state is aware of the identity of the
child. The per capita normative state support for minority education can be very
well traced; moreover, the declarations of identity cannot be destroyed given
their importance in accounting for the extra normative before the State Audit
Office. Similar is the situation with other forms of support where minority identity is a precondition of providing the support. If the state is to follow consequently the premises of its minority protection system, according to which
sometimes special treatment is due to minorities in order to achieve their equality of opportunity, it has to identify in some way or other the members of its target group. Otherwise either the idea of special treatment has to be dropped or
the risk of over-inclusiveness of the policy undertaken.

It is exactly this problem that surfaced in the field of election of minority self-
governments. The 1993 Minority Act declares the right of ethnic and national
minorities to establish self-government as a special community right, either at
the local or national level. Basically the contention revolves around the question
of defining the active and passive electorate in the election of minority self-governments. On the one hand, since the system of self-governments is explicitly
created to ensure the representation of conscious members of national or ethnic

37. Article 18(3)a, article 43.
38. Article 70/A (3).
39. Article 45 (2).
40. Article 44, Article 55 on additional normative support for minority education.

minorities, it would seem straightforward that only individuals consciously self-identifying with one of the 13 national or ethnic minorities recognized in Hungary could elect and be elected, and each in the election for the self-government of his/her group of belonging. Yet, given the priority that the legal system accords to the inalienable and exclusive right to declare national or ethnic identity is also understood to include the possibility of refusal of making such a declaration, and deriving from this right the avoidance of registration of minority members in Hungary, it is practically impossible to define the passive and active electorate of minority elections. As a matter of fact, the Hungarian constitution states that everybody can elect and can be elected in minority self-government elections, regardless of their ethnic or national belonging.[41] This led to quite paradoxical results in the October 1998 elections, when much more votes were cast for minority candidates than the total number of minority group members (using the highest estimate available for such numbers). This resulted in the absurd situation in which the representatives of the minorities were not elected by the groups themselves. The obvious fear here was, that if exercising the special minority right to self-government requires declaration of identity, this would either lead to the creation of some kind of state-owned registry containing sensitive data or would render elections invalid, because minorities would stay away from elections due to their fear of being registered as such. The contradiction between providing special rights and benefits for members of national and ethnic minorities and the principle of necessity of state ignorance as far as ethnic data is concerned, inherent in the Hungarian legal system is a major contradiction.

Another contradiction that shall be mentioned mainly concerns one of the minority groups in Hungary: the Roma minority. One of the features which contributes to the distinctiveness of this minority in Hungary is its visibility. In case of persons belonging to the Roma minority, declaration of identity is in most cases not necessary for identification and abuse. The premise of the Hungarian data protection system is that the sensitive data does not exist until it is registered in some way. The purpose of this volume is to examine how litigation of racial discrimination[42] cases or research on the phenomenon of racial discrimination can be conducted within the framework of the existent data protection systems. If thinking about racial discrimination in Hungary, its patterns of occurrence, the ethnic identity of the large majority of victims, it becomes clear that the

41. Article 70 (1). For an analysis see Andrea Krizsán (2000) "The Hungarian Minority Protection System: a flexible approach to the adjudication of ethnic claims" *Journal on Ethnic and Migration Studies* Vol.26, No.2:247-262.
42. I use racial discrimination as an umbrella term for discrimination on grounds of national, ethnic or racial origin.

above premise of the Hungarian data protection system is wrong at least as far as racial discrimination is concerned. The abuse the system tries to avoid is, on the one hand, abuse that has historically occurred; on the other hand, it is a matter of principle, and concerns the neutrality of state. Meanwhile the most present abuse against the largest minority group in Hungary, the Roma, does not derive from registration of sensitive data, but it may occur just as well within the frame - work of the careful, "colorblind" data protection system. The ethnic data is pre - sent at the level of personal interactions, is present in the employment situations, in schools, in provision of services, in the activity of local authorities (be that housing, distribution of social benefits, child support, community work or any - thing else). At the local level, especially in small settlements, everybody knows who is Roma and who is not; moreover, this knowledge has nothing to do with informational self-determination. The public knowledge of being a member of the Roma minority does not have to overlap with personal self-identification. In such circumstances it is rather deceitful, at least as far as this minority group is concerned, to say that by avoiding the registration of sensitive data we avoid abuse of it. Moreover, as far as litigation or proof of racial discrimination cases is concerned, it seems that whereas the absence of any kind of ethnic statistics at the local level (meaning the practices of the particular employer, of the local authority, of the school, or of the service provider) does not manage to avoid abuse based on ethnicity (since at the local level ethnicity is not a matter of pri - vacy); it more or less makes impossible proof of discrimination by those who try to challenge it (public interest law firms, Minority Commissioner etc.) and who rarely are in possession of such local knowledge, or even if they are they may not resort to it lawfully.

The right not to be discriminated against on grounds of race, national or eth - nic origin is a basic constitutional right and the necessity of its enforcement makes this contradiction one of vital importance for the Hungarian legal system, the solution of which is required not only by the Constitution but also by sever - al international documents referring to the right not to be discriminated against, and ratified by Hungary.

Concerning regulation of racial discrimination in Hungary, the following can be said. First the Hungarian Constitutional context is permissive though not requiring from the point of view of the right not to be discriminated against on racial grounds.[43] The relationship established by the Constitutional Court between the right not to be discriminated against and the right to human digni - ty allows for a very inclusive constitutional definition of discrimination. Also the

43. Constitutional Court Decision ABH 431/E/1996.

provision of paragraph 3 of Article 70/A concerning the promotion of equal opportunities makes void a debate about unconstitutionality of positive discrimination[44] void. Moreover, Article 7 of the Constitution brings in at constitutional level as valid domestic law the international obligations undertaken by the state. These international obligations also require of Hungary, even if some of them are at a quite general level and without effective sanctions, a comprehensive approach to racial discrimination in all fields of life where it might occur. Some of these international documents go further then just requiring abstaining from acts of discrimination to requiring positive steps on the side of the state to prevent and sanction discrimination committed by actors other than the state.

Yet regulation of racial discrimination at the statutory level in Hungary is rather unsatisfactory in light of the above requirements. Most fields of law contain general prohibitions of discrimination, however, no detailed definition of discrimination is available in any of them, not to speak of the absence of a definition generally applicable to all fields. Most fields lack provisions concerning the special procedural requirements necessary for the proof and evidence and sanctioning of discrimination. As a consequence, only challenges of facially discriminatory acts make it to the courts and even those are challenged mostly under legal provisions not explicitly made for prohibition of discrimination. In the current legal context in Hungary, in violation of international obligations undertaken by the state[45], only individual disparate treatment cases of discrimination can be challenged in which only the individual complainant can get redress for explicit, intended acts of racial discrimination. In these circumstances the real need for using ethnic statistics in challenging and litigation of racial discrimination cases has not surfaced yet in court procedures.

In Hungary there are no facially discriminatory regulations. However, as already mentioned, the interpretation of discrimination of the Constitutional Court does not include indirect or disparate impact discrimination. Thus, based on a definition of discrimination which includes this form of discrimination as well, one could argue that there are certain seemingly neutral regulations in Hungary, the disparate impact of which burdens national or ethnic minorities, and has no objective justification.[46] In the absence of ethnic statistics, however,

44. A very much debated issue under the Equal Protection Clause of the US constitution.
45. NEKI submission to the Constitutional Court on 29. October 1999. The Constitutional Court turned down the case in December 2000. ABH 45/2000 (XII.8.)
46. Definition used by the EC Directive: "indirect discrimination shall be taken to occur where an apparently neutral provision, criterion or practice would put persons of a racial or ethnic origin at a particular disadvantage compared with other persons, unless that provision, criterion or practice is objectively justified by a legitimate aim and the means of achieving that aim are appropriate and necessary." Article 2.2.b.

it is very difficult to argue this, except in the obvious cases where the disparate impact is so outrageous that discrimination can be argued even without numbers.

The Minority Parliamentary Commissioner uses a concept of discrimination which includes indirect discrimination, as well. Thus his investigations often have to address the issue of the lack of ethnic statistics. In one of the cases that came before his office[47], he argued that a local government decree concerning the collection of waste was indirectly discriminatory because it primarily impacted on the local Roma population. The decree set a disproportionate sanction for collection of waste from the garbage cans on the streets. The decree was neutral; it banned all persons from collection of garbage, yet the disadvantage has fallen on Roma exclusively. The Commissioner grounded his argument on a statement made by the head of the local Roma self-government, according to whom all sanctioned people were Roma.

Probably there are several other similar local regulations that could be challenged if the concept of indirect discrimination would be explicitly available at constitutional level.

The Commissioner also found indirectly discriminatory the regulation of Roma minority education. The legal provisions in this field result in a situation in which minority education for Roma means in practice special catch-up classes having only Roma students but having no special Roma curricula. In most cases these classes are organized in the absence of the informed consent of the parents to enroll their children to minority education, yet they make use of the extra per capita financial normative provided by the state for special minority education.[48] The regulation shifts together elements of minority education with elements of special catch-up education, which results in schools disregarding the minority education elements and enrolling all Roma in catch-up education. The disparate impact is obvious here: in some schools only Roma children end up in catch-up classes, whereas no Roma children are educated in normal classes.

It can be argued that the recent amendment of the 1993 Act LXXVIII on Lease and Sale of Apartments and Other Premises[49], according to which eviction can take place without court decision, falls with disproportionate burden on members of the Roma minority. However, in the absence of ethnic statistics it is difficult to see first whether the number of Roma victims of eviction is indeed larger than their proportion in the relevant pool of the population. Second, it is impossible to see in the absence of statistics whether discrimination occurs here due to the discriminatory implementation of the law (i.e. only Roma are evicted,

47. 5887/K/1999.
48. 3008/K/2000.
49. Act XLI. of 2000.

while non-Roma in similar situations are not, even though the law refers to them, as well) or the law is indirectly discriminatory (i.e. there is a much larger proportion of Roma who are going to be affected by this law, and as such the amendment burdens this group with a disproportionate impact).

Until now no Constitutional Court or other court decisions were brought regarding the availability or use of ethnic statistics. Ethnic statistics have not been used so far in court decisions.

Besides the Data Protection Commissioner's interpretation, recommendations concerning collection, processing and use of ethnic statistics, the practice of the Minority Commissioner shall also be examined here. The Minority Commissioner has used ethnic statistics in some of the cases investigated by his office. He utilized ethnic data for proof of systemic racial discrimination. In the case of one complaint referring to the discriminatory practices of the local authority in the distribution of social benefits[50], the Commissioner asked the local authority to provide data on the share of the Roma population in the overall amount of social benefits distributed. The local authority answered accordingly: they provided the necessary data (data that was probably registered and collected in an unlawful manner), showing that despite the fact that only 19% of the population belongs to the Roma minority, their share among the recipients of different social benefits is 50-68%. Similar data was provided by the local authority in another case.[51] In both cases the Commissioner grounded his argument refuting the suspicion of discrimination on these ethnic statistics. In none of these cases is it clear how the local authority has collected the data, whether the ethnic monitoring followed the rules set by the Data-protection Act. The Commissioner, however, did not call the attention of the authority to the problem, and did not question the lawfulness of the statistics. Obviously this omission derived from the point of view of the Commissioner according to which availability of statistical data is crucial for the proof of discrimination and for the monitoring of discriminatory procedures. As such it can be argued that this omission is morally acceptable even though it has no legal support.

A question is raised, however, by the interpretations of these ethnic statistics: what is the proper way to understand these statistics? The question is whether it is sufficient that at least the same proportion of social benefits should go to the Roma, as their proportion is within the overall population, or some other measure should be applied? Given the fact that the Roma population is multiply disadvantaged, and a much larger proportion of the Roma is dependent on social benefits vis a vis the non-Roma, it is clear that statistics have to be used differ-

50. 3630/1996/K.
51. 6240/1996/K.

179

ently. The overall sample against which the share of social benefits has to be measured should not be the entire population of the settlement, but rather only those who qualify for social benefits in general: the population which has a pre-carious financial situation, above average number of children, bad housing con-ditions etc. The proportion of Roma in this group will certainly be much larger that their proportion in the overall population. The share of social benefits will have to follow this proportion in order to be non-discriminatory in racial terms. As such, the application of the concept of systemic disparate impact was mistak-en here.

In another interesting case not ethnic statistics but control cases have been used (Roma and non-Roma). The office of the Minority Commissioner trans-ferred a complaint of discrimination (Roma persons where not allowed to enter a disco) to the Consumer Protection Authority, which, in cooperation with the local Roma self-government, organized an experimental team of four Roma per-sons. The fact that none of them was allowed to enter was perceived as proving the case of discrimination. The Consumer Protection Authority issued an injunction for the disco.[52]

International Obligations

Article 7 (1) of the Hungarian Constitution says "The legal system of the Republic of Hungary accepts the generally recognized principles of international law, and shall harmonize the country's domestic law with the obligations assumed under international law."

First, with respect to discrimination The International Covenant on Civil and Political Rights[53] refers to discrimination in two articles: Article 2 and Article 26. Article 2 formulates the prohibition of discrimination as a derivative right: that is, all rights in the covenant shall be provided without discrimination. Article 26 extends the previous formulation. It says: "All persons are equal before the law and are entitled without any discrimination to the equal protection of the law. In this respect the law shall prohibit any discrimination and guarantee to all persons equal and effective protection against discrimination on any ground such as race, color, sex, language religion, political or other opinion, national or social origin, property, birth or other status." Article 26 thus formulates a general prohibition of discrimination, not only one that is in relation to the rights provided for by the Covenant; it prescribes a positive duty for the states to provide for *an equal*

52. OBH 7178/K/1998; decision 1293/1999 of the Consumer Protection Authority of Szabolcs-Szatmár-Bereg county.
53. Promulgated in Hungary by Law Decree No.8 of 1976.

and effective protection against discrimination for all persons beyond the general prohibition of discrimination.

Similarly, until lately Article 14 of the European Convention for the Protection of Human Rights and Fundamental Freedoms[54] defined discrimination in relation to the other rights protected by the Convention ("the enjoyment of the rights and freedoms set forth in this Convention shall be secured without discrimination on any grounds such as..."). In June 2000 the Council of Europe Committee of Ministers adopted Protocol No.12 to the European Convention which provides for a general prohibition of discrimination. This Protocol removes the restriction of Article 14 on the right to be free from discrimination and provides a guarantee that no one shall be discriminated against on any ground by any public authority. The Protocol was opened for signature to member states in November 2000. Once signed and ratified by a sufficient number of countries and the Hungarian state, Protocol 12 will allow for a more extensive protection against discrimination pursued by the European Court for Human Rights and Fundamental Freedoms.[55] Hungary has signed Protocol 12 on the 4th of November 2000. Since the 5th of November 1992, complaints against violations of rights defined in the Convention can be raised against the Hungarian state before the European Court for Human Rights and the Commission. Until 1999[56] 26 complaints went before the European Court for Human Rights or the Commission. Two referred, among other violations, to discrimination on grounds of ethnic origin. However, the Commission found these claims unsupported.

More extensive protection against discrimination is provided by the International Convention on the Elimination of all Forms of Racial Discrimination.[57] Article 1(1) of the Convention gives the definition of discrimination according to which "any distinction, exclusion, restriction or preference based on race, color, descent, or national or ethnic origin which has the *purpose or effect* of nullifying or impairing the recognition, enjoyment or exercise, on an equal footing of human rights and fundamental freedoms in the political, economic, social, cultural or any other field of public life." The scope of this definition is wide, on the one hand, because of the actions to which it refers: distinctions, exclusions, restrictions or preferences. On the other hand, because it

---

54. Promulgated in Hungary by Act XXXI. of 1993.

55. Protocol 12 says: (1) The enjoyment of any right set forth by law shall be secured without discrimination on any ground such as...(2) No one shall be discriminated against by any public authority on any grounds such as those mentioned in paragraph 1.

56. Report of the Republic of Hungary concerning the implementation of the Framework Convention. Government Decree 2023/1999 (II.12.)

57. Promulgated in Hungary by Law-decree No.8 of 1969. The declaration under article 14th of ICERD was made by Hungary on 13 September 1992. Since than complaints againts violation of rights defined in the Convention can be made before CERD.

does away with the requirement of discriminatory intent, any action that has the purpose or at least the effect of impairing equality is discriminatory. The Convention also allows for affirmative action if it is temporary and does not lead to the maintenance of separate rights for different groups. Article 2 of the Convention provides both for negative and positive duties of the state parties: state parties condemn discrimination and undertake to pursue by all appropriate means and without delay a policy of eliminating racial discrimination in all its forms and promoting understanding among all racial or ethnic groups.[58] Thus states signatory to the Convention are expected, beyond refraining from discrimination, to have comprehensive anti-discrimination policies that prohibit and sanction discrimination and, moreover, promote understanding between groups. A separate article prohibits forms of segregation and apartheid.[59]

No complaints were brought against Hungary to CERD before the present day. Hungary submitted to CERD its eleventh, twelfth and thirteenth periodic report on the 6th of March 1996.[60] The CERD, concluding observations and comments on Hungary[61], stated the following: "the absence of demographic data on the minorities in different districts of the country makes any evaluation of activities intended for their benefit difficult. Equally, the lack of data on the representation of minorities in the local authorities and the lack of recent data on the situation of minorities in the fields of education, culture, the media and employment is regretted."[62] The Committee made two recommendations relevant to our purposes here. It recommended that "adequate indicators and other means of monitoring the economic and social conditions of this group [the Gypsies] should be developed"[63] and "that the State party provide in its next report, statistical data on the minorities in the different districts, on their representation in the local authorities, as well as recent data on their situation in the fields of education, culture, the media and employment."[64]

The Framework Convention for the Protection of National Minorities[65] also formulates a general prohibition against discrimination on grounds of member-

58. "No state organ shall engage in racial discrimination; state shall not sponsor, defend or support racial discrimination by any persons or organizations; states shall take effective measures to review governmental, national or local policies and to amend rescind or nullify any law and regulations which have the effect of creating or perpetuating racial discrimination wherever it exists; state shall prohibit or bring to an end by all appropriate means ... racial discrimination by any persons, group or organization; shall encourage integrationist, multiracial organizations and movements."
59. Article 3.
60. CERD/C/263/Add.6.
61. CERD/C/304/Add.4.
62. Paragraph 16.
63. Paragraph 21.
64. Paragraph 22.
65. Promulgated in Hungary by Act XXXIV of 1999.

ship in national minority groups in its Article 4. It provides that state parties shall guarantee the right to equality before the law and equal protection of the law, that is, prohibit any discrimination based on membership in a national minority. In the second paragraph of the article the Convention provides for a positive duty of the state parties to "adopt, where necessary, adequate measures in order to promote in all areas of economic, social, political and cultural life full and effective equality between persons belonging to a national minority and those belonging to the majority." The last sentence of the paragraph, "In this respect they shall take due account of the specific conditions of the persons belonging to national minorities," provides for the recognition of differences between groups, a recognition that can form the grounds for recognition of systemic disparate impact as a prohibited form of discrimination and also for necessity of preferential treatment for the members of national minority groups in the form of affirmative action plans, both requiring the use of ethnic statistics for implementation. The Convention also states: "every person belonging to a national minority shall have the right freely to choose to be treated or not to be treated as such and no disadvantage shall result from this choice..."[66] Hungary has submitted to the Secretary General of the Council of Europe its first country report under the Framework Convention in January 1999.

The second European Commission against Racism and Intolerance (ECRI) report on Hungary shall be mentioned here.[67] It analyzed the situation in Hungary as regards racism and intolerance and made suggestions and proposals about how to manage the identified problems. Issues relating to ethnic data and ethnic monitoring are referred to in three parts of the report. The first is connected to the administration of justice. The report states that there is evidence that there is discrimination against Roma in the administration of justice (such as pre-trial detention for longer periods and more frequently than in case of non-Roma). Connected to this worry, the report notes the difficulty in evaluating this situation due to the absence of records of ethnic origin.[68] Referring to the monitoring of the situation, ECRI writes: "While acknowledging the fact that the collection and utilization of data on ethnic origin is restricted in Hungary for valid reasons, ECRI is concerned that the lack of reliable information about the situation of the various minority groups living in the country makes evaluation of the extent of possible discrimination against them or the effect of actions intended to combat such discrimination difficult. ECRI recommends that the Hungarian authorities might consider ways of monitoring the situation in this

66. Article 3.
67. ECRI. Second Report on Hungary. Adopted on 18 June 1999. CRI (2000)5.
68. Paragraph 14.

respect, with due attention to the need for protection of data and of privacy. For example, carefully prepared studies which respect the anonymity, dignity and full consent of persons involved may allow the situation in some areas of life to be evaluated." [69] Finally the report mentions, among issues of particular concern, with reference to discrimination against Roma in the field of employment, the unlawful registration and use of ethnic data by some employment offices. [70]

Finally a document shall be mentioned, which is only indirectly relevant at the moment for Hungary. The Council of the European Union Directive imple-menting the principle of equal treatment between persons irrespective of racial or ethnic origin[71] entered into force in the European Union on the 19th of July 2000. Even though Hungary is not a member of the EU (it is only an associated state), the long-term aim of the Hungarian State to integrate sets the require-ment of legal harmonization in this field, as well. In this sense the new Directive sets the path that has to be followed by Hungary in the realm of regulating racial discrimination.

The EC Directive aims to implement the general prohibition of discrimina-tion contained in Article 13 of the Amsterdam Treaty. The Directive defines the concept of racial discrimination very widely. The definition as formulated in Article 2 includes direct discrimination, indirect discrimination, harassment and instruction to discriminate[72]. Article 9 also prohibits victimization. [73] Direct dis-crimination, the directive says, "shall be taken to occur where one person is treated less favorably than another is, has been or would be treated in a compa-rable situation on grounds of racial or ethnic origin." Indirect discrimination is defined as when "an apparently neutral provision, criterion or practice would put persons of a racial or ethnic origin at a particular disadvantage compared with other persons, unless that provision, criterion or practice is objectively justified by a legitimate aim and the means of achieving that aim are appropriate and nec-essary." Racial harassment is also considered as one form of discrimination and is defined as "an unwanted conduct related to racial or ethnic origin [that] takes place with the purpose or effect of violating the dignity of a person and of creat-ing an intimidating, hostile, degrading, humiliating or offensive environment." The scope of the directive is extended to employment and all activity connected to employment, including promotion, selection criteria and recruitment, hier-archy, access to vocational training and guidance, retraining, working condi-

---

69. Paragraph 26.
70. Paragraph 41.
71. Council Directive 2000/43/EC of 29 June 2000 published in the *Official Monitor of the European Communities* on 19.7.2000. L 180/22.
72. "An instruction to discriminate against persons on grounds of racial or ethnic origin shall be deemed to be discrimination…"

tions, dismissals and pay, to membership in professional organizations and trade unions, to social protection, social security and health care, to social advantages, to education and, finally, to access to supply of goods and services, to housing. Article 5 of the Directive also allows for positive action "to prevent of compensate for disadvantages linked to racial or ethnic origin."

The Directive prescribes for the member states the general duty to provide for judicial and administrative procedures and remedies in order to enforce its provisions. In procedural terms it is important to mention that the Directive provides in its Article 8 for the shift of burden of proof to the respondent in discrimination cases once a presumption of discrimination can be made from the evidence brought by the plaintiff. The only exceptions from this rule are criminal procedures and proceeding in which the court or some competent body is responsible for investigating the facts.[74] The other procedural details concerning the implementation of the directive and the promotion of equal treatment are left to the member states. The Directive only provides for general guidelines such as the necessity to disseminate information concerning the directive, promoting social dialogue for the implementation of the principles of the Directive or dialogue with non-governmental organizations. A final requirement of the Directive concerns the obligation states undertake to designate a specialized body or bodies for the promotion of equal treatment on grounds of race or ethnic origin.[75]

The relevance of the Directive for Hungary and the importance political actors have assigned to it is best shown perhaps by the project of anti-discrimination law proposed by the Office of the Minority Commissioner. The Directive, as mentioned, was ratified on the 19th of July, 2000. Beginning in September 2000, the Minority Commissioner's Office started the preparations of a project of anti-discrimination law for regulating racial discrimination in Hungary. Beginning in November 2000, the project (in a rather premature form) reached the Ministry of Justice and the parliamentary Committee for Human Rights. The project has been debated in the Committee on the 21st of November and the proposal for having a unified anti-discrimination law in Hungary gained its almost unanimous support.[76] The Directive and the stan-

---

73. "Adverse treatment or adverse consequences as a reaction to a complaint or to proceedings aimed at enforcing compliance with the principle of equal treatment."

74. Shifting the burden of proof is introduced because of the typically unequal relationships, which characterize cases of discrimination (employer-employee, local authority-individual citizen). When the Court or some competent body stands for the investigation of facts and proof of discrimination the unequal relationship is no longer present thus making the shift of the burden of proof unnecessary.

75. Chapter III, Article 13.

76. Only the MP of the far right party has voted against it.

dards set by it were widely referred to during the debate. During the first months of 2001, two more projects of anti-discrimination law were prepared in Hungary.[77]

Concerning data protection: Hungary is a signatory to and has ratified the Council of Europe Convention for the Protection of Individuals with Regard to Automatic Processing of Personal Data.[78] Article 6 of the Convention provides with regard to special categories of data (sensitive data in Hungarian terminology): "personal data revealing racial origin, political opinions or religious or other beliefs, as well as personal data concerning health or sexual life, may not be processed automatically unless domestic law provides appropriate safeguards. The same shall apply to personal data relating to criminal convictions." The Hungarian legal framework for regulating the right to informational self-determination satisfies all the requirements of the convention.

The European Directive 1995/46/EC on the protection of individuals with regard to the processing of personal data and on the free movement of such data as to the 2000/43/EC equal treatment directive, has only an indirect effect on Hungary. However, under this directive the situation of Hungary is somewhat better than under the Equal Treatment Directive analyzed above: the Hungarian legal framework for data protection has been deemed generally adequate under the Directive (as a third country which may receive personal data), meaning that there is no need to decide about adequacy in case of each export of data. The European Commissioner, deciding on the level of protection (under Art. 29 of the Directive), found Hungary's[79] data protection level especially adequate because of its general validity for both public and private sector.

Future Prospects, Possibilities for Legal Reform

As far as the enforcement of the right not to be discriminated against on grounds of national or ethnic origin is concerned, a solution could be found even within the present legal framework as it is provided for by the Data Protection Act. The Article 3.2 provision, which authorizes processing of sensitive data also in cases when it is needed for the enforcement of a constitutional right, seems to allow for processing of sensitive data for the purpose of enforcement of the right not to be discriminated against. The required data is certainly not data of personal character, but anonymized data of statistical character. The problem thus becomes technical: what are the ways and conditions which are to be respected

---

77. One by the the party of Free Democrats and one by two MPs of the Socialist party.
78. Ratified in Hungary by Act VI. of 1998.
79. And also Switzerland's.

within the present legal framework in the process of collection of ethnic data? The Data Protection Commissioner could develop and provide good practice codes for different institutions where ethnic monitoring could be important from the perspective of an efficient anti-discrimination policy (schools, employ - ers having more than a given number of employees, public employers especial - ly, local authorities as far as distribution of benefits or housing is concerned, police, attorneys' offices, courts). Such good practice codes should contain meth - ods for ethnic monitoring which are in accordance with the principles of data protection, data safety, and especially depersonalization of ethnic data, as soon as possible. Also, good practice codes should contain advice concerning the law - ful methods for collecting the data: questions to be included in questionnaires, categories from which the data subjects may choose, and obviously the voluntary nature of data provision. Voluntary data provision cannot and shall not be modified. However, consciousness of the concerned minorities should be raised— especially of Roma, who are the most prominent victims of racial dis - crimination in present day Hungary— concerning the importance of ethnic monitoring in implementation of an efficient anti-discrimination policy. With an increased awareness of the importance of ethnic monitoring and by securing adequate safeguards against the abuse of the collected data the hindering nature of the requirement of voluntary data provision can be decreased. This is obvi - ously a long process in which the necessary legal modifications and provision of the good practice guidelines require the smallest effort: the larger effort will be required for changing the approach of minorities toward ethnic monitoring, and for convincing the relevant bodies, state or non-state, to collect the data, and start any meaningful monitoring of the relevant processes.

With regard to the provision of special minority rights and entitlements (among them the right to form minority self-governments) it seems that the reg - istration of sensitive personal data of the beneficiaries cannot be avoided. In fact, the Data Protection Commissioner's point of view, as formulated in one of his recommendations[80], is that if a minority benefit is to be granted, the respective member of the minority can be obliged to declare her identity, obviously upon being assured that her data will be kept in a way that respects the rules of data protection. The same principle can be applied for the election of minority self-governments or for any other special minority right or entitlement. Everybody has to have the possibility to identify with a minority, and upon such identification to exercise the minority rights to which she is entitled according to the Constitution and the Minority Act. However, if someone chooses not to

80. The case concerning the obligation to declare identity for the purposes of receiving special minority grants. 611/A/1996.

declare her identity, that person cannot make a claim to those special rights. Based on this argument voting lists could be created, based on voluntary registration, for the purposes of minority elections. Or else, before casting the ballot in the minority election, everybody could be obliged to make a declaration on identity. The resulting lists would obviously have to be temporarily maintained, only for the period of election, and would be maintained by the concerned electoral bodies, and not made public or accessible to any other state organ. The principle behind them would not be any different that the principle existent behind the different minority grants, or behind the minority education system.

II. Uses of Ethnic Data and Statistics in Practice

Registration of Data on Minorities

In the pre-data protection act period, schools registered ethnic data. The 1992-93 school year is the last one for which ethnic statistics are available on school attendance/performance of students belonging to national or ethnic minorities.

Since the promulgation of the Data Protection Act, personal data on national or ethnic origin is not registered in any state-maintained centralized registry.

However, declarations on national or ethnic identity may be collected in connection with special minority rights and benefits, especially for the purposes of different educational programs. In order to ask for minority education, parents have to make a written declaration about the identity of their child. Also, such declarations are needed in case of applying for minority grants (see, for example, the above analyzed case investigated by the Data Protection Commissioner). These declarations are given on a voluntary basis, however, they are in most instances necessary for exercising the special minority entitlements. These declarations can be perceived as forming an indirect registry of data on ethnicity. Also, lists of students attending minority educational programs can be perceived as indirect registries of ethnic data. The written consent of the parents of children belonging to minority groups certifying the identity of their child is not accessible legally to anybody except the State Audit Office, which may review the declarations as proof for the lawful utilization of the per capita minority education normative given to minority educational programs by the state.

As far as illegal registration is concerned, the above-mentioned Minority Commissioner investigations apply, in which it became clear that the local authorities had, in fact, data about the ethnic composition of their welfare recipient population. It wasn't clear whether the small c (standing for cigány) by the name of each recipient of social benefits was only registered for proving to the Commissioner that the practice wasn't racially discriminatory, or that the eth - nic data was registered anyway. It is possible that such illegal registries exist in Hungary and are used for the internal purposes of the bodies which have them. Such possible abuses are signaled by the second ECRI report on Hungary.[81] It mentions that in Hungary "some employment offices screen applicants based on ethnicity and maintain files noting the ethnicity of Roma/Gypsy clients."[82]

A well known abuse of the right to informational self-determination dates back to the pre-transition period of Hungary. Ethnicity was registered by police before 1989. The term "Gypsy crime" was used by police at that time for the purposes of showing the tendency of the Roma population towards crime.

In a 1997 communication between the Budapest Police Department and met - ropolitan Roma organizations, a high ranking police officer, after stating that he was not using the expression "gypsy crime," referred to "exact and reliable data" on the proportion of crimes committed by Roma.[83] At the end of the meeting one of the representatives of the Roma organizations questioned the legality of the statement and the registration that possibly stood behind it. The police officer claimed that the statistics were prepared on the basis of names. The Minority Commissioner investigated the case and recommended that the police avoid the continuation of unlawful use of ethnic data and ethnic statistics. The Police accepted the recommendation.

So far no other abusive registrations of ethnic data have become public or were sanctioned.

In the absence of ethnic data in registries in Hungary, the available ethnic sta - tistics have been produced based on censuses and scientific research. Other avail - able statistics concerning education are from before the 1993 promulgation of the Data Protection Act. In reports concerning education, the ethnic data and statistics collected before 1993 are still often referred to.[84]

Sometimes ethnic statistics based on the approximation of minority organi - zations or other relevant bodies are used, as well. NEKI, for example[85], uses in some of its cases estimates of local minority self-governments.[86] Estimated data

81. CRI (2000)5. Adopted on 18 June 1999. Paragraph 41, pp. 14.
82. No other information is available on this issue.
83. 5636/K/1997.
84. See for example "A Kisebbségi Ombudsman jelentése a kisebbségek oktatásának átfogó vizs - gálatáról" (Report of the Minority Commissioner on the Comprehensive investigation of the Education of Minorities.) 1998.
85. Legal Defense Bureau for National and Etrhnic Minorities. Public interest law firm which rep - resented Roma plaintiffs before courts in all the major discrimination cases.
86. See for example Fehér Füzet (White Booklet) (1998) NEKI. pp. 41.

on minorities (estimation of minority organizations) is often used by authorities. The Minority Commissioner in one of his indirect discrimination cases has used the local minority self-government as a source of information on ethnic data. [87]

The Report *No. J/3670 of the Government of the Republic of Hungary to the National Assembly on the situation of national and ethnic minorities living in the Republic of Hungary. 1996*, prepared by the governmental Office for National and Ethnic Minorities for presenting the situation of minorities in Hungary before the parliament, also uses estimates. The same is true about the Governmental Report submitted to the Council of Europe concerning the implementation of the Framework Convention.[88] These reports not only contain the census data concerning national and ethnic minorities, but also list the estimations of minority organizations concerning the size of these minority groups and also note the problems that occurred with regard to the 1990 census.[89]

Where authorities are known to have kept data on ethnicity, the terminology varied. Sometimes accurate descriptive terminology was used, but other times, as in the already mentioned Minority Commissioner case, codes were used for registering minority status ("c" stood for *Cigány*).

Census

Official Hungarian censuses have contained questions on native language since 1880, and on nationality since 1941.[90]

In Hungary the last census took place in February, 2001. The previous census was in 1990. The census provides national-level data and data broken down to settlement level. Answering the census questions referring to sensitive data was voluntary in the last census. The census data did not include name and exact address. Statistics based on census data are public.[91]

At the last census the following questions were asked concerning ethnicity from the subjects:
– What nationality do you identify with?
– To the cultural values, traditions of which nationality you are attached?
– What is your mother tongue?

87. 5887/K/1999/ The Commissioner argues based on the estimations of the Roma Minority Self-government that a certain local government decree falls with a disparate impact on the local Roma minority.
88. Governmental decree 2023/1999. II.12.
89. Chapter on Demographic features of Hungary. URL: *www.meh.hu/nekh/*
90. *1990. évi Népszámlálás. Magyarország nemzetiségi adatai megyénként.* (The 1990 Census. Ethnic Data in Hungary by Counties) (1992) Budapest KSH.
91. Article 2. of Act XLVI. of 1993 on statistics.

– What language do you use generally among friends or family?

As far as other sensitive data is concerned, a separate question was asked con - cerning religion. There was no checklist, however, for religion, the category was open-ended. There were two separate categories mentioned, namely: "I do not belong to any church or religion" and "I do not want to answer." There were three separate questions concerning disability: the type of disability, the gravest disability (if more than one), and the cause of disability.

Regarding ethnic data, the questionnaire provided a checklist for the answers. In the case of the first two questions, the checklist consisted of all 13 national or ethnic minorities recognized by the Minority Act in Hungary, the category "Hungarian" and an "other" category which was open-ended (the subject could specify which other group she belongs to).

In the case of the second two questions, those referring to language, the check - list consisted of 16 categories and the open-ended "other" category (similar in form to the one described above). The 16 categories were: the languages spoken by the 13 national and ethnic minorities recognized in Hungary, with 3 languages mentioned for the Roma (Gypsy language, Beash and Romani), and the Hungarian language. Nationalities and languages listed under the "other" category are not melted up during the processing of the census data, but processed separately.

Respondents were allowed to have more than one ethnicity and more than one language, but no more than three in either case. Persons who listed more than one ethnicity will be reported in primary publications under each category that they listed. In the long term the Central Statistical Office also plans to pub - lish data according to multiple identities as such, and a listing according to the combination or coupling of identities is to be done, as well.

It is important to mention that the census questionnaires in 2001 were trans - lated into all the languages spoken by national and ethnic minorities in Hungary and the translated versions were made available as reference material to the cen - sus takers.

No censuses have been officially rendered invalid in Hungary thus far. However, the data gathered by the 1990 census regarding membership in national or ethnic minority groups is generally neither accepted nor referred to as accurate by anybody (not even by the state).[92] The reason for this is twofold.

---

92. Organizations of national and ethnic minorities kept using their estimated data for the size of the groups they represented. Győri Szabó, R. (1998) *Kisebbségpolitikai rendszerváltás Magyarországon*, (Minority policy transition in Hungary) Budapest, Osiris Századvég. pp. 50. The Office for National and Ethnic Minorities uses the census data together with the estimations provided by the Minority organizations in all of its reports, see for example *Report No. J/3670 of the Government of the Republic of Hungary to the National Assembly on the situation of national and ethnic minorities living in the Republic of Hungary. 1996.* Also Report on the implementation of the Framework Convention. 1999.

On the one hand, in 1990 there was no possibility for listing multiple identities; on the other hand, the fear of abuse was very much present in 1991, and the rel - evant part of the census was not voluntary. At that time, in the census question - naire there were two questions concerning ethnicity: one referred to belonging to a national or ethnic minority, the other referred to mother tongue.

Finally, according to the law the data collected in the census can only be used for statistical purposes.

Research and Surveys

Despite the official collection of data on national and ethnic origin in the cen - sus, this data on Roma cannot be considered accurate. Neither their answers to the language questions nor answers to the nationality question can be trusted. The assimilation of Roma in language terms is relatively advanced[93], but rarely do Roma declare their identity in censuses. Surveys try to gather more accurate data on the Roma in Hungary and on the different aspects of their lives.

A comprehensive representative nationwide survey on Roma was conducted in 1971 by Kemény and the Sociological Research Group of the Academy.[94] In the survey 2% of all the Roma population of Hungary was interviewed. The aim of the survey was to gather information about the size of the Roma population, its geographic and linguistic distribution, its objective living conditions. This survey defined as Roma all those who were considered Roma by their non-Roma surroundings.

In 1992-1994 research was conducted by the National Statistical Office on Hungarian households. The interviewers had three options: data subject is sure - ly Roma, the data subject is surely not Roma, the data subject is "suspect" (i.e. not sure whether she is Roma or not). The interviewers made their assessment based on outlook, behavior and assessment of the environment. The researchers who conducted the survey argued that this method is more advantageous than using the assessment of local people because it uses "experts"; interviewers, due to their extensive experience with meeting people, will be more apt for an objec - tive assessment than local people would be.[95]

93. Mészáros Árpád — Fóti János (2000)"A cigány népesség jellemzői Magyarországon" (Main char - acteristics of the Roma population in Hungary) in Horváth, Landau, Szalai eds. *Cigánynak születni*. Aktiv Társadalom Alapitvány — Új Mandátum. Budapest. pp. 285.
94. Kemény István, Rupp Kálmán, Csalog Zsolt, Havas Gábor (1976) *Beszámoló a magyarországi cigányok helyzetével foglalkozó 1971-ben végzett kutatásról* (Report on the 1971 survey on the situation of Roma in Hungary) MTA Szociológiai Kutató Intézetének Kiadványai. Budapest and Kemény István *A ma - gyarországi cigány lakosság*. (The Roma population in Hungary) URL: *www.romapage.c3.hu/konyvtar*
95. *A cigányság helyzete, életkörülményei*. (The situation and lifeconditions of Roma) (1994) Budapest. KSH.

Kemény István, Havas Gábor and Kertesi Gábor also conducted a representative national survey on Roma in the winter of 1993-94. [96]

The Ministry of Welfare survey in 1993 on Roma families [97] used two types of data collection: declaration of the family and self-identification of the child. The families were chosen by local experts (employees of local government, teachers, social workers).

In 1993 Ivan Szelényi and Donald Treitman conducted a survey which used a combination of self-identification and external identification by the interviewer for defining who are the Roma. [98]

TARKI, the Sociology Department of the University of Economics and the Central Statistical Office, has also conducted a nationwide survey called Hungarian Household Panel which also contained data referring to the Roma population of Hungary (1992-1997). [99] The questionnaires contained no question on ethnicity, and there was no personal data in the questionnaires. The interviewers were the ones that assessed the ethnicity of the data subjects.

In 1996 one of the public opinion research companies in Hungary, Szonda-Ipsos, also conducted research in which the interviewers assessed the data subjects' ethnicity. [100]

Szelényi and Ladányi conducted a comparative survey on poverty and Roma in countries of Central Europe in 2000. The part on Hungary was a representative national survey with demographic and sociological purposes. Nothing has been published so far on the findings of the survey. The survey used the method of self-identification for Roma.

Data has been collected in several other cases as well, for purposes of scientific research. As far as I know, this was not on a nationwide basis and not comprehensive but only for analyzing certain aspects of life.

Debates Concerning Registration of Ethnic Data

The most important debate concerning the use of data on minorities was connected to the above-analyzed issue of the necessity of registration of members of national or ethnic minorities for the purposes of election of minority

96. Kemény István, Havas Gábor (1995)„A magyarországi romákról" (About Roma in Hungary) in *Szociológia* 1995/3 and Kertesi Gábor, Kézdi Gábor (1998) *A cigány népesség Magyarországon* (The Roma Population in Hungary) Szoció-Typo.
97. Bánlaky Pál (1993) *Cigánycsaládok vizsgálata.* (Research on Roma families) Népjóléti Minisztérium család-, gyermek- és ifjúságpolitikai f_osztály családpolitikai osztálya.
98. Ladányi János és Szelényi Iván (1997) "Ki a cigány?" (Who is Gypsy?) in *Kritika*, December.
99. See Sik Endre (1995)"A longitudinális cigány." (The longitudinal Roma) In *Replika* 1995/17-18.
100. Ladányi János and Szelényi Iván op.cit.

self-governments. As mentioned in the October 1998 elections, many more votes were cast for minority candidates than the total number of minority group members, leading to the situation in which representatives of the minorities were not elected by the groups themselves. Even more paradoxically, in some cases the individuals elected did not belong to the minority group for the self-government of which they were running. According to the Minority Act it is sufficient to collect five supporters in order to run in the minority elections. Several candidates run for positions as belonging to more than one minority group in more than one minority self-government. As a result of the investigation started by the Minority Parliamentary Commissioner concerning this issue, the solution was found in separating local elections from minority elections, having a separate date for the minority elections. The idea of registration of those who can vote in the minority election was dropped because of the massive opposition of the minority organizations and the argument that the data protection legislation would not permit such a registration. During the debate the issue of the necessity of external confirmation of the minority identity of the candidates for minority self-governments was also raised. Among others the Minority Commissioner also seemed to have favored this solution.[101] However, it seems that if only minority voters would vote in these elections, and sympathy votes would be excluded, then the possibility for non-minority candidates to win seats would also decrease. Thus the rather non-liberal method of external identification could be dropped.

Another important debate that shall be mentioned here concerns the question of how Roma can be identified for the purposes of research. Two standpoints, both represented by established Hungarian scholars dealing with the issue, clash here. First, for the purposes of research a Roma is the person who declares identity as a Roma.[102] However, since self-identification is influenced by different factors, such as the undesirability of being a member of a low prestige minority group, or fear of possible abuse, this cannot produce accurate results and as such cannot be trusted. Thus, according to this first point of view, research has basically no means available for identifying who is Roma. Second, Roma can be identified beyond the self-identification, also based on the external identification of the community in which he or she lives or of the unbiased interviewer.[103] The debate is reflected in the approach of the different surveys that were conducted in Hungary on the social situation of Roma. Both approaches

---

101. Office of the Minority Parliamentary Commissioner *A kisebbségi önkormányzatok kézikönyve.* (Guiding Booklet of Minority Self-Governments) Budapest 1999, pp. 106.
102. Szelényi and Ladányi.
103. Standpoint represented by Havas, Kemény and Kertesi.

were used in practice.[104] The present framework set by the Data Protection Law obviously favors the first approach, the one based on self-identification.

The debate concerning the possibilities for gathering ethnic statistics with the purpose of monitoring and improving the situation of the Roma minority in Hungary is ongoing. A good illustration of the issue is the roundtable discussion concerning this issue with the participation of sociologists working in the field, data protection experts (among them the Data Protection Commissioner) and representatives of the Roma minority published in a Hungarian monthly in 2000.[105] The debate illustrated well the impasse at which experts are with regard to this problem, and the fact that they perceive the issue as unsolvable.

The above makes clear that the nature of the issue of ethnic monitoring and gathering of ethnic data is such that it cannot be addressed without the active participation of the minorities themselves. According to the Minority Act[106] the National Minority Self Governments have the right to express their opinion on all projects of law, including decrees of metropolitan and county level general assemblies, that concern the minority which they represent. They may request the administrative agencies to supply information on matters affecting the minority they represent, may submit proposals to these bodies, may initiate mea-sures that fall under the jurisdiction of these bodies. Similarly the National Minority Self Governments have the right to express their opinion on all minor-ity education matters relevant to the group they represent; they participate in the professional supervision of all levels of education of the minority they stand for.

The Minority Parliamentary Commissioner in one of his recommenda-tions[107] wrote to the President of the Parliament that in order to achieve the meaningful application of this provision, the official bodies that shall ask for the opinion of the Minority Self Governments have to send them the projects of laws and decrees in due time. Otherwise this prerogative of the Minority Self Governments becomes an empty provision.

Thus, at least in principle, representatives of minorities have the opportuni-ty both to propose measures concerning processing and collection of ethnic data and also to give their opinion on measures that are being prepared concerning this issue.

104. For the debate see: Havas Gábor, Kemény István and Kertesi Gábor (1998) "A relatív cigány a klasszifikációs küzdőtéren" in *Kritika*, March. Kertesi Gábor (1998) "Az empirikus cigánykutatások lehetőségéről" in *Replika*, 29. Ladányi János and Szelényi Iván (1997) op. cit. Ladányi János and Szelényi Iván (1998) "Az etnikai besorolás objektivitásáról." (On the objectivity of ethnic classifications) in *Kritika*, March.
105. "Megszámolhatóság kontra megszámozhatóság" (Ethnic Statistics versus Ethnic Registries) in *Beszélő* March 2000. Vol.5/3. pp.8-24.
106. Article 38.
107. 8761/K/1997.

National Minority Self-Governments, together with the governmental Office for National and Ethnic Minorities, the Minority Commissioner and the Data Protection Commissioner participated intensively in the preparation of the census questionnaire. The possibility of marking multiple identities and the anonymity of the questionnaires were actually proposed by the minority self-governments. The depersonalization of the address data was recommended by the Data Protection Commissioner.

If thorough ethnic monitoring is to be started for the purposes of the enforce-ment of the right not to be discriminated against, or some other minority right beyond the above formal channels, other channels will also have to be used for involving minorities in the process.

III. Methods and Means of Collecting and Processing Data Relating to Minorities

In Hungary different methods and primary data are being used for collecting and processing minority data by researchers. Four such methods shall be men-tioned:

1. Collection of ethnic data based on self-identification. A good example for the application of this method is the 2001 Census, which allowed for voluntary self-identification of the data subjects.

2. Collection of ethnic data based on the assessment of the interviewer (not a local person). Example: 1992-94 research on Hungarian households. The inter-viewers had three options: data subject is surely Roma, the data subject is surely not Roma, the data subject is "suspect" (i.e. not sure whether she is Roma or not). The interviewers made their judgment based on outlook, behavior and the assessment environment. The researchers who conducted the survey argued that this method is more advantageous than using the assessment of local people because it uses "experts"; the interviewers, due to their extensive experience with meeting people, will be more apt for an objective assessment of ethnicity than local people would be.[108]

3. Collection of ethnic data based on the assessment of the people of the sur-rounding social environment. The standpoint grounding this approach is that a Roma is the person who is regarded as such by people in the surrounding area. Several surveys used this method.[109]

108. See Sik Endre op. cit.
109. For example the 1983 national registration of the Roma population; the already mentioned 1971 national survey; 1994 survey by Kemény and others; the 1992-97 household panels.

4. Since the Data Protection Law entered into force, estimates of proportions of the Roma population are also being used sometimes. Estimations can be provided by local people: school directors, local minority self-governments etc.

The Minority Commissioner conducted an investigation on research performed with method (2).[110] He suggested that even though in the absence of personal data that could be used for identification of data subjects, the research method cannot be deemed unlawful; the research method which is based on subjective external identification of belonging to the Roma minority should not be used in the future. According to the Commissioner surveys conducted with this method cannot provide accurate data on such important aspects of life as employment, income, unemployment and poverty, or household life strategies. Meanwhile, the report of the investigation recognizes the inaccuracy of research grounded on self-identification and does not suggest any more reliable alternative method.

In order to reach their potential data subjects for personal interviews or data collection, interviewers have to use indirect strategies. As seen, no lists or registries are available (at least legally), which would contain personalized ethnic data that could be used for approaching people personally for interviews. Thus, using intermediaries or personal contacts is basically the only way to find data subjects. The most appropriate and accurate source for information is local minority self-governments. For example, in a case of discrimination against Roma by a disco the Consumer Protection Authority organized its test with the help of the local minority self-government.[111]

*Guarantees used for protecting information
privacy/ensuring data protection*

In collection of data for statistical purposes the personal data which may allow personal identification of data subjects (identification data: name, address) has to be destroyed at the end of data processing, after checking whether the data is

110. 4061/K/1997.
111. 7178/K/1998; decision 1293/1999 of the Consumer Protection Authority of Szabolcs-Szatmár-Bereg county.
112. Act on Statistics, Article 19.
108. See Sik Endre op. cit.
109. For example the 1983 national registration of the Roma population; the already mentioned 1971 national survey; 1994 survey by Kemény and others; the 1992-97 household panels.
110. 4061/K/1997.
111. 7178/K/1998; decision 1293/1999 of the Consumer Protection Authority of Szabolcs-Szatmár-Bereg county.

complete and consistent, but no later than 1 year after the collection, in case of transfer of data even before.[112] For the purpose of time series analysis after one year, the identification data should be replaced with an internal identifier which is not appropriate for identification of the data subjects. The identification data has to be processed separately from the data basis. If new data has to be collect-ed, the identification data can temporarily be connected to the data basis.

Data quality is ensured by collecting the data, where possible, directly from the data subjects. Where registration is needed for state purposes, such as in case of identification data, or non-sensitive census data, registration is made compul-sory. Compatibility is in principle ensured by using the same questions and answer categories throughout the years. However, in practice, given the changes in the legal system, the change in the perception towards the sensitive parts of the census, and other statistical collections of data, less attention has been paid lately in Hungary to the compatibility and comparability of ethnic data.

Conclusion

As a conclusion it can be said that in Hungary the data protection legal con-text is interpreted so as to ban any type of ethnic monitoring for the purposes of the enforcement of the right not to be discriminated against, except the census data. No field-specific ethnic statistics are available, especially not accurate ones, that could be used for the efficient monitoring of the situation of minorities, of the enforcement of their rights.

The debate around starting the gathering of such statistics is ongoing, how-ever, it has not achieved any results yet. It seems that the recognition that minorities should be involved in the debate is present, and channels for such an involvement are available.

The following factors seem to be necessary for starting to move towards the process of efficient and lawful ethnic monitoring:

– The data protection legislation shall be understood properly, so as too allow within given limits the gathering of anonymized ethnic statistics at all nec-essary levels.
– The technical solutions have to be worked out which, on the one hand, allow for meaningful collection of ethnic statistics, on the other hand respect the rules of data protection, and assure minorities that their data will not be abused.

112. Act on Statistics, Article 19.

– Minorities have to be made aware of the fact that gathering of ethnic statistics, if properly done, serves the purposes of a more efficient enforcement
of their rights.
– State and non-state actors have to be convinced of the necessity of ethnic
monitoring, the use of such data for the implementation of equal opportunity policies. Meanwhile, they will also have to be taught the ways in which
such data can be gathered and handled safely, with due regard to the rules
of data protection.

These factors signal the necessity of a well-considered state level public policy with regard to the issue of ethnic monitoring. Without such a state public
policy initiative it is difficult to see what would give the green light to changes in
the field.

Ethnic Statistics and Data Protection: The Case of Spain

Ina Zoon and Daniel Wagman

I. Legal framework

Constitutional Provisions

The Constitution of Spain does not recognize national minorities. It affirms the "Spanish nation," pledges to protect all Spaniards and "peoples of Spain in the exercise of human rights, their cultures and traditions, languages, and institutions." [1] The existence of the "peoples of Spain" is further confirmed by the constitutional category of autonomous regions ("autonomous communities")[2], whose statutes contain terms such as the "Basque people," the "Catalan people," the "Galician nationality." Statutory law does not recognize minorities either.

Freedom of information was first recognized in Spain as a distinct right from the freedom of expression[3] by the 1978 Constitution which protects "the right to receive and communicate freely accurate information by any means of dissemination" [4] and provides protection against any interference of public authorities in the exercise of the right.

As far as access to information is concerned, the Spanish Constitution does not expressly state that governmental and administrative acts should be public. However, in order to fulfill its duties, the administration must permit, within certain limits, access to documents. The law shall regulate "access by citizens to the administrative archives and registers except where it affects the security and defense of the State, the investigation of crimes, and the privacy of persons." [5]

---

1. Constitution of Spain (1978), Preamble.
2. Constitution of Spain (1978), Article 2: "[...] the Constitution is based on the indivisible unity of the Spanish people, the common and indivisible land of all Spaniards." The same article recognizes and guarantees the right of autonomy of nationalities and regions and "the solidarity of all of them."
3. The Constitutional Court repeatedly confirmed the separate existence of the two rights, see, for example, Constitutional Court Decisions (*Sentencias del Tribunal Constitucional*) STC 6/1981 and STC 107/1988.
4. Constitution of Spain (1978), Article 20(1) let. d).
5. Constitution of Spain (1978), Article 105 let. b).

The right to honor as well as the right to privacy are also guaranteed constitutionally.[6] The Constitution requires[7] the adoption of specific legislation for the
limitation of the use of information, in order to guarantee personal and family
honor, the privacy of citizens, and the full exercise of their rights. The
Constitutional Court's jurisprudence establishes the existence of the right to
control the information included in a file and to oppose the use of personal data
for purposes different from those for which it was collected.[8] Data protection
laws ensure the enforcement of these rights.[9] Defamation[10] and false accusa-
tions[11] are traditionally sanctioned by the criminal law as crimes against honor.
Civil protection of the right to honor is ensured also by a special organic law
called the Law for the Civil Protection of the Right to Honor, Privacy and
Image.[12]

There is an explicit prohibition of discrimination on the basis of racial or ethnic origin in the Constitution, which states that "Spaniards are equal before the
law, without any discrimination on the basis of birth, race, sex, religion, opinion
or any other personal or social condition or circumstance." [13]

At first sight the abundant anti-discrimination jurisprudence[14] of the Spanish
Constitutional Court does not include significant race or ethnicity related
cases.[15] The constitutional case law, however, recognizes and frequently addresses both direct and indirect discrimination. Statistical evidence presented in
building *prima facie* cases of discrimination was not only accepted but considered
necessary by the Spanish Constitutional Court in gender discrimination cases.

---

6. Constitution of Spain (1978), Article 18(1): "The right of honor, personal, and family privacy and
identity is guaranteed."
7. Article 18, paragraph 4.
8. Constitutional Court Decisions STC 30/1999, STC 44/1999 and STC 45/1999.
9. See below: Data Protection Legislation.
10. The Spanish Criminal Code (Organic Law No. 10/1995), Articles 208 *et seq.*
11. The Spanish Criminal Code, (Organic Law No. 10/1995) Article 456 and 457.
12. Law for the Civil Protection of the Right to Honor, Privacy and Image, No. 1/1982 from 5th of
May 1992 [*Ley Orgánica de Protección Civil del Derecho al Honor, a la Intimidad Personal y Familiar y a
la Propia Imagen.*]
13. Article 14.
14. For example, one of every five complaints filed within the *amparo* procedure with the
Constitutional Court alleges a violation of the anti-discrimination clause, see Constitutional Court's
Annual Report 1999, section. V.1.a.
15. A selection of the most significant constitutional decisions related to the non-discrimination principle made by the Constitutional Law Department of the University in Valladolid covers the following areas:
• equality before the law: (STC 25/1999 and STC 75/1983 age);
• gender discrimination: i) affirmative action -STC 128/1987; ii) indirect discrimination — STC
  145/1991; iii) direct discrimination STC 126/1997;
• other reasons: children born out of wedlock (STC 80/1982) and adopted children (STC 46/1999).
Source: *www.der.uva.es/constitucional/verdugo/14.html*

"It should be noted that, according to the jurisprudence of the Constitutional Court [...] when it is alleged that the right not to be discriminated against on one of the grounds protected by article 14 C.E. has been violated, it is not always necessary to have a *tertium comparationis* to prove the existence of an discriminatory treatment, especially in indirect discrimination cases. In these cases not individuals, but social groups are compared and their characteristics statistically evaluated; in other words groups formed by persons belonging to one of the categories especially protected by article 14 V.E. — in our case the women. [...]

[W]hen a differentiated treatment is invoked before the court — and the invocation is made precisely by a person belonging to a group traditionally affected by this type of discrimination — in this case the women — the judicial body cannot limit itself to examine if the difference in treatment has, *in abstracto*, a reasonable and objective justification, but must analyze if the formulation which appears reasonable does not hide, or permits the hiding, in reality, of discrimination prohibited by article 14 C.E. (STC 145/1991). For this, the court should necessarily consider the "data provided by statistics" (STC 128/1987). This is consistent with the jurisprudence of the Tribunal of Justice of the European Communities." [16]

Discrimination

Beyond the constitutional provisions and constitutional case law, civil, labor and criminal law also address the issue of racial discrimination. The Spanish labor legislation contains clear-cut anti-discrimination provisions. The Workers' Statute prohibits discrimination on all the grounds mentioned in Article 13 of the Amsterdam Treaty.[17] However, the burden of proof is reversed only in gender discrimination cases, when the complainant makes a prima facie case of indirect discrimination. The employer must prove that the measures adopted respect the principle of proportionality and have an objective, reasonable and sufficiently proved justification.[18] The court may require and take into consideration the opinion — including statistical data — of the competent *public bodies.*[19]

16. Decision from February 9th, 1999.
17. "Article 4(2)(c) of the Workers' Statute (Workers' Statute. Revised text. Royal Legislative Decree No 1/1995 of 24 March 1995).
18. RD 2/1995, from 7 April 1995, approving the amended text of the Labor Code, Article 96.
19. RD 2/1995, from 7 April 1995, approving the amended text of the Labor Code, Article 95(3): "when, during the trial, a gender discrimination issues has been raised, the judge or the court may ask for the opinion of the competent public bodies."

The Penal Code[20] imposes imprisonment or fines on persons who are responsible for employment discrimination on any of the above mentioned grounds. [21] The criminal law penalizes the incitement to discrimination, hate or violence against groups or associations, on racial or anti-Semitic grounds or on other grounds related to ideology, religion, beliefs, family situation, belonging to a race or to an ethnic group, national origin, sex or sexual preferences, disease or disability.[22]

The fundamental rights and freedoms and the principle of non-discrimination contained in Section Two, Title 1 of the Constitution are protected in two ways. First, they are binding on all public authorities. [23] Second, any citizen may make a claim to enforcement of these rights before the regular courts and the Constitutional Court.[24] Regular courts deal with such claims in a preferential and speedy procedure called "ordinary recourse of *amparo*." Appeal before the Constitutional Court is possible by way of "constitutional recourse *de amparo*" after all available judicial remedies have been exhausted. It is important to notice, however, that not all rights may be defended within the *amparo* procedure, but only those covered by a certain section of the Constitution[25] (e.g. the constitutional recourse of *amparo* is not applicable to allegations of violation of property rights.) [26]

Affirmative action is permitted by the Constitution, which says: public authorities may take positive action measures to achieve the material equality of certain disadvantaged groups.[27]

20. Criminal Code, Organic Law No. 10/1995 of 23 November 1995.
21. Articles 314 and 512 Spanish Criminal Code.
22. Article 510.1 Spanish Criminal Code.
23. Constitution of Spain (1978), Article 53 (1): "The rights and liberties recognized in the second chapter of the present Title are binding on all public authorities. Only by law, which in every case must respect their essential content, could the exercise of such rights and liberties be regulated, and they shall be protected in accordance with the provisions of Article 161 (1) b)."
24. Constitution of Spain (1978), Article 53(2): "Any citizen may make a claim to the liberties and rights recognized in Article 14 and the first Section on the Second Chapter [n.a. the section on fundamental rights and freedoms] before the regular courts through a process based on the principles of preference and speed and through the recourse before the Constitutional Court [...]."
25. Constitution of Spain (1978), Article 53 (2). "Any citizen may make a claim to the liberties and rights recognized in Article 13 and the first Section of the Second Chapter before the regular courts through a process based on the principles of preference and speed and through the recourse before the Constitutional Court. This last recourse shall be applicable to objections of conscience recognized in Article 30."
26. See, *inter alia*, Constitutional Court's Annual Report 1999, Presentation by the President of the Constitutional Court, Pedro Cruz Villalón.
27. Constitution of Spain (1978), Article 9(2): "It is the responsibility of the public authorities to promote conditions so that liberty and equality of the individual and the groups he joins will be real and effective; to remove those obstacles which impede or make difficult their full implementation, and to facilitate participation of all citizens in the political, economic, cultural, and social life."

The 1999 Law on Data Protection guarantees and protects individuals' fundamental rights and freedoms, especially the right to honor, to family and private life, in relation to personal data processing.[28] The law applies to *personal data*[29] processed both by *public and private* data controllers.[30]

The law *does not* apply to[31] files kept by private persons exclusively for their personal and domestic use, files subjected to regulations on classified materials[32], and files created for the investigation of terrorism and serious forms of organized crime.

Some specific types of data files are governed by other, specific legislation. These are electoral files[33], files maintained for statistical purposes[34], personal files of Army members[35], criminal records[36] and video-files created by security forces.[37]

The Law on Data Protection provides special protection to several types of data called *especially protected data*. Within the especially protected category there are two sub-categories: data that require maximum protection and data that require medium protection. Maximum protection data are those concerning ideology, trade union affiliation, religion or beliefs.[38] Nobody can be obliged to provide information about these matters.[39] They can only be processed with the express written consent of the data subject.[40] The entity that collects the information has the obligation to inform the person concerned about his/her right to refuse to provide information.[41]

---

28. Article 1, Law on Data Protection No. 15/1999.
29. "Personal data" is defined as any information related to an identified or identifiable person (Article 3 let. a), Law on Data Protection No. 15/19).
30. Art. 2(1), Law on Data Protection No. 15/1999.
31. Art. 2(2), Law on Data Protection No. 15/1999.
32. The meaning of the term "classified materials" is defined under the Law on Official Secrets (Law 9/68 as subsequently amended) as matters about which general knowledge might be damaging or threatening to the security or defense of the state.
33. These files are governed by electoral laws: Law No. 5/85 as amended by Law No. 13/94, see: Data Protection Agency, "Practical Guide for Citizens," *www.agenciaprotecciondatos.org/data2.htm* (site in Spanish).
34. Governed by Law 12/89 on Public Statistic Function and relevant legislation of autonomous communities.
35. These are the files that contain the information from the personal qualification reports regulated by laws on the Regime of the Personnel of the Army Forces, see: Data Protection Agency, "Practical Guide for Citizens."
36. Individual files from the Central Criminal Record Register (*Registro Central de Penados y Rebeldes*).
37. The files containing images and sounds obtained by the Security Forces are regulated by special norms.
38. Data Protection Agency, "Practical Guide for Citizens."
39. Article 7(1), Law on Data Protection No. 15/1999.
40. Article 7(2), Law on Data Protection No. 15/1999.
41. Article 7(1), Law on Data Protection No. 15/1999.

Medium protection data refers to data on racial origin[42] health and sexual life.[43] Medium protection data can be gathered, processed and transmitted only if a law permits it for public interest reasons, *or* the person concerned explicitly agrees with processing this type of information (existence of consent).[44] It is prohibited to create files aimed *exclusively* at storing personal data on subjects' race or ethnic origin.[45] In case of maximum protection data, the law requires previous express written consent[46] while for the medium protection data the law requires only the express consent.

The responsible entities have the obligation to take, before June 2001[47], high security level measures[48] in order to protect all electronic files that contain information on ideology, religion, beliefs, health, racial origin and sexual life.

However, Security Forces can process personal data, including data on racial/ethnic origin, obtained for police purposes, without the consent of the person concerned, if it is required by public security needs, or is necessary to prevent a real danger or a criminal offense.[49] Furthermore, processing data on racial origin is permitted if necessary for medical prevention or diagnosis, health care, medical treatments or management of health care services provided that the person who deals with the information respects the legal obligation to preserve confidentiality.[50]

The Law on Data Protection introduces, through exceptions, significant differences between the public administration's obligations and private persons' obligations with respect to controlling and processing personal data. For example, the law requires all entities to inform expressly, precisely and unequivocally the persons concerned about the existence of a file, its objective, the addressee (recipient) of the information[51], compulsory or optional character of the answer[52], consequences of data collection or consequences of refusal to provide

---

42. The notion of "race" is understood as covering also ethnic grounds.
43. Article 7(3), Law on Data Protection No. 15/1999.
44. Article 7(3), Law on Data Protection No. 15/1999. If the person concerned is physically or legally unable to consent, data may still be processed if is in his or her vital interest or in the vital interest of another person, see Article 7(6), Law on Data Protection No. 15/1999.
45. Article 7(4), Law on Data Protection No. 15/1999.
46. *Consentimiento previo, expreso y por escrito*
47. Article 29(2), RD 994/1999 on Security Measures Pertaining to Electronic Files that Contain Personal Data, from 11 June 1999. Henceforth RD 994/1999.
48. Article 3(3), RD 994/1999.
49. Article 22(2), Law on Data Protection No. 15/1999.
50. Article 7(6), Law on Data Protection No. 15/1999. The person who process the information may be a health professional subjected to medical confidentiality rules or another person subjected to equivalent obligations.
51. Article 5(1) let. a), Law on Data Protection No. 15/1999.
52. Article 5(1) let. b), Law on Data Protection No. 15/1999.

information[53], about the existing possibilities to exercise the right to access, modification and cancellation[54], and about the identity and the address of the responsible entity.[55] When written forms are used for data collection this information has to be printed in a clearly readable manner.[56]

However, the public administration may collect data without complying with the obligations described above in cases when informing the data subject impedes or creates serious difficulties in exercising the control and verification functions of the public administration *or* affects national defense, public safety *or* the investigation of criminal or administrative offenses.[57]

Also, private and public files are created differently. Those created by the public administration must be registered in BOE[58] while private files may be created without registration in BOE, only notifying the Data Protection Agency.[59]

Access, rectification and cancellation of personal data are possible. The *right to access* to personal data is regulated by the Data Protection Law.[60] Under this Law the person concerned or his legal representative[61] has the right to review personal data (including information related to race or ethnicity), as well as to know the entity that created the file and all performed or expected transmission of such data.[62] The right to access personal data is limited to data included in electronic files.

The right to access may be exercised *once a year*, except when the person concerned has a legal interest to obtain the information more often.[63] The responsible entity[64] must decide and respond to all access requests within one month from their receipt.[65] If granted, *de facto* access must be ensured within ten days from the decision.[66] Impeding or blocking the exercise of the right to access, and refusal to provide information to rightful applicants constitute serious offenses.[67]

---

53. Article 5(1) let. c), Law on Data Protection No. 15/1999.
54. Article 5(1) let. d), Law on Data Protection No. 15/1999.
55. Article 5(1) let. e), Law on Data Protection No. 15/1999.
56. Article 5(2), Law on Data Protection No. 15/1999.
57. Article 24(1), Law on Data Protection No. 15/1999.
58. Article 20(1), Law on Data Protection No. 15/1999. BOE (*Boletin Official del Estado*) — is the Official Monitor.
59. Article 26(1) and (3), Law on Data Protection No. 15/1999.
60. The access right is regulated by Law on Data Protection No. 15/1999, RD 1332/1994 and by Instruction 1/1998 of Data Protection Agency.
61. The legal representative has the right to access personal data only in cases where the person concerned is a minor or is unable to exercise his right on his own (Article 11(2), RD 1332/1994).
62. Article 15(1), Law on Data Protection No. 15/1999.
63. Article 15(3), Law on Data Protection No. 15/1999.
64. The "responsible entity" is defined as the "legal or physical person, of public or private nature, or administrative organ, competent to decide over the finality, content and use of the information" [Article 3 (d), Law on Data Protection No. 15/1999].
65. Data Protection Agency, "Practical Guide for Citizens, Part V, section 4 (c).
66. Data Protection Agency, "Practical Guide for Citizens, Part V, section 4 (c) final.
67. Article 44 (3) (e), Law on Data Protection No. 15/1999.

When these types of actions are of a systematic nature, they constitute very seri-ous offenses.[68]

Individuals cannot have access to the personal data of the others.[69] Under the data protection law individuals only have access to *personal* information; access to information about communities or other groups is not allowed.

The specific conditions in which the rights to access, rectification and can-cellation of personal data might be exercised depend on the character — public or private — of the file. There are a number of differences with respect to access of individuals to information stored by the state and information stored by non-state bodies. There are more restrictions of individuals' access to public files as compared to private files. If the file is private, access may be denied only if the request is not formulated by the person concerned.[70]

If the file is created by a public authority access can be denied in certain specific cases. First, access to files created by Security Forces, for police necessi-ties, which contain personal data, may be denied if the exercise of the right to access could represent a threat to the state defense; public safety; protection of rights and freedoms of the others or needs of an on-going police investigation.[71] Second, access to Tax Office files may be denied if the exercise of the right might impede the fulfillment of tax obligations *or* the person concerned is subjected to tax inquiry.[72] Third, access to public administration files in general may be denied on public interest grounds or where the interest of a third party deserves more protection.[73] The responsible authority must issue a *reasoned* decision and to inform the applicant on his right to challenge it before the director of the Data Protection Agency.[74] The individual whose right to access has been denied, total-ly or partially, may file a complaint with the competent authority.[75]

Individuals have *the right to rectification and cancellation* of *their* personal data — including information on race or ethnicity — unlawfully processed, incorrect or incomplete.[76] The responsible entity must introduce the changes or deny the request within ten days.[77]

---

68. Article 44 (4) (h), Law on Data Protection No. 15/1999.
69. According to Rule 1, Instruction 1/1998 issued by the Data Protection Agency, the access requests formulated by other persons but the person concerned or his/her legal representative shall be rejected.
70. Data Protection Agency, "Practical Guide for Citizens, Part V, section 4 (d).
71. Article 23(1), Law on Data Protection No. 15/1999.
72. Article 23(2), Law on Data Protection No. 15/1999.
73. Article 24(2), Law on Data Protection No. 15/1999.
74. Article 24(2) final, Law on Data Protection No. 15/1999.
75. The competent authority is the Data Protection Agency or the equivalent agency in each autonomous community, or the authorities with competence over files maintained by police forces or autonomous tax administration authorities.
76. Article 16(2), Law on Data Protection No. 15/1999.
77. Article 16(1), Law on Data Protection No. 15/1999.

When cancelled, personal data is not erased immediately, but kept at the disposal of public administration, judges and courts, to be used for the determination of responsibilities for unlawful processing until the prescription term elaps-
es.[78] If the canceled or rectified information has been previously transmitted, the
third party that received it must be informed and, at its turn, must rectify or can-
cel the information.[79]

The exercise of rectification and cancellation rights is free of charge.[80]
Persons whose rights of rectification or cancellation have been violated may file
a complaint with the Data Protection Agency, respectively with the competent
autonomous community's agency. The decision of the Director of the Agency
can be challenged within the contentious administrative procedure.

Cancellation of information from both private and public files may be denied if
the operation might affect negatively the person concerned or a third party.[81]
Again there are some distinctions as far as *public* files are concerned. Rectification
or cancellation of information included in Security Forces files, created for
police necessities, may be denied if these operations could represent a threat to
the state's defense, public safety, protection of rights and freedoms of others or
a threat against an on-going police investigation.[82] In the case of Tax Office files,
rectification or cancellation may be denied if the exercise of the right might
impede the fulfillment of tax obligations or the person concerned is subjected to
tax inquiry.[83] Finally, rectification or cancellation of data from public administration files may be denied on public interest grounds or where the interest of a
third party deserves more protection.[84] The responsible authority must issue
here, as well, a *reasoned* decision and inform the applicant on his or her right to
challenge it before the competent authority.[85]

As a rule, *transmission of personal data* to a third person or entity requires the
consent of the individual concerned.[86] However, there are many exceptions to
this rule.[87]

Between two organs of public administration transmission is always possible, provided that the two bodies have the same competence, *or* the information is trans-

78. Article 16(3), Law on Data Protection No. 15/1999.
79. Article16 (4), Law on Data Protection No. 15/1999.
80. Article 17(2), Law on Data Protection No. 15/1999.
81. Data Protection Agency, "Practical Guide for Citizens," see: *www.agenciaproteccióndatos.org/data2.htm*.
82. Article 23(1), Law on Data Protection No. 15/1999.
83. Article 23(2), Law on Data Protection No. 15/1999.
84. Article 24(2), Law on Data Protection No. 15/1999.
85. Article 24(2) final, Law on Data Protection No. 15/1999.
86. Article 11(1), Law on Data Protection No. 15/1999.
87. Article 11(2), let. a) to f), Law on Data Protection No. 15/1999.

mitted for historic, statistical or scientific purposes, *or the* transmission of data has been established from the creation of the file, *or* so establishes a legal regulation.[88] Information obtained or elaborated by one administrative organ for another may always be transmitted.[89] The consent of the interested person is not required in such cases.[90]

The information contained in private files may be transmitted only provided that, at the first transfer, the person concerned is informed about the objectives of the new file, the type of information that was transferred, the name and the location of the entity that administrates the new file.[91] There are several exceptions to this rule (e.g. when the destination of the information is the Ombudsman, the Prosecution Office, the courts; when the transmission of information serves historic, statistic or scientific purposes, etc).[92]

Internationally, personal data from Spain can be transmitted, with the authorization of the Director of the Data Protection Agency, only to countries where the legislation ensures a comparable level of protection.[93] Again, there are many exceptions to this rule: (e.g. when the interested person expressly agrees with the transfer, when the transmission is based on a treaty ratified by Spain, when the country of destination is another EU member state, when the information is necessary for a medical treatments, diagnosis, or administration of health care services, etc.)[94]

In Spain the national authority which plays the role of an independent supervisory authority for data protection is the Data Protection Agency (DPA).[95] The DPA is a public entity, independent from the administration[96] and mandated to control the implementation of data protection legislation. The Director is appointed by its Consultative Council.[97]

The Data Protection Agency has a "General Register of Data Protection" that may be consulted, free of charge, by any interested person.[98] The register contains descriptions of public and private files (e.g. structure, objective, location, the entity that administrates it) but does not contain the individual data as such.[99] Therefore, the individual concerned can only find out from the register

---

88. Article 21(1), Law on Data Protection No. 15/1999.
89. Article 21(2), Law on Data Protection No. 15/1999.
90. Article 21(4), Law on Data Protection No. 15/1999.
91. Article 27(1), Law on Data Protection No. 15/1999.
92. Article 27(2), Law on Data Protection No. 15/1999.
93. Article 33 (1), Law on Data Protection No. 15/1999.
94. Article 34 (a) — (k), Law on Data Protection No. 15/1999.
95. Created by Law 5/1992, from 29 October 1992, Regulating the Treatment of Personal Data (LORTAD).
96. Article 35(1), Law on Data Protection No. 15/1999.
97. Article 36(1), Law on Data Protection No. 15/1999.
98. Article 14, Law on Data Protection No. 15/1999.
99. Article 39(2), Law on Data Protection No. 15/1999.

the addresses and the entities that keep a certain type of data and then apply for access with each of these entities. The process is lengthy and difficult if the person does not know from the very beginning which file he or she wants to access.

Apart from the national agency, each autonomous community may create its own data protection agency.[100] To date, however, only the Community of Madrid has such an agency.[101] The attributions of the local agencies are more limited; they cannot order the cancellation of files, ending data processing, cannot impose sanctions and cannot regulate the international transfer of data.[102]

The law defines three types of offenses related to personal data processing: simple (*infracciones leves*), serious (*infracciones graves*) and very serious (*infracciones muy graves*). Processing race or ethnicity related information in the absence of a law that specifically allows it for public interest reasons or without the consent of the person concerned or creating files aimed exclusively at processing information on people's racial or ethnic origin are very serious offenses.[103] The regime of sanctions depends on the type of the file, whether public or private. When the offense has been committed in connection to a *private file* the sanction is a fine between 100,000 and 10 million Pesetas for simple offences; 10,000,001 to 50 million Pesetas for serious offences; 50,000,001 to 100 million Pesetas for very serious offences. The prescription terms are one, two and three years respectively.[104]

When the offense is committed in a *public file*, there are no financial sanctions.[105] The Director of the Data Protection Agency establishes, through resolution, the measures that must be adopted to stop and/or correct the effects of the offense.[106] He notifies the authority that processes the data, its supervisory body and the person(s) affected.[107] The responsible public authorities have the obligation to inform the Agency about the measures adopted according to the resolution.[108] The Director may initiate disciplinary procedure under the relevant administrative law.[109] Furthermore, he has the obligation to inform the *Defensor del Pueblo* (the Ombudsman)[110] about the activities and resolu-

---

100. Article 41(1), Law on Data Protection No. 15/1999.
101. The Data Protection Agency of the Community of Madrid was created by Law 13/1995 as subsequently amended, see: "The New Law from Madrid Data Protection Agency's Perspective," *SIC* [*Revista Seguridad en Informática y Comunicaciones*] April 2000.
102. Article 41(1), Law on Data Protection No. 15/1999.
103. Article 44(4) (c), Law on Data Protection No. 15/1999. All offenses are listed by article 44 of the Law 15/1999.
104. Article 47(1), Law on Data Protection No. 15/1999.
105. Article 43(2), Law on Data Protection No. 15/1999.
106. Article 46(1), Law on Data Protection No. 15/1999.
107. Article 46(1), Law on Data Protection No. 15/1999.
108. Article 46(3), Law on Data Protection No. 15/1999.
109. Article 46(2), Law on Data Protection No. 15/1999.
110. Spain has an Ombudsman at national level (Constitution 1978 article 54). Each autonomous community may also have its own Ombudsman.

tions issued in relation to offenses committed by public authorities.[111]. In case of both *public* and *private* files, the Director of the Data Protection Agency may ask the responsible entity to stop the use or the transmission of personal data that seriously impede the exercise of fundamental rights or hinders the free development of personality.[112] If the concerned entity fails to respect the request, the Director may block, through reasoned resolution, the files in ques - tion.[113]

Legislation on Data of Statistical Nature

In Spain, according to the Constitution, the state holds exclusive competence over the statistics for *state purposes*. [114] The collection of statistical data at the *national level* is governed by the Law on Public Statistic Function. [115] On the regional level, communities may assume, in their autonomy statutes, compe - tences related to statistics *for the needs of the community*[116] and may adopt laws on statistics and statistic plans.[117]

Although Spain does not recognize the existence of national minorities, the law on statistics expressly provides for the possibility to collect *data on ethnicity*, with the previous and informed consent of the individuals concerned. [118]

There are also certain statistical data, which may provide information indi - rectly on certain ethnic groups. For example, the Law on Statistics in Andalucia permits, within the field of "social statistics," the collection of data on pre-uni - versity school systems[119], which may include the so-called data collection on the "compensated education" attended mainly by Roma children or statistics on

111. Article 46(4), Law on Data Protection No. 15/1999.
112. Article 49, Law on Data Protection No. 15/1999.
113. Article 49, Law on Data Protection No. 15/1999, final.
114. Constitution of Spain (1978), Article 149(1), (31).
115. Public Statistic Function Law No. 12/1989, from 9th of May 1989, published in BOE from May 5, 1989. Henceforth Public Statistic Function Law No. 12/1989.
116. See, for example, the Autonomy Status of the Community of Valencia, Article 31; the Autonomy Status of the Community of Andalucia, Article 13.34, etc.
117. See, for example, Law 4/1998, from October 1st, 1998, on the Statistic Plan of Andalucia 1998-2001;
Law 23/1998, from 30 December 1998 on Statistics in Cataluna; Law 6/1997, from 31 July 1997 on the Statistic Plan of Galicia 1998-2001, etc.
118. Public Statistic Function Law No. 12/1989, Article 11(2): "In all cases it will be strictly volun - tary and in consequence only can be gathered with previous consent of the interested parties data which can reveal *ethnic origin*, political opinions, religious or ideological convictions and in general any information which can affect personal and family privacy."
119. Law 4/1998, from October 1st, 1998, on the Statistic Plan of Andalucia 1998-2001, Annex 1, Sub-Section 3.1.2 or Law 7/1996, from the 8th of November 1996, approving the Basque Statistic Plan on the period 1997/2000, Code 0601, "Statistics Concerning the Activity of the Schools."

"social marginalization" [120] or "social behavior" [121] which may also touch upon, without naming it, the Roma population.

Some of the regional regulations establish that data included in administra - tive files and used for statistical purposes are subjected to data protection laws. [122] The Law on Public Statistic Function regulates in detail the type of information, which may be collected for national statistical purposes. Limitations imposed by the regulations on statistics do not impede, however, the administration, both at national and community level, to realize *qualitative* inquiries, studies and reports necessary for their activity. [123]

The legislation related to the elaboration of statistics for *community purposes* contains few or no limitations on collecting racial and/or ethnic data. The fol - lowing examples are illustrative: In the Autonomous Community of Andalucia, the law requires the written consent of the individual only when providing infor - mation on "ideology, political, religious and philosophical options" and not on ethnicity.[124] This law contains no references to "race." In Canarias, the law pro - vides only that statistical activities must respect relevant constitutional provi - sions.[125] The laws in Cantabria and Galicia prohibit questions "directly con - nected to the right to honor, private life, religious and political beliefs of the interested person" but do not expressly prohibit questions related to ethnicity or race.[126] In Cataluna, the law requires that the respondent is adequately informed on his rights and duties, but does not prohibit the collection of data on ethnici - ty or race.[127] In the community of Madrid and in the Basque Country, sensitive

120. Law 4/1998, from October 1st, 1998, on the Statistic Plan of Andalucia 1998-2001, Annex 1, Sub-Section 3.3.3.
121. Law 4/1998, from October 1st, 1998, on the Statistic Plan of Andalucia 1998-2001, Annex 1, Sub-Section 3.4.3.
122. See for example, Law 4/1998, from October 1st, 1998, on the Statistic Plan of Andalucia 1998-2001, Annex 1, final paragraph.
123. Public Statistic Function Law No. 12/1989 (*exposicion de motivos*).
124. Law 4/1989, from 12 December 1989 on Statistics in the Autonomous Community of Andalucia. "Information related to ideology, religious or political options cannot be collected. This information may be gathered only with the express and written consent of the interested per - son."
125. Law 1/1991, from 28 January 1991, on Statistics in the Autonomous Community of Canarias, Article 21: "The statistic activity regulated by this law will be carried on with the respect of Articles 16.2 and 18 paragraphs 1 and 4 of the Constitution."
126. Law 3/1990, from 21 March 1990 on Statistics in Cantabria, Article 20: "The questionnaires cannot include questions directly related to the right to honor, private life and the religious or polit - ical beliefs of the respondent. The questionnaires shall respect, in all cases, the Article 18 of the Constitution of Spain." The text of Article 20, of the Law 9/1988, from 19 July 1988 on Statistics in Galicia is rigorously the same.
127. Law 23/1998, from 30 December 1998, on Statistics in Cataluna, Articles 38 and 39.

data, including data on ethnicity or race, may be collected if the respondent pro‑
vides it voluntarily. [128]

Ethnicity or race has never been included as a variable in any government census, nor is it planned to be in the upcoming census. [129] In a report submitted to the United Nations Committee on the Elimination of Racial Discrimination (CERD) in 1995 the Spanish government stated that "the censuses carried out by the National Statistics Institute contain no data on racial or ethnic identity, a subject which it is not authorized to investigate. Consequently, there are no official data on Spain's Gypsy or Jewish populations." [130]

International Law

International human rights conventions ratified by Spain are part of the inter‑ nal legal order and they are directly applicable by national courts. [131] Moreover, domestic courts must follow interpretations of the authoritative international bodies, which implement treaties to which Spain is a party (e.g. the European Court of Human Rights) and should use the interpretation of non-authoritative bodies (e.g. the UN Human Rights Committee), as interpretative guides in applying domestic law. [132] The EC directive on data protection [133] is implement‑ ed in Spain through the recently adopted Law on Data Protection. [134] The European Convention on Human Rights entered into force on Spanish territo‑

---

128. Law on Statistics of the Community of Madrid, from 21 April 1995, Article 23(3): "Individuals are not obliged to provide information to which Articles 16(2) and 18(1) +(4) of the Constitution of Spain refer to. In these cases the collaboration is always voluntary." and Law 4/1986, from 23 April 1986 on Statistics in the Autonomous Community of the Basque Country, Article 10(1): "[...] sup‑ plying information that refers to individual data [...] in relation to the right to honor and privacy is voluntary [...]."
129. National Statistic Plan 2000-2001.
130. "Thirteenth periodic reports of States parties due in 1994: Spain," CERD/C/263/Add. 5 from 3 May 1995 (State Party Report), paragraph 6.
131 Constitution of Spain (1978), Article 96(1): "Validly concluded international treaties once officially published in Spain shall constitute part of the internal legal order. Their provisions may only be abolished, modified, or suspended in the manner provided for in the treaties themselves or in accordance with general norms of international law."
132. Constitution of Spain (1978), Article 10(2): " The norms relative to basic rights and liberties which are recognized by the Constitution shall be interpreted in conformity with the Universal Declaration of Human Rights and the international treaties and agreements on those matters ratified by Spain."
133. "Directive 95/46/EC of the European Parliament and of the Council of 24 October 1995 on the protection of individuals with regard to the processing of personal data and on the free movement of such data."
134. Law 15/1999 from 13 December 1999, on Protection of Personal Data. [*Ley Orgánica 15/1999 de 13 Diciembre, de Protección de datos de Carácter Personal]*. Henceforth Law on Data Protection No. 15/1999. Spain participates in the Working Group created by the EC directive, which monitors the level of incorporation of the directive in the internal legislation of the member states.

ry in 1979. The declaration under Article 25 of the European Convention on Human Rights was made in 1985. Spain also ratified Council of Europe's Convention for the Protection of Individuals with regard to Automatic Processing of Personal Data (ETS No. 108).[135] The International Convention for the Elimination of all Forms of Racial Discrimination entered into force in Spain on January 4, 1969.

Future Prospects, Possibilities for Legal Reform in the Field

According to the Deputy Director of the Data Protection Agency, political leaders and the administration feel that the 1999 Spanish data protection law is quite adequate.[136] Consequently, there is no public debate regarding legal reforms in this area. There are, however, two important elements to consider regarding the future. Except for a few academics and some Roma organizations, the question of ethnic data gathering is basically not a concern in Spain at this time. On the other hand, the legislation is almost universally misunderstood to prohibit any kind of ethnic data gathering, storing or use. However, as has been described above, the law does not prohibit gathering ethnic data; it only impos -es special guarantees for its processing and transfer. Thus new proposals for fur -ther ethnic data gathering can be carried out without legal reforms.

The second consideration is more general. According to numerous experts, the increasingly powerful information technology makes more and more viable the collection of extremely detailed information about all individuals.[137] It is also believed that in spite of the enforcement of data protection laws there is a real danger of growing illegal collection, storing, transfer and use of intimate dat.[138] These practices are particularly attractive for direct product marketing, or exclu -sion of specific consumer groups, and ethnic data in some such cases could be a valuable variable.

135. The Convention was ratified on January 31, 1984 and entered into force on Spanish territory on the 1st October 1985 after being ratified by five countries.
136. Interview with the Deputy Director of the Data Protection Agency, September 2000.
137. "The informatics ... might be used to violate the privacy or aimed to all types of discrimina -tion." Fernández Calvo, as cited by the newspaper El Pais "A new ethics in the use of technologies.", 20 November 1991.
138. "With these powerful and modern computers is every day easier to obtain and transfer sensitive data on the economic situation, ideology, beliefs diseases, criminal records, y in several years from now, data on people's genetic configuration." R. Ryssdal, President of the European Human Rights Court, as cited by the newspaper El Pais in "The harassed privacy, " 26 October 1991.

II. Ethnic Data and Ethnic Statistics and their Use in Practice

According to information published by the Data Protection Agency there are 85 public entities, which maintain specially protected databases containing information on racial origin.[139] The Agency does not reveal the responsible entities for these files. However, it is necessary that they be approved by law and then announced in the Official Monitor of Central or Autonomous Governments.[140]

Each of the 17 autonomous communities of Spain has its own official bulletin. These 85 data bases registered with the DPA are assumed to be registered within the autonomous communities. When a database is developed the relevant Official Bulletin refers to a series of questions in connection to it, such as the entity responsible for the database, the name of the database, type of controlled data, the finality, etc.

Out of an estimate of 6 million data bases in Spain only around 400.000 are registered with the Data Protection Agency.[141] The Distribution of files containing sensitive data, as registered in the General Register for Data Protection and published by the Agency, is presented below[142]:

	Public files	Private Files
Specially Protected Data	62	368
Ideology	39	167
Beliefs	18	40
Religion	13	189
Other Specially Protected Data	2059	3822
Racial Origin	85	60
Health	1840	3803
Sexual Life	352	113
Data Related to Offenses	1235	-
Criminal Offenses	727	-
Administrative Offenses	842	-

139. Catalogue of Files, 2000, CD-ROM issued by the Data Protection Agency, "Distribution of files containing sensitive data, registered in the General Register for Data Protection."
140. Article 20, paragraph 1, Data Protection Law 15/1999.
141. Interview with the Deputy Director of the Data Protection Agency, September 2000.
142. Catalogue of Files, 2000, CD-ROM issued by the Data Protection Agency, "Distribution of files containing sensitive data, registered in the General Register for Data Protection."

A computer search carried out by the authors in BOE (Official State Bulletin) found no examples of *central* government ethnic data collecting, but the decrees that created six such data bases (out of the 85 in the table above) were found in the Official Bulletin of Madrid Autonomous Community.

1. The database called "Computerized Social Conflict" of the Madrid Institute of Youth and Family includes information on youth with judicial records and includes data on racial origin. Providing data is compulsory. The declared finality is the elaboration of statistics.[143]

2. Database of Personal and Family Clinic History of users of the Center "North Residence" for Adolescent Mothers. This center is under the direction of the Department of Women's Affairs (*Dirección General de la Mujer*) of the CAM. Included is data on racial origin, and its finality is "sanitary control of users," and for medical and scientific investigations.[144]

3. The Shelter Database (*Centro de Acogida*) of the Department of Women's affairs whose users are mothers and children, also maintains data on racial origin in order to know the personal, social, work, and family situation of the women, and thus orient their demands for social, judicial, psychological and family resources.[145]

4. Women's Social History database of the same department also includes data on racial origin. This database includes women who require services of the department of women's affairs because of being in a situation of exclusion or social risk. The finality is to carry out social intervention with women and children in situations of exclusion or social risk. In these three cases providing race or ethnicity related data is voluntary.[146]

5. Database of "Marginal and shantytown (Chabola) population" covered by the *Instituto de Realojamiento e Integracion Social* (IRIS). Data is included regarding racial origin for the goal of proportioning housing to persons in situations of social exclusion. The data is voluntary.[147]

6. Database of the Center of Sports Medicine of the Education and Cultural Department of the Community of Madrid, where racial origin is included. The goal is described as "to gather all the necessary data for a correct prevention, diagnostic treatment, and follow-up of patients and athletes in

143. Decree 90/1999, of June 10, 1999. BOCM No.146, from 22 June 1999, page 26.
144. Decree 87/1999 of June 10, 1999, Annex, BOCM No. 147 from 23 June 1999, page 24.
145. Decree 87/1999 of June 10, 1999, Annex, BOCM No. 147 from 23 June 1999, page 25.
146. Decree 87/1999 of June 10, 1999, Annex, BOCM No. 147 from 23 June 1999, page 26.
147. Decree 80/1999 of June 3, 1999, Annex 1, BOCM No. 137 from 11 June 1999, page 41.

order to develop medical reports, statistical studies, and with permission of those affected, investigative work." [148]

Apart from the legally registered and maintained databases, several bodies (state and private) are known or presumed to control databases that contain eth - nic data, and which are not registered with the Data Protection Agency.

State Actors

The fact that the police have targeted certain ethnic groups, and continue to do so for control, is no secret in Spain. *Presencia Gitana*, a Spanish NGO work- ing on Roma rights, revealed the existence, in 1986, of an order of the chief of police in Madrid region that established, "among the permanent attributions of police agents the examination of hotel registers, control of small packages and vigilance concerning *national ethnic groups*" and included "permanent preventive control and vigilance concerning ethnic national groups suspected of drug trafficking" in the police action plan. [149]

More recently, the press revealed three cases of local police departments ille - gally gathering ethnic data in three different localities: Valencia, Arganda del Rey and Alcobendas. In 1995 in Valencia it was discovered that the police were keeping files where they identified suspicious people by color, ethnic group, sex - ual orientation, and accent. There were over a 1000 persons in these files when the district attorney began an investigation. The chief of local police, who elud - ed any responsibility by blaming three of his subordinates, was appointed, one year later, General Director of the Spanish Police. [150]

According to the press, in Arganda del Rey and Alcobendas, two municipali - ties in the community of Madrid, the police were classifying people by race (e.g. European, Latino, African, Roma) by appearance (normal, rude, educated, affected), by accent, by health (Aids, parasites, hepatitis), by dress (rags, normal, travesty) or by other aspects (prostitutes, homosexual, transsexual, pimps). [151] The Data Protection Agency inspected the police files. In Arganda del Rey it was found that an order to collect information related to race, sexual life and health existed, but the investigation was closed because the Data Protection Agency could not prove the existence of individual files in the possession of the police. [152]

---

148. Decree 49/1999 of April 8, concerning personal databases of the Department of Education and Culture of the Autonomous Community of Madrid.
149. "Roma before the law and the administration," *Presencia Gitana*, 1991.
150. "The files are the suspects," see: *members.es.tripod.de/mojual/104.htm.*
151. "The files are the suspects," see: *members.es.tripod.de/mojual/104.htm.*
152. Annual Report of the data Protection Agency, 1999, pp. 160.

In Alcobendas, out of 1905 police files inspected, 415 contained information on race, health and sexual life of individuals who were not related to any concrete police investigation.[153] The director of the agency ordered the municipality to immediately put an end to the illegal use of specially protected data, but the order was not respected. He reacted by ordering the destruction of the information concerning race, health and sexual life and initiating administrative procedures against the police.[154] The case is pending.[155]

In the penal system a recent private study did a count of Roma women in Spain's twelve largest prisons.[156] This was done through informal counts by persons working in each center, except one center where the director had compiled, ad hoc, a list of names of the Roma prisoners, which was given to the investigation team. In this study data has been used to denounce alarming over-representation of Romani women in Spanish prisons, and to detect possible discriminatory practices in the criminal justice system.[157]

The school systems in some (if not all) Autonomous Communities carry out regular anonymous counts of Roma and immigrant students, and how many are in special education programs center by center. Apart from the count, each center must fill out a nominal list of Roma students, immigrant students, and special education students. This second list is only used to insure that the anonymous count is correct, and this data is not introduced into any database, or centrally maintained. The Ministry does not consider that these files must be registered with the Data Protection Agency.[158] The statistics published by the Central Education Ministry indicate that this entity also has statistical information regarding the total number of Romani children in Spanish Schools.[159]

Data collected by Madrid Education Department has been used to document disparities: in the first place the fact that the majority of Roma students are centered in very few public schools (sometimes being a majority); there are very few in private subsidized schools. In the second place it demonstrates the over-representation of Roma children in special education classes. These data are oriented to correcting these inequalities.[160] The anonymous school data for Madrid are tabulated on a centralized basis in Madrid; the nominal lists are kept in the

153. Annual Report of the data Protection Agency, 1999, pp. 160.
154. Annual Report of the data Protection Agency, 1999, pp. 159-160.
155. Interview with the Deputy Director of the Data Protection Agency, September 2000.
156. Baraní, an investigation of "Roma Women and the Spanish Criminal Justice," February 2000, see: *personales.jet.es/gea21*.
157. Baraní, an investigation of "Roma Women and the Spanish Criminal Justice," February 2000, see: *personales.jet.es/gea21*.
158. Interview with the Head of Madrid Special Education Department, September 2000.
159. "Inequality in Education in Spain," MEC and CIDE, 1999.
160. Interview with the Head of the Madrid Special Education Department, September 2000.

regional educational offices and are not incorporated into any database. The Ministry of Education of Spain claims that data from autonomous communities are not gathered and centralized.[161] The Madrid Education Department data regarding distribution of Roma children has been cited by the press.[162] The school-by-school ethnic breakdown data is restricted and available only upon written request and depending on the purpose for which it is requested.

Various central health data bases checked by the Data Protection Agency did not contain ethnic or race related data.[163] There are cases of individual doctors who have carried out investigations in health centers or clinics recording ethnic data for comparative purposes. For example, Dr. Felipe Reyerta has collected data on 5000 Roma patients in southern Madrid.[164]

It has also been reported that the Madrid Social Services Office (IMI), which gives small welfare grants to low income people, indicates ethnicity in individuals' case files. Four years ago immigrants became eligible for these grants and the eth - nic category now includes immigrants and Spanish Roma together. According to IMI representatives, this is not information voluntarily given by the clients, but is a "professional evaluation" made by caseworkers, being understood that a request for welfare is a tacit permission to note and use this data.[165] This data is treated as specially protected data, maintained in a computerized centralized database, and it is used for statistical studies.[166] The ethnic data gathered by social workers in the Madrid IMI Office can help to better orient Roma clients to the most appropriate programs of integration and education.[167] The administrative databases contain - ing information on race registered in the Official Bulletin are obviously "central - ized" at the level of the community of Madrid. Data from evaluations of social workers in the Madrid IMI Office are computerized anonymously by the Madrid Central Welfare office files and are treated as specially protected data.[168] The Madrid Social Services office has produced statistics of Roma clients.[169]

A rather peculiar database is formed by the files kept under the Franco regime under the Law on "social danger"[170] (*peligrosidad social*). This database contained (and still contains) at the local level the data of over 50,000 persons defined as

---

161. Interview with the Head of the Madrid Special Education Department, September 2000.
162. *El Pais* June 11, 2000.
163. Data Protection Agency, Annual Report on 1999, pp. 164-187.
164. Felipe Reyrta, paper delivered at the "Jornadas de ASGG," October 1999.
165. Interview with sub director of Madrid IMI grant office, September, 2000.
166. Interview with sub director of Madrid IMI grant office, September, 2000.
167. Interview with the Deputy Director of Madrid IMI grant office, September 2000.
168. Interview with the Deputy Director of Madrid IMI grant office, September 2000.
169. Paper delivered by Nieves Alonso, Head of IMI office, in ASGG Conference, October 1999.
170. Law 16/1970, from the 4th of August 1970, on social dangerousness and rehabilitation. [BOE, No. 187 from 6 August 1970, pp. 12551-12557].

social deviants. Roma, drug addicts, prostitutes and homosexuals were some of the collectives who were targeted under this law, which was kept in force for sev-enteen years after Franco died, until the reform of the Spanish Criminal Code, in 1995. Antonio Ruiz recently won a court suit in Valencia and his file, opened in 1976, under Franco's regime, which indicated that he was homosexual, was destroyed.[171] This was just an individual case, where it was proved that the infor-mation from the files still existed in the police archives. As a rule, the files are considered of historic interest and protected by the Law on Patrimony.[172] Some of them are kept in judicial, police, or administrative premises.[173] Some organi-zations believe that the information from these files could have been introduced into the databases of the police.[174] Indeed, the press publishes cases where peo-ple have been deprived of liberty after the police, consulting databases, discov-ered that they are labeled as socially dangerous for being homosexuals.[175] The Data Protection Law prohibits the consultation of the files without the consent of the interested person or before fifty years have passed from their creation.[176]

Numerous studies have been carried out in the last decade by regional gov-ernments regarding Roma population.[177] "White paper: the Spanish Gypsies," prepared by the Institute of Applied Sociology of Madrid in 1978, was the first nationwide study on Roma. In 1983, the Senate Commission on Human Rights and Relations with the Ombudsman collected data on Roma population and its social situation. In 1987, the Ministry of the Interior carried out a sociological investigation on anthropology and demography in Spain's Roma community, although the results were not published.[178] In 1990 the Ministry of Social Affairs supported a sociological study on the Roma community in Spain.[179]

---

171. "Antonio Ruiz is not a "social danger" anymore," *El Pais*, 27 September 2000, pp. 88.
172. Law 16/1985, from 25 June 1985, on Spanish Historic Patrimony.
173. In Extremadura the files were kept in the General Archive of the Administration, see "Keeping or destroying the files on social dangerousness?" in Documents in Information Science, see: *dois.mimas.ac.uk/DoIS/data/Articles/julilfkijy:1999:v:9:i:31:p:38.html*.
174. "Proyecto Memoria," Cabinet of Studies and Publications of the Foundation Triangle, see: *www.redestb.es/triangulo-gep/cvgeppm1.htm*.
175. "People on whom the Franco regime was keeping files are new less dangerous," *El Mundo*, 29 March 1999, see: *www.el-mundo.es/1999/03/29/sociedad/20N00051.html*.
176. The Third Additional Provision of the Law on Data Protection No. 15/1999 provides that the files created under the law on Lazy People from 1933 [*Ley de Vagos y Maleantes*] and under the Law on Dangerousness and Social Rehabilitation from 1970, "which contain information that might affect the right to security, honor, privacy or the right to imagine, may be consulted only with the express consent of the interested person or after fifty years from their creation."
177. "Thirteenth periodic reports of States parties due in 1994: Spain," CERD/C/263/Add. 5 from 3 May 1995 (State Party Report), paragraph 34.
178. "Thirteenth periodic reports of States parties due in 1994: Spain," CERD/C/263/Add. 5 from 3 May 1995 (State Party Report), paragraph 34.
179. "Thirteenth periodic reports of States parties due in 1994: Spain," CERD/C/263/Add. 5 from 3 May 1995 (State Party Report), paragraph 34.

A major statewide study was carried out by the Group PASS in 1992 [180], which included an estimate of the total Spanish Roma population. [181] One of the most detailed regional studies was carried out in Valencia, interviewing almost 2000 Roma.[182] In these cases Roma people were located by a mixture of contacts from public offices who work with Roma, usually regarding housing relocation pro - grams, Social Services, school systems and by networking among friends and family of members of Roma associations. Names were encoded when introduced into databases and the original survey forms were kept a certain period of time after completion of the studies and then destroyed. [183]

Non-state Actors

The overwhelming majority of the unions, churches and associations con - tacted by the authors maintained that they are not collecting ethnic/racial data. It is important to note that a number of public and private organizations main - tain data on nationality, a category, which is not, protected information under the data protection legislation. In some cases, however, nationality might pro - vide a strong indication of the race of the person.

The Permanent Observatory on Migrant Farm workers keeps data on workers, classifying the following groups: Roma, Portuguese Roma or Portuguese Non- Roma, immigrants from East Europe, other immigrants, and Spanish non-Roma. [184]

With regard to religious organizations it is interesting to note that the Tax Office requires, according to the law, [185] the evangelical churches to provide the names of their members who have made tax deductible donations to their church. There is peculiar potential for an indirect ethnic database here, in that most Protestant Roma are in one church — the Church of Philadelphia — and there are very few non-Roma in this church.[186] Additionally, according to the president of the

180. "Social anthropological analysis of the situation of the Roma community in Spain," Association Secretariado General Gitano, (ASGG) 1992.
181. Official estimates on the number of Spanish Roma do not exist. Various studies cited by the gov - ernment indicate between 325,000 and 450,000. [See: "Thirteenth periodic reports of States parties due in 1994: Spain," CERD/C/263/Add. 5 from 3 May 1995 (State Party Report), paragraph 34.]. A study published in 1999 by the Associacion Secretariado General Gitano (ASGG) in 1999 estimates that actually there are 600,000 Roma in Spain. "Data on Roma population in each autonomous com - munity," ASGG, October 1999.
182. "Situation and social economic problems of the Roma people resident in the Autonomous Community of Valencia," January 1991, Grupo Emer.
183. Interviews with investigators who carried out some of the cited studies, September 2000.
184. Interview with the Head of the Department of Attention for Farm workers of Caritas, September 2000.
185. 16885, Order from 30 July 1999, published in BOE No. 186, from August 5, 1999, pp. 29044.
186. "Structure and Composition of the Federation of Evangelical Religious Entities of Spain," FEREDE, 1999.

Federation of Spanish Evangelical Churches (FEREDE), another governmental entity, the Office of Religious Affairs, has, at times, verbally requested the list of members of new churches who applied to be legalized as religious organizations. [187]

Arthur Anderson, a large consulting firm, recently published a study on the neighborhood of Vallecas, Madrid, where they included exact numbers of Roma children in the schools. [188] However, the source of this information is rather unclear. [189]

In 1993, a part of an unpublished study elaborated by a student in sociology for a research institute was been destroyed because it contained personal data and lists with names and addresses of Roma families in Huesca (Aragon). The author maintained that all information was provided voluntarily by the persons interviewed and that there was no racist intention in data processing. [190] However, the association SOS Racismo argued that the families who refused to answer the questions were told that the inquiry was a municipal census and would be taken into consideration for the distribution of social benefits. [191]

As far as use of the above ethnic data is concerned in theory, registers where - by a person's ethnicity can be identified are covered by the Data Protection Law and can only be used by the department which has developed the data base, fol - lowing the security regulations of this law and for the finality for which it has been gathered. Statistical data can be gathered from these registers and made public. Individuals have the right to see their own files.

However, in practice several abuses have become known. Good examples of abuse are the cases cited above of police gathering ethnic data in various munic - ipalities in Spain, or the use of information contained in files created during Franco's regime on certain ethnic groups, homosexuals, etc.

A few years ago Rafael Vera, by then Secretary of State for Security Matters, declared before a parliamentary commission that 70% of the heroin market in Spain is "controlled by gitanos." [192] This statement was severely criticized by

187. Interview with Mariano Blazquez, President of the Spanish Federation of Evangelical Churches (FEREDE), September 10, 2000. The FEREDE, however, recommends the new churches not to facilitate to the government the lists with their members.
188. "Study on the social and economic re-equilibrium in the districts of Villa de Vallecas, y Puente de Vallecas, 2000. Commissioned by the Office of the President of the Community of Madrid." Arthur Anderson Consultancy Firm, 2000.
189. The consulting firm told the authors that the Madrid government supplied the information on Roma children while this body denied it. According to the Data Protection Agency the majority of the complaints received in 1999 referred to the transfer of information from the public administra - tion files to private entities. (Data Protection Agency, *Annual Report on 1999*, pp. 161-162.)
190. "The justice destroys the Roma census to protect privacy," *Meralbo de Aragon*, 3 July 1993.
191. "A census of the Roma population marked by discrimination and racism," *Meralbo de Aragon*, Zaragoza, 19 June 1993.
192. "The police orders to count all delinquents gitanos in Lleida," *Segre*, Lerida, 11 November 1991.

Romani organizations, which qualified it as "racist, unconstitutional and legally condemnable" because it identified Roma with the drogues.[193] Later Vera corrected his statement, affirming that only 1000-1500 "gitanos" are drug dealers, which represents no more than 0.3% of this population.[194] However, he allegedly requested all municipal police stations to send him statistics of Roma involved in drug trafficking.[195] Police Departments in Cataluna reportedly received similar orders from the Police Headquarters in Barcelona.[196]

Meanwhile, beyond the possibility for abuse one can also see the advantages of having ethnic statistics. The sociological studies mentioned above produced a wealth of statistics in Spain, regarding such important questions as income, age, education, housing situation, and in some cases comparisons with non-Roma population. For example, there are available figures on what percentage of welfare recipients in Madrid are Roma (17-18%)[197], on the distribution of Roma children in schools and their participation in special education classes[198], on the representation of Romani women within total prison population (25%)[199], or on the percentage of agriculture work force who are Roma.[200] The Ombudsman's annual report on 1999 notes that "the ghettoisation is a phenomenon that affects mainly the Romani people; the discrimination in the housing field is obvious: more than 90% of those who live in ghettoes belong to this ethnic group."[201]

Methods Used for Collecting and Processing Minority Data

Where authorities and/or non-state actors are known or suspected to keep data on ethnicity, the descriptive terminology is mostly coded. In the case of Madrid IMI Welfare Office they use the general category of "ethnic" which includes without distinction[202] Roma and immigrants. The Madrid Department of Education uses the word "gitano."[203] Other offices use codes. Gitano when

193. "Roma representatives consider Vera's words revolting," *El Independiente*, Madrid, 26 October 1991.
194. "The police orders to count all delinquents gitanos in Lleida," *Segre*, Lerida, 11 November 1991.
195. "Counting the Gitanos," *El Diario Montanes*, 14 November 1991.
196. "The Catalan Police censes the delinquents of Roma ethnicity," *La Region*, Orense, 12 November 1991.
197. Paper delivered by Nieves Alonso, Head of IMI office, in ASGG Conference, October 1999.
198. "General Data on Ethnic Minorities," Programming Unit of the Education Department of Madrid Regional Community, December 1999.
199. Barani, an investigation of "Roma Women and the Spanish Criminal Justice," February 2000, see: *personales.jet.es/gea21*.
200. Interview with the Head of the Department of Attention for Farm workers of Caritas, September 2000.
201. Ombudsman's *Annual Report 1999*, section 14.2.5. Source: See: *www.defensordelpueblo.es*
202. Interview with the Deputy Director of Madrid IMI grant office, September 2000.
203. "General Data on Ethnic Minorities," Programming Unit of the Education Department of Madrid Regional Community, December 1999.

used is a noun, and not a qualifier. Sometimes the category used is "member of an ethnic group" and can include Roma and immigrants.

The administration, which may collect data on race or ethnicity (i) obtains directly the statistical data (e.g. the above mentioned data on compensated education is gathered by school inspectors who go to every center and have teachers make a count. Madrid Social Service workers make an individual evaluation of their clients and so on); (ii) uses other administrative sources; or (iii) uses other statistics and recompilations.[204]

Several methods can be used by researchers or administrative bodies for reaching potential data subjects: using name and address lists; using information from intermediaries (community leaders, schoolteachers, neighbors etc.); using stochastic methods; or using their personal knowledge and contacts. All methods are used in Spain; information from intermediaries (community leaders, schoolteachers, neighbors etc.), stochastic methods, personal knowledge and contacts. It seems that the names are collected on a personal informal basis, for instance social workers will provide contacts among the Roma people they know. These can be provided by people in public administration, from NGOs, and Associations. In the Baraní study, conducted in prisons, the guards introduced the investigators to the Roma women inmates. Lists of non-ethnic categories, which might contain an important representation of Roma, can be used (people with street vendor licenses for example) and personal contacts are used to remove non-Roma names from the lists.

In the sociological investigations mentioned above, investigators worked through public data and contacts suggested by public workers. It does not appear that they used officially ethnic databases kept by administration but rather used lists of people who live in sub standard housing, street vendor registers or lists of welfare recipients, where there might be a high percentage of Roma. Contacts are also made through Roma associations. Interviewers also collect data directly from individuals.

An important area for contacting a large mass of Roma people would be through the Philadelphia Church (*Iglesia de Filadelfia*), which has up to 150,000 members, although it is not known which bias would be implicit there.

As far as guarantees for protecting information privacy and ensuring data protection are concerned, throughout the processing of ethnic data in the sociological studies data from the survey forms are incorporated in computer programs eliminating names and addresses. The original survey forms are stored for a period of time and then destroyed. The Madrid Education Department

204. National Institute for Statistics, Inventory of Statistical Operations performed by the General Administration of the State (IOE), see: *www.ine.es/ioe/defininv.htm*.

maintains their database on only one computer, which can only be accessed in their office.

Major Debates and Arguments on Using Data on Minorities.

According to the Deputy Director of the Data Protection Agency, there are no on-going debates on using data on minorities within the Spanish administra - tion.[205] As mentioned above, many officials insist that collection of ethnic data is discriminatory and anti-constitutional, while in practice gathering such data is legal and the administration does it, publishing the creation of databases in the Official Monitors.

Some members of academia affirm that it would be useful to have ethnic data for comparative studies, but mostly with regard to immigrant populations.[206] The Baraní Project develops certain analysis around the usefulness of ethnic data gathering and critiques of certain arguments against ethnic data gathering based on the idea that this data can increase discrimination.[207]

For years the Association Presencia Gitana has been defending the need for a Roma Census. "It is both interesting and even necessary to know the total pop - ulation of the Roma community... to guarantee the quantification and the qualification of the coordinates of the Roma universe." [208] A proposal for Cultural Autonomy implicitly requires a Roma electoral census when it states that "the Institutions which Represent the Roma nation must be elected by uni - versal suffrage by the Spanish Roma." [209]Some Roma lawyers understand the need for statistics for anti-discrimination litigation purposes.[210]

The idea of the census has been misused in several instances by local admin - istrations, in attempts to control particular ethnic groups. For example, in 1995 the Department of Social Services in Leon declared its intention to prepare lists of all Roma families in the municipality in order to "avoid that new families occupy deserted flats in the city." [211] The socialist party (PSOE) stated that the plan, which would have permitted the police to control the spontaneous Roma

---

205. Interview with the Deputy Director of the Data Protection Agency, September 2000.
206. Interviews with Javier de Lucas, Universidad de Valencia, Cesar Manzano, Universidad de Pais Vasco, Vitoria, Mario Gaviria, Universidad de Navarra.
207. Baraní, an investigation of Roma women in Spanish Prisons, February 2000, see: *personales.jet.es/gea21.*
208. "Report on the Roma Question," (*Informe sobre la Cuestión Gitana*), Ed. Presencia Gitana, 1991.
209. "Duma Romani: a socialist proposal to the Roma Question," November 1998.
210. Interview with Carmen Santiago Reyes, Romani Lawyer, member of the Council of Europe MG-S-ROM group, October 2000.
211. "The City Hall will not elaborate a Roma census without consulting with the Secretariat," *El Diario de Leon*, 2 August 1995.

settlements, had "purely Hitlerist connotations." In September 1995, Madrid regional government announced its intention to cense all Roma living in Madrid's ghettoes in order to "facilitate their social integration." [212]

Other Roma spokespeople are very hesitant about ethnic data gathering. They argue that ethnicity is not an objective category and that ethnic data gath-ering can reinforce mistaken beliefs about "ethnic homogeneity." There is also a historical remembrance of the use of ethnic data by the Nazis, as well as in ear-lier moments of Spain's history, which required registering of Roma citizens. In other cases there is fear that data which indicates over-representation of Roma people in certain areas, such as prison populations, can reinforce negative stereo-types. [213]

No provisions were made for the inclusion of minority groups in decision making about the gathering, storage and use of data on ethnicity. One exception can be mentioned: the participation of Roma spokespeople in some debate in Valencia regarding a public financed study about Roma population. [214]

212. "The Community will cense the Roma population," *Ya* -Madrid, 12 September 1995.
213. Interview with Manuel Bustamonte, MP, Valencia Parliament, and Head of the office for Roma Affairs, September 2000.
214. Interview with Manuel Bustamonte, MP, Valencia Parliament, and Head of the Office for Roma Affairs, September 2000.

Ethnic Statistics and Data Protection in Latvia

Boris Koltchanov

I. Legal Framework

The peculiar feature of the Latvian situation is the institutionalization of eth-nicity. Continuing the Stalinist tradition, every individual has to register his or her ethnic origin with the state authorities by means of the population registry and the census. Ethnic origin is also registered on a mandatory basis in the iden-tification documents issued by Latvian authorities.

Relation to the Stalinist practice is especially evident as the registration of "nationality" in the registry, the census and the identification acts refers not to the person's self-identification (or even mother tongue), but to the ethnic origin of the parents and grandparents of the data subject.

Registration of ethnic origin is regulated by a number of legal provisions.

Passports

About one-quarter of Latvia's population is still denied Latvian citizenship. Therefore, it is important to consider regulations concerning passports of both citizens and non-citizens of Latvia.

The Governmental Regulations on the Passports of Latvian Citizens[1] require registration of ethnic origin in the passports of Latvia's citizens.[2] Latvian citizens are supposed to receive a passport upon reaching 16 years of age. In this case the person's ethnic origin is recorded in accordance with the registered ethnic ori-gin of either his or her mother or father, depending on the person's choice[3] The name and surname has to be written according to Latvian language grammar rules. Citizens are also entitled to have their names and surnames recorded in their "original form" upon presentation of supporting documents.[4] However, this non-Latvian form of the name will be typed in the "special notes" box and

---

1. Adopted on 2 November 1995.
2. Article 5.
3. Article 18.
4. Article 6.

only the Latvian version will be considered as the officially valid name. Should a citizen have changed his or her ethnicity (see below), the Regulations require such an individual to submit documents for changing his or her passport within one month following the change of ethnicity.[5]

Similarly, the Governmental Regulations on the Passports of Latvian Non-citizens[6] also require the registration of ethnic origin in the passports of persons who are not Latvian citizens. This record is placed on a separate page of special notes, together with "color of eyes", "height" and unspecified "distinctive marks." Non-citizens are also required to receive passports upon reaching the age of 16 and their ethnicity is also determined based on the ethnicity of their parents.[7] In case of change of ethnicity, persons are obliged to submit documents for changing their passports within one month following the change of ethnicity. Names and surnames of Latvian non-citizens are to be typed according to Latvian language grammar rules.[8] Individuals can also request to type their names in original form (either in Latin or in Slavonic letters,) on the page of "special notes."

Changing Ethnicity

The Law on Changing the Registered Name, Surname or Ethnicity[9] reinforces the ascription of an individual's ethnicity by the "blood principle." Provisions of the Law equally apply to Latvia's citizens and non-citizens. Individuals seeking to change their ethnicity in the records have to provide evidence that one of their parents or grandparents was of the desired new ethnicity.[10] Besides, individuals seeking to change their ethnicity to Latvian have to prove their highest command of the state language.[11] If an individual seeks to change ethnicity to Liv, but is unable to provide evidence that one of his or her parents or grandparents were Livs, an opinion by a Liv NGO, acknowledging the person's ethnic origin as Liv, should be attached to the application.[12] The Civil Registry Department of the Ministry of Justice will decide to grant or refuse applications for changing ethnicity and their refusal can be appealed in court.[13] Ethnicity can be changed only once.[14]

---

5. Article 13.
6. Adopted on 21 January 1995.
7. Articles 5 and 28.
8. Article 11.
9. Adopted on 5 July 1994.
10. Article 9, paragraph 1.
11. Article 11, paragraph 2.
12. Article 11, paragraph 3.
13. Article 13.
14. Article 9, paragraph 2.

The Law on the Residents' Register[15] requires information about an individual's "ethnic origin" to be entered into the data of the Register.[16] In cases where information about the person's parents is not existent in the Register, the Law requires such information to be entered into the database, including the information about the parents' ethnic origin.[17] The Law also stipulates that information about the person's race or complexion, religious conviction or affiliation with a church, political conviction, sexual orientation or health status shall not be included in the Register.[18]

The Law on the Residents' Register regulates registration of personal data in the Residents' Register. The data are entered into the Register upon completion of a standard primary registration form.[19] An official of the Citizenship and Migration Department completes the form on the basis of documents submitted by the data subject.[20] The data subject has to confirm the data in the completed registration form with his or her signature.

Census

The Law on Population Census[21] does not directly require that questions concerning "ethnicity" be included in the census questionnaire. The Law stipulates that the census shall provide "information about all inhabitants of the state, necessary for the society and state government." [22] The census is conducted according to the Census Program, which in particular includes questions of the census questionnaire. The Program is developed by the Central Statistics Authority and approved by the Cabinet of Ministers.[23] The latest census, conducted in 2000, required individuals to define their "ethnicity," "mother tongue" and "second language."

Article 9 of the Law on Population Census regulates the process of gathering personal data in the census. It provides that census data has to be collected by authorized census takers and obliges residents of the country to provide accurate information concerning their data to them. Census takers can request individu-

16. Article 10, paragraph 1(9).
17. Article 10, paragraph 3 (5).
18. Article 12.
19. Articles 4 and 6.
20. Article 8.
21. Adopted on 16 December 1999.
22. Article 1.
23. Article 6.

als to show their identification documents in order to make sure that the provided census data is accurate.

Recent Initiatives

Taking into consideration the above legal context, the issue of personal data protection with respect to ethnic data should have an especially important role in Latvia. However, the issue of personal data protection had occurred only recently in the agenda of Latvian legislators. Latvia signed on 31 October 2000 (albeit still has not ratified) the Council of Europe Convention for the Protection of Individuals with Regard to Automatic Processing of Personal Data. The Law on Personal Data Protection was adopted on 23 March 2000. The Law explicitly prohibits processing of "sensitive personal data" [24], including data referring to an individual's race, ethnic origin, philosophical and political beliefs, health or sexual life. The Law is applied both to the state and non-state databases. However, it does not apply to two exceptional cases:

– databases of natural persons where personal data are processed for personal or family purposes and are not accessible to other persons;
– Databases of the state institutions in the areas of security and criminal law.

It remains to be seen how these measures will affect the current situation. Apart from being rather recent, these measures are not only in conflict with some other legal provisions, but they are also in contradiction with the ongoing practices and the deep-rooted convictions prevalent among state and municipal functionaries, many politicians, as well as large segments of the population.

Rights of Data Subjects. Access to Data. Transfer, Altering and Deleting Data

Articles 8 and 9 of the Law on Personal Data Protection regulate the registration process of personal data. Article 8 refers to cases where the personal data is acquired directly from individuals. It is envisioned that unless legislation allows personal data processing without disclosing its goal, the data controller has to ensure that the data subject is informed about:

– Title and address of the data base;
– The envisioned purpose and justification for collection and processing of personal data;
– Possible receivers of the data;

---

24. Article 11.

– The individual's rights to access his/her personal data and the possibility to alter or delete the data;
– Whether providing the data is voluntary or mandatory and whether any sanctions are envisioned for refusal.

Article 9 of the same act regulates cases in which the personal data is not acquired directly from the individual. It provides that before data is being released to a third party, the data base supervisor is obliged to inform data sub- ject about:

– Title (name) and address of the database;
– The envisioned purpose of data processing;
– Possible receivers of the data;
– The source of personal data;
– The individual's rights to access his or her personal data and possibility to alter and delete the data.

This provision is not applicable if the law permits personal data processing without the consent of the individual, or personal data is processed for scientific, historical or statistical studies, and if delivering this information to every data subject requires disproportionate efforts or is not possible.

The Law on Personal Data Protection provides for the right to access to information on personal data included in any database, except in situations explicitly mentioned by the law.[25] Such information shall be released to the indi- vidual within one month after application, though not more often than two times a year.

The Law on Personal Data Protection stipulates that in certain cases defined by law, the data controllers have to give out personal data to officials of the state and municipal institutions. No such cases are defined by the Law, however. Otherwise, the Law does not provide individuals the right to access to other data from the databases.

The Law on the Residents' Register provides for all data subjects the right to "request two times a year, free of charge, information on data concerning him- self/herself as well as on his/her children under 16" from the Register.[26]

The Law on the Residents' Register[27] also allows natural and legal persons to access the data contained in the Register "upon a substantiated request." However, the latter term is not specified in the Law. Neither it is clarified if the information to be given is of personal or of general/statistical character. Article 21 deals specifically with statistical information and other information of gener-

25. Article 15.
26. Article 18.
27. Article 19.

al character that does not make possible the identification of the data subjects. It entitles authorities, companies, organizations and natural persons to receive such information from the Register. The Law also entitles the state and other bodies to whom the state has delegated administrative functions, courts and the public prosecutor's office, to obtain personal data from the Register within the limits of the competence of these institutions.[28]

Transborder transfer of personal data contained in the Register is permitted by the Law in accordance with international agreements, or in special cases if approved by the Minister of Foreign Affairs and the Minister of the Interior.[29]

The Law on Population Census[30] limits accessibility of personal data collected from individuals. Such information cannot be released to natural and legal persons. At the same time, such information can be used for statistical purposes only.

Data subjects have the right to demand correction of their personal data contained in the Resident's Register, including data on ethnicity. If a person discovers that the Register contains his or her personal data illegally, he or she has the right to demand deleting such information.[31]

Article 16 of the Law on Personal Data Protection also gives individuals the right to demand modification or correction of their personal data, as well as to demand that the data controller stop processing their personal data or delete it.

Legal Sanctions

The Law on Personal Data Protection provides that the State Data Inspection of the Ministry of Justice shall supervise the enforcement of the right to informational self-determination.[32] The State Data Inspection ensures compliance of data processing and controlling with the Law, reviews complaints of data protection violations, and registers databases. If it finds violations of the Law, the Inspection can refuse registration of a data base, as well as demand blocking of data, deleting or eliminating erroneous or illegally acquired data, can rule permanent or temporary ban on data processing. The Inspection can also submit applications to courts over violations of the Law on Personal Data Protection.

---

28. Article 22.
29. Article 23.
30. Article 15.
31. Article 20 of the Law on the Residents' Register.
32. Article 29.

Minority rights in Latvia are formulated rather vaguely. However, there is one provision in the Latvian legislation concerning minority rights, which contradicts the principles of protection of personal data. The Law on Unrestricted Development of National and Ethnic Groups of Latvia and the Rights to Cultural Autonomy[33] declares the right of every person to have indicated in identification documents "national belonging" (i.e. ethnicity) according to the "national self-determination and national origin, in accordance with the law." First, the underlying idea of this provision (indication of ethnicity in IDs) interferes with the right to informational self-determination, even though certain freedom to choose is envisioned. Second, the choice of affiliation is limited by the individual's national origin.

Discrimination on grounds of national, ethnic or racial origin can be mostly observed in three areas: citizenship, language requirements for employment in both private and public sectors, and employment in the decision-making bodies and state apparatus.

Citizenship legislation[34] adopted soon after restoration of Latvia's independence recognized as citizens only those persons who possessed citizenship in the inter-war republic and their direct descendants. Although this decision was formulated in purely legalistic terms, it had enormous effect on the ethno-political balance of the country: two-thirds of persons belonging to minorities were refused Latvian citizenship, and thus any possibility to influence the political decision-making process of the country.

Language legislation requires graduates of minority schools to pass special language examinations to receive a state-language proficiency certificate. Without such a certificate graduates of minority schools cannot be employed legally, neither in the public nor in the private sector of the economy. Although this requirement is not defined by the ethnicity or race of individuals, it discriminates against minorities, as an overwhelming majority of adult ethnic Latvians are graduates of schools with Latvian language of instruction and thus, do not face any difficulties when required to pass language examinations

Employment practices in the decision-making bodies and the state apparatus are another area prone to discrimination. In short, although no legal norms overtly discriminate against ethnic minorities, minorities are heavily under-rep-

33. Law adopted on 19 March 1991. Article 2. Source:
www.riga.lv/minelres/NationalLegislation/Latvia/Latvia_CultAut_English.htm
34. Resolution on The Renewal of the Rights of Citizens of the Republic of Latvia and Fundamental Principles of Naturalisation, Adopted 15 October 1991.

resented in these areas of employment. Latvia has neither formal nor informal mechanisms ensuring minority representation. While minorities constitute more than 40% of the total population, their share in the decision-making bodies and state apparatus is negligible. The assessment of the level of minority representation can only be made on the basis of rare pieces of official information and on the basis of surveys. Information is available for example about the judiciary. This shows that out of 152 judges in January 1994, 142 were ethnic Latvians [35] The Parliament approves the appointment of judges and it is worth noting that ethnicity is mentioned in the CVs of all candidates for the judge positions. [36] Of 48 judges approved by the Parliament in 1999, only one was ethnically non-Latvian. All judges of the Supreme Court are ethnic Latvians. Not a single Russian-speaker has ever been a member of the National Council on Radio and Television Broadcasting — a supervisory body which determines the strategy of electronic media development, issues licenses and monitors compliance with the legislation in the field. The staff of Latvia's ombudsman-like institution — the National Human Rights Office — is also entirely ethnic Latvian. Minorities' share in the country's legislature and municipalities is also far below their share amongst the relevant population. Survey data indicated that in 1996, 31% of all employed ethnic Latvians were employed by "non-market employers" (i.e. state and municipal bureaucracy, military, state health-care sector, education etc.), while only 12% of employed minorities were working within this sector. [37] Latest surveys also suggest that within the working age population, unemployment among ethnic Russians is twice the rate among ethnic Latvians. [38]

No legal norm requires the usage of race or ethnic statistics in Latvia. However, ethnicity is institutionalized and in many cases data on the ethnicity of individuals is part of the data that has to be provided on a mandatory basis. For example, the application form for employment in the Ministry of Foreign Affairs[39] requires, among other data, the applicant's ethnicity, the way of acquiring citizenship (i.e. whether a natural-born or naturalized citizen of Latvia), the ethnicity and citizenship of relatives, including spouse, parents, siblings, chil-

35. *Latvijas Vestnesis* (The Official Gazette), 29 January 1994.
36. It is revealing that ethnicity is mentioned in the CVs of all candidates for the judiciary submitted for approval to parliament. When asked about the necessity of this record, the Minister of Justice explained that "mentioning ethnicity is not prescribed by any normative act," and that the Ministry "simply forwards to the parliament all data, which the candidate him/herself considers relevant." See Reply of the Minister of Justice, Mr. V.Birkavs, to an enquiry of MPs of "For Human Rights in Integrated Latvia" faction on 7 October 1999. Enquiry No. 8/4-6119.
37. Richard Rose (1997) *New Baltic Barometer III: A Survey Study*, University of Strathclyde, Glasgow. pp. 3.
38. Aasland, A. (2000) *Ethnicity and Poverty in Latvia*. Riga, Jumava. pp.37.
39. Approved by the Cabinet of Ministers on 25 June 1997

dren, spouse's parents and siblings. This offers unscrupulous state functionaries the possibility to "single out" and refuse the applications of individuals of "unde -sired" ethnicity.

No governmental or independent body supervises in Latvia the protection and implementation of minority rights.

II. Data on Individual Members of Minority Groups and Minority Groups as a Whole and the Uses of such Data and Statistics in Practice

Registration of Data on Minorities

The Residents' Register as described above is a uniform system of registra -tion of Latvia's citizens and non-citizens, as well as foreigners and stateless per -sons with residence permits in Latvia. Among other information, individuals' ethnicity is also included into the data maintained in the Register. Every indi -vidual is assigned a personal identity number after his/her data is entered into the Register. The Citizenship and Migration Department is in charge of running the Register.

The advantage of the personal identity number, assigned to every data sub -ject in the Register, is that it helps in relation with other state services, e.g. health-care, insurance, social benefit payments, taxation etc. The information of the Register can also be used for statistical and other research purposes.

However, the mandatory record of ethnicity in the Register and the iden -tification documents of all persons living in Latvia constitutes a violation of the right to privacy and the right to informational self-determination and offers an opportunity for abuse of members of ethnic minority groups by nationalistic bureaucrats. However, no cases of this kind were ever brought before courts in Latvia.

Statistical data of the Register are regularly published in the mass media and are available free of charge. Also, statistical data of latest population census have been widely publicized. Statistical data from both the Resident's Register and Census database are available online free of charge.

The statistical data on ethnicity, produced by the Resident's Register is some -times referred to by members of the political parties in the Parliament. For example the governmental party "For Fatherland and Freedom" made its argu -ments against allowing naturalization of non-Latvians based on the data coming from the Resident's Register, according to which "non-Latvians" constituted more than 40% of the population. They also argued that it is their deep conviction that ethnic minorities are disloyal to Latvia.

Census

In the latest census held on 31 March 2000, respondents were asked about *"Your ethnicity"* and were offered the possibility of a combination of "checklist" and "blank space" answers. Respondents had to either choose between three the largest ethnicities of Latvia (Latvian, Russian and Belarusian) or to fill in the "other" blank space.[40]

Only one ethnicity can be reported. Census takers have to make sure that the data obtained throughout the census interview is "precise." This way, as already mentioned, census takers can request individuals to give "accurate information," show identification documents to prove or "make more accurate" the provided information. Existing identification documents envision only one ethnicity, thus it is not possible to report more than one.

The ethnicity of the Latgalians, the native population of Latgalia (eastern region of Latvia) is a matter of dispute. The official view is that they are a subgroup of ethnic Latvians and they speak a dialect of Latvian. Some Latgalians believe that they are a separate ethnic group, speaking a separate language. During the 1920s Latgalian was taught in schools, and newspapers and books were published in this language. Following the breakdown of democracy in 1934, and throughout the Soviet era, the Latgalian language was suppressed and by now it is only spoken by people belonging to the older generation.

The final results of the census do not mention "Latgalian" ethnicity and language. It is impossible to verify how many individuals insisted on having "Latgalian" ethnicity during the last census. "Latgalian" ethnicity cannot be reported, since neither the Soviet nor the present-day Latvian authorities recognize it and "Latgalian" is not registered in identification documents either.

The issue of language was treated separately in the last census. The question asked for *"Your native language"* separately from ethnicity.[41] Similarly to the question on ethnicity, respondents had either to choose between three languages (Latvian, Russian and Belarusian) or to fill in the "other" blank space.

"Latvian," "Russian" and "Belarusian" ethnicity and languages are among the most widespread in Latvia and were not merged with (melted into) other categories. Apart from "Latgalian," any other ethnicity and language is listed in the detailed official results of the census.

---

40. Point 3 of the census form.
41. Point 4 of the census form.

After the collection of data, functionaries of the Central Statistics Board process the obtained data. The Central Statistics Board confirms the completion of the census forms and the total census outcome, which has to be made public within six months after the census.

Major Debates and Arguments on Using Data on Ethnic Minorities

There has been debate on whether to abolish the mandatory record of ethnic origin in passports in Latvia. One of the proposed ways out of the situation was to make this record a matter of voluntary decision for the passport holders. Thus, an individual could simply leave blank the "ethnic origin" box in his or her passport. This solution would not require many changes to the legislation or any additional investment, as it does not require changing the existing layout of the internationally recognized Latvian passport. This solution to the mandatory record of ethnicity was also suggested by the OSCE High Commissioner on National Minorities, Max van der Stoel, in his letter to the Minister of Foreign Affairs of the Republic of Latvia, Valdis Birkavs, on the 21st of November 1996.

Upon receiving the Commissioner's letter, the Ministry of Foreign Affairs has discussed the suggestion with other relevant ministries, the Naturalization Board and the Consultative Council on Nationalities. While the officials sup-ported the underlying idea of the suggestion, its actual implementation was rejected, with reference to technical difficulties. In particular, in his official answer on 27th of February 1997, the Minister cited the following reasons:

"the present passport of citizens of Latvia is internationally recognized, including the fact that information is given under all headings; implementation of the present proposal would require a considerable number of amendments to Latvian legislation, which might be a lengthy process."

The sustainability of the official argument is rather doubtful. Firstly, the proposed solution does not require changing the internationally recognized Latvian passports. Secondly, Latvian legislation in general does not differentiate rights, freedoms and entitlements of individuals depending on their ethnic origin, and thus, its abolition should not result in any legal problems.

Ethnic Statistics and Data Protection
Some Related Practices in Romania

Florin Moisa

I. Legal Framework

Constitution

In December 1991, Romania, after decades of communism and a violent transformation of its situation, adopted a new Constitution. Article 1 of the Romanian Constitution states that Romania is a nation state, sovereign and independent, unitary and indivisible. Romania is a democratic and social state, governed by the rule of law in which human dignity, citizens' rights and freedoms, the free development of human personality, justice and political pluralism represent supreme values and shall be guaranteed.

Article 6 (1) of the Constitution states with respect to national minorities: "The state recognizes and guarantees the right of persons belonging to national minorities to the preservation, development and expression of their ethnic, cultural, linguistic and religious identity."

Article 20 (1) states the respect for human rights: "Constitutional provisions concerning the citizens' rights and liberties shall be interpreted and enforced in conformity with the Universal Declaration of Human Rights, with the covenants and other treaties Romania is a party to"; and (2) "where any inconsistencies exist between the covenants and treaties on fundamental human rights Romania is a party to, and internal laws, the international regulations shall take precedence." Individual rights are also guaranteed constitutionally: among them the right to privacy (Articles 26, 27, 28), freedom of religion (Article 29), freedom of expression (Article 30), the right to access to information (Article 31), the right to education (Article 32), freedom of association (Article 36, 37). However, despite the constitutional intent, several rights remain merely at a declarative level, Romania not being able to reach a decent standard of life.

A distinction shall be made between "citizenship" and "nationality/ethnicity." The Law on Romanian Citizenship[1] says, "Romanian citizenship is the connection and the membership of a natural person to the Romanian state. Romanian citizens are equal before the law; only they can be admitted in civil and military public functions." The term "nationality/ethnicity" is used to refer to membership in an ethnic group officially recognized by the state. Usually ethnic groups in Romania are referred to as "national minorities" and they are understood to be the historical minorities of Romania. There are 18 ethnic minorities officially recognized by Romanian law and according to the Law on the Election of the Chamber of Deputies[2], the organizations belonging to these minorities are entitled to one deputy's seat in case they are not attaining the 5% threshold.

The Romanian Government adopted in 2000 an Ordinance for Prevention and Punishment of all Forms of Discrimination, a legal document that was inspired by the most important international regulations in the area. According to this document[3], discrimination shall encompass any difference, exclusion, restriction or preference based on race, nationality, ethnic origin, language, religion, social status, beliefs, sex or sexual orientation, belonging to a disfavored category or any other criterion, aiming to or resulting in a restriction or prevention of the political, economical, social and cultural fields or in other fields of public life. This recent Ordinance will probably bring to the public attention cases of discrimination, especially related to employment.

Until December 2000, the main authority concerned with the protection of national minorities was the Governmental Department for the Protection of National Minorities[4], an institution set up in January 1997 that operated under

1. Act 21/1 March 1991, Article 1.
2. Law 68/1992, Article 59 (2).
3. Ordinance No. 137/September 2000 on Prevention and Punishment of all Forms of Discrimination, Article 2.
4. The main functions of DPNM are to:
– prepare the draft laws and other regulatory instruments within its sphere of responsibility;
– approve draft laws and other regulatory instruments affecting the rights and duties of persons belonging to national minorities, based on the recommendation of the Council for National Minorities (the Council of National Minorities is a DPNM's advisory board);
– oversee the implementation of legislation concerning protection of persons belonging to national minorities;
– promote and organize programs concerning the preservation, expression and development of the ethnic, cultural, linguistic and religious identity of persons belonging to national minorities;
– establish and maintain relations with governmental and non-governmental organizations at home and abroad, which are concerned with protecting the rights of persons belonging to national minorities.

the authority of the Prime Minister. After the general election in November 2000, the problem of minorities was allocated to the new Ministry of Public Information under the Department of Interethnic Relations.

The Department of Interethnic Relations (former Department for the Protection of National Minorities) is not directly involved with issues of data protection; its responsibility is to oversee the implementation of legislation con-cerning protection of persons belonging to national minorities.

The institution of Ombudsman[5] was set up in March 1997 with the mandate to defend the rights and freedoms of the citizens against unlawful or abusive interference by the public authorities. The Ombudsman's Office is now fully operational with a staff of approximately 70 persons. The Office registered 4,372 complaints in 1999, up from 2,985 in 1998 and 1,168 in 1997. Being a relatively new institution, the Ombudsman's role and the procedures utilized are not fully known to the public yet. Many complaints were rejected by the Ombudsman because they were related to problems with the judiciary and not the adminis-tration; several of them had as a subject allegations of racial discrimination.

Data Protection

Romania does not have at the moment a special law concerning data protec-tion. In November 2000, after the change of the government, a Public Information Ministry was established in Romania. This new Ministry has among its tasks the preparation of a law concerning access to public information law; the act is already on the agenda of the Parliament and it is expected to be fully in place by the end of 2001.

There are, however, different legal guarantees concerning the protection of personal data collected by the state and non-state bodies.[6] Personal data is con-sidered to have a confidential character in most cases. According to the legal reg-ulations[7], the statistics services, the staff involved, official staff or public services

5. *Avocatul poporului* in Romanian.
6. Ordinance No. 9/1992 on Organization of Public Statistics, Article 1 (2) "The law on organiza tion of official statistics is applicable to all natural and legal persons that are active on the Romanian ter-ritory." Article 3 (3) "According to the principle of confidentiality, the statistic services and the sta-tistic personnel have the obligation to adopt and to ensure during statistical research — from the stage of collection of data to the stage of publication — protection measures for the data referring to the individual statistical subjects (natural or legal persons), data gathered directly by statistical research or indirect from administrative or other sources."
7. Ordinance No. 9/August 1992 on Organization of Public Statistics, amended by Ordinance 111/31 August 2000, Article 14 (1) "The official statistic services have to adopt administrative, orga-nizational and technical measures in order to ensure the confidentiality of the individual statistical data, to prevent the unauthorized access to the data, to prevent the distorted transmission of the sta-tistical data and intentional or unauthorized destruction of the data."

that have access, according to their legal status, to the content of the statistical data have to ensure the confidentiality of the data. In the case of personal data, the data has a confidential character and cannot be transmitted to other natural persons or legal persons and cannot be used for other purposes except the statis - tical ones.

In case of opinion polls, both as a legal obligation and a technical/scientific rule, the data subjects are informed about the confidentiality and anonymity of the data collected and the computerized statistical programs support the priva - cy of the data.

According to the Ordinance[8] public statistics activities are based on the fol - lowing principles: autonomy, confidentiality, transparence, specialization, pro - portionality and statistical deontology. The Ordinance is applicable to *all the nat - ural and legal persons* that are acting on the territory of Romania, but at the same time to all the Romanian natural and legal persons acting on the territory of other states. In order to ensure the objectivity, transparency and scientific char - acter of the methods, indicators and techniques used in statistical activity, the "Council for Coordination of the Statistical Activity" [9] is set up. This is a con - sultative body that has as its main task the strategic development of statistics. The decisions made by this Council are binding for all the actors concerned, including the private ones.

The National Institute for Statistics and Economical Studies is the main state institution responsible in the field of statistics. It is established and functions based on Government Ordinance on the Organization of Public Statistics.[10] The National Institute for Statistics and Economical Studies organizes and coordi - nates the public statistics activity in Romania. Its major tasks are: providing to the general public and to the public authorities information on the social-eco - nomic situation of the country; supplying to the all interested users the statisti - cal information data resulting from statistical surveys and research; creating and maintaining the national statistical data fund of social, demographic, economic,

8. Ordinance 9/1992, Article 3 (1).
9. Ordinance No. 9/August 1992, modified by Ordinance 111/August 2000, Article 4 (1) "In order to ensure the objective, transparent and scientific character of the methodologies, indicators, labels and classifications used in statistical activity, the Council for Coordination of Statistic Activity is set up, as a consultative body that has, in principle, as main objective the analysis and approval of the development strategy of the national statistic system, of the reports of the National Institute for Statistic and Economical Studies and of the annual program for statistic research and economical studies."
10. Ordinance No. 9/7 August 1992 on Organization of Public Statistics, modified by Ordinance No. 111/31 August 2000 on Organization of Public Statistics, Article 2 (1) "The official statistics in Romania are organized and coordinated by the National Institute for Statistics and Economical Studies, which is the specialized structure of the central public administration subordinated to the Government, and funded from the state budget."

financial and legal nature; setting up the statistical working tools; setting up and exploitation of the statistical information system; providing statistical studies, analyses and publications and their dissemination; coordinating of the scientific research activity.

Breaking the law concerning abusive storage, transmission and use of the information attracts disciplinary, administrative, civil or penal responsibility, depending on the situation. The Ordinance on Public Statistics states: "The fol-lowing constitute contravention, unless considered crimes in accordance with penal law: … e) breaking, by the official statistic services personnel of the legal provisions on the preservation of the confidential character of the individual sta-tistical data and information…".[11]

Romania has a National Informational System for evidence of the popula-tion[12] maintained by the Ministry of Internal Affairs. Part of the National Informational System is the "Permanent Registry of the Population Evidence."[13]

The Registry serves as a unique support for delivering data to all the systems of the central and local administration that are using personal data. It is struc-tured at the local, county and national level. The data is organized in the fol-lowing categories (Article 5):

– main personal data: name and surname, sex, birth date, place of birth, names of the parents, personal code number, husband/wife and children support-ed, civil status, nationality;
– general personal data: education, occupation, military situation;
– address: county, town, street, number, apartment;
– papers issued by public authorities: identification card, birth certificate, marriage certificate, death certificate;
– emigration and immigration data;
– data concerning death, place, year;
– color photo.

Each individual receives at birth a personal numerical code that will be used in all official acts including the permanent registry for data.

The Permanent Registry of Population Evidence defines as beneficiaries of the data collected by the Romanian Government and its institutions; they can

11. Article 19.
12. Law No. 105/25 September 1996 on Evidence of the Population and Identity Card.
13. Law No. 105/25 September 1996, Article 2: (1) "The Permanent Registry of the Population Evidence is component part of the National Informational System on Population Evidence and is established based on the personal evidence data. Its purpose is to facilitate information on the num-ber, structure and movement of the population on the country's territory. (2) Creation, actualization and utilization of the data … is made by the Ministry of Foreign Affairs, based on its organs of pop-ulation evidence."

have access to the data upon request only for activities that are classified as being of a *general interest*. [14] Usually, the general interest is connected with public order, criminality, national security and defense.

The Government Decision on Content, Actualization and Utilization of data from the Permanent Registry of Population Evidence [15] states: "(1) The data provision for the local and central interest activities will be ensured by a contract between the Ministry of Internal Affairs by its county police inspectorates or by General Police Inspectorate and the beneficiary. (2) the contract will refer to the destination of data, their structure, [...] the data protection and security measures adopted [...]" The same Decision states: "the beneficiaries mentioned at article 9 (b), (c) and (d) will sign a commitment letter by which they oblige themselves to use the data only for the destination established and to ensure their confidentiality and protection." [16]

According to the Act on the Evidence of the Population and Identity Cards, individuals have the right to access and review their personal data, upon written request to the local registry. [17] The local head of the registry must approve the request and the applicant will have to pay a fee for processing the request.

In certain cases individuals can have access to others' personal data upon a written request made to the local registration authority. [18] The local head of the registry must approve the request and a fee shall be paid for its processing. In case that *proof of a legal reason* exists, natural persons can have access to others' personal data upon written request. A contract must be signed by the registration authority and the beneficiary in order to ensure the destination of the data, their structure, the necessary data protection measures and the costs of the service.

As far as individuals' rights to demand altering or deleting data or other records being kept about their person are concerned, all the modifications con-

14. Romanian Government Decision No. 113/April 1997 on Content, Actualization and Utilization of data from Permanent Registry of Population Evidence, Article 9: "The beneficiaries of the data from Permanent Registry of Population Evidence may be: ...c) local public authorities, for the data of natural persons or for applications of local interest, based on a legally justified reason; d) central public authorities, for the data of natural persons or application of a central interest, based on a legally justified reason; e) the Romanian Government, for activities of a general interest."
15. Article 13.
16. Article 14.
17. Law No. 105/25 September 1996, Article 8: (1) "The organ of population evidence, according to the residence of the data subject can communicate, upon request, data recorded in its personal files. (2) The organ of population evidence can communicate, upon request, to a natural or legal person, civil status data, residence or address of another natural person, only after a written consent of the concerned was obtained. (3) The consent mentioned in (2) is not necessary when a legal reason exists for accessing the data."
18. Romanian Government Decision No. 113/14 April 1997 on Content, Actualization and Utilization of Data from the Permanent Registry of Population Evidence, Article 9. b.

cerning the data should be subject to a court decision.[19] In order to change or delete the data, the court ruling must be requested, depending on the case, by the concerned person, by the local public authorities, by the County Council or the Public Attorney's office.[20] The request can ask for deletion, modification, rectification, or completion of the civil status acts and any data included.

There are certain norms for storage, processing and controlling of data in the registry of personal data. Breaking up these norms will bring *civil and penal measures*, depending on the gravity of the facts.

International Obligations

International treaties ratified by the Parliament are part of the national law in Romania.[21] In case of conflict between covenants and treaties on fundamental human rights to which Romania is a party to and internal laws, the international regulations shall take precedence. The Council of Europe Framework Convention for the Protection of National Minorities was ratified by the Romanian Parliament in 1995.[22]

Romania has signed several important human rights conventions among them the Convention for the Elimination of all Forms of Racial Discrimination, the Convention on the Rights of the Child, the International Covenant on Civil and Political Rights and its Optional Protocol, the International Covenant on Economic, Social and Cultural Rights and the European Convention on Human Rights and all its protocols.

In 1993 Romania signed the Association Agreement with the European Union, and there are regular reports on the Romanian progress towards *aquis communautaire*.

---

19. In accordance with Law 119/16 October 1996 on Civil Status Documents, Article 57 (1).
20. Article 57 (2).
21. Romanian Constitution, Article 11: (1) "The Romanian State is obliged to fulfill accordingly and in good faith its obligations coming from the treaties to which it is signatory. (2) The treaties ratified by the Parliament are, according to the law, part of the internal legislation."
22. Law 33/29 April 1995.

II. Data on Individual Members of Minority Groups and Minority Groups as a Whole and the Uses of such Data and Statistics in Practice

Registration of Data on Minorities

Religious groups are quite diverse in Romania, from orthodox to Catholics, Protestants, Jews or Muslims. Many of the denominations can be connected directly to ethnicity (for example, while Romanians are mostly Orthodox, Hungarians are either Catholic or Protestant). The 1992 census has collected data on the historical denominations (those recognized under the provisions of a 1948 decree). All the religious groups collect data on their believers. Churches register all the important religious moments: baptism, marriage and death. The registration is made based on the official papers presented: birth certificate for baptism, marriage certificate for religious wedding, and inhumation certificate in case of death. We can also make a connection between ethnicity and the religious affiliation.

The data collected by the churches is usually available upon request from the data subject — being a natural or a legal person. All the data has an unofficial character, but, according to the legislation mentioned before, the confidentiality rules are applicable. The religious services (burial and marriage) delivered in the absence of official documents are contraventions.

The existence of such data may be used for the verification of the data existent in the state registry, but it can also be used in the recreation of lost data or for supporting the property restitution claims of different minorities of personal, group and religious nature.

The Romanian Police are known to be registering ethnic data on perpetrators and several times it published crime statistics imputing specific offenses to Roma. The only other group to be singled out by police, except Roma, is non-Romanian citizens that commit crimes in Romania.

The Romanian Ministry of Education also collected data on students, including data on their ethnicity and mother tongue. For example, the web site of the Ministry of Education contains data on Roma students. The school, high school and university departments are also keeping records on the different minority language classes and students attending them.

The Ministry of Health collected data concerning patients during their professional investigations. In both previous cases the data is used for professional purposes.

The Ministry of Internal Affairs and the police form one example of abuse regarding registration of ethnic data, namely data on the Roma minority. The Ministry in the previous years was able to provide very detailed statistics on Roma criminality, data that was not available on other national or ethnic groups. This kind of data is stored and used in the Police reports and most of the times taken over by the media and used on different occasions. Several times the representatives of the Police talked about the "gypsy mafia" (*mafia tiganeasca*) and about the high criminality rate within this ethnic group.

Census

The next official census will be held in March 2002.[23] The details of the organization of the census will be established later by a new legislative act, but in general it can be stated that the census will register all persons having Romanian citizenship and permanent residence in Romania, and also all non-Romanian citizens who are permanent or temporary residents of Romania.

The registration of data will be performed based on the declaration of the household head, having a full legal capacity. The registration staff has to confront the data with the identity cards, passports or birth certificates. Any other documents can be used only with the consent of the data subject. Persons without legal capacity will be represented by other members of the household or by a legal representative.

Refusal to provide the information requested in the census questionnaire or provision of inaccurate information is a contravention. In "exceptional situations" the person can go before the local census commission in order to provide the data.

Based on the previous census (1992) organization details, the following data will be registered:
  - identification data: name, surname, name and initials of the father;
  - geographical data: permanent address, residence address, place of birth;
  - socio-demographic data: sex, date of birth, civil status, number of children born, year of marriage (for women on first marriage), citizenship, nationality/ethnicity, maternal language, religion, education;
  - relationship to the household head;
  - economical data: economic situation of the person, occupation, occupa-

23. Romanian Government Decision No. 827/September 2000 on Population and Household Census in Romania.

tional status, main job, sector, working time, transportation means to work-place, unemployment.

The census questionnaire is still under construction, but already at this stage it is clear that language and ethnicity will be separated (they were not merged in the 1992 census either).

The Romanian census system is a mixed one, both with blank spaces and checklists. The registration staff fills in the data that the respondents declare.

Each person is allowed to declare one nationality/ethnicity. There were 16 historical national minorities registered in Romania during the last census: Hungarians (1,620,199), Roma/Gypsies (409,723), Germans (119,436), Ukrainians (66,833), Russians/Lippovans (38,688), Turks (29,533), Serbs (29,080), Tartars (24,649), Slovaks (20,672), Bulgarians (9,935), Jews (9,107), Czechs (5,800), Poles (4,247), Croatians (4,180), Greeks (3,897), Armenians (2,023). Data subjects can specify an ethnicity that is not officially recognized either. The registration of nationality is according to the declaration of data sub-ject. The 1992 census recorded 8,420 persons that declared an identity different than the recognized ones. This included Carashovenians (2,775) and Csangos (2,165). Another 1,047 persons did not declare any ethnic identity.

The information collected by the census will be processed electronically, based on statistical programs. All the personal data is considered confidential. The census data and information cannot be used as evidence before courts or as a means for establishing rights or obligations for the respective data subjects.

Human rights organizations and the organizations representing national minorities can delegate observers for the whole period of the census. [24]

For the 2002 census, the National Commission for Statistics has not yet con-sulted the organizations representing national minorities with respect to the specific problems related to their registration. This is partly due to the postpon-ing of the census from 2001 to 2002, which leaves some more time for the prepa-rations. Some representative organizations belonging to the Roma minority offered to help the registration process in places where compact Roma popula-tion exists, but they have received no official answer yet. In the case of Roma, it is known that in the previous censuses a large proportion of people did not declare their belonging to this minority. The reason for this was their fear from the stereotypes and prejudices existent towards this ethnic group. A study made by the Research Institute for Quality of Life Bucharest on Roma population in

24. Romanian Government Decision No. 878.October 1999 on Organizational Measures for the Population and Household Romanian Census in 2001, Article 9: "Legally set up organization that have as their objective the defense of human rights and the organizations of national minorities, members of the Council of National Minorities, may delegate observers for the whole period of the census. ..."

Romania (1997-1999) shows that approximately 900,000 people will declare their belonging to the Roma minority in the next census, which would mean an important improvement.

Research

Research institutes and other private institutions using statistics are known to collect and publish data, including data on ethnicity/nationality. Data is collected in public opinion pools, political barometers, in economical surveys, or with the occasion of marketing studies. The purpose for data collection is scientific.

Several surveys were organized in Romania, mostly covering general aspects of the social life and giving information on the distribution of the population at the national level, regional opinions and attitudes etc. These surveys are using the census and the electoral lists in order to design the samples. The most important are the following:

- Open Society Foundation Romania: Public Opinion Barometer — "Way of living and Social Structure in Romania" (two surveys each year, usually May and October). The main subjects of the Barometer include: political options and notoriety of main political parties and personalities, life quality and life standard, social and economic policy of the government, evaluation of institutions, social capital and sociability resources, human and physical capital, life styles, religion and faith, labor ethics, income and expenses. www.osf.ro.
- Ethnocultural Diversity Resource Center, Cluj Napoca: Ethnobarometer. The Ethnobarometer is designed as a series of periodical surveys, focussed on issues such as: monitoring and evaluation of the interethnic situation in Romania, self-perception and perceptions of otherness, dynamics of representation and stereotypes of different ethnic groups, construction and assertion of ethnic and national identities, knowledge and impact of public policies regarding ethnic minorities in Romania, rhetoric on minorities developed in various contexts and situations. One important future focus will be the correct estimation of the number of ethnic minorities living in Romania.
- Research Institute for Quality of Life Bucharest: "Resource Center for Social Action," a project aiming at the collecting, studying and dissemination of the relevant data concerning the problems faced by the Roma population in Romania and the public policies designed for these problems. The project will offer a complex diagnosis of the social situation of the Roma across the country on the following topics: socio-demographic char-

acteristics, living conditions, school education, economic standards, occupations, health, tolerance and prejudice towards Roma, social exclusion, migrations. The research report will be published soon by the Research Institute for Quality of Life Bucharest. The Research Institute for Quality of Life Bucharest conducted a comprehensive study on the situation of the Roma minority in Romania in 1993 and repeated it in 1997-1999 (funded by Open Society Foundation Romania).

– A research conducted in 2000 by Ioan Durnescu and Cristian Lazar in Romanian prisons shows that the Roma are approximately 17.5% to 20% of the total prison population (based on self-identification of subjects). The objective of the study is to estimate the proportion of Roma in Romanian penitentiaries and to identify their socio-cultural characteristics in order to design policies for the social inclusion of the Roma prisoners. Also, the proportion of Roma minors in the re-education centers is around 39.5%.[25] It is important to mention that Roma represent approximately 5%-6% of the Romanian population, according to sociological estimations.

Major Debates and Arguments

The Romanian Constitution defines Romania as a national state, sovereign and independent, unitary and indivisible.[26] The national character of the state has been questioned on several occasions, especially by the representatives of the Hungarian minority. The national character of the state (based mainly on the composition of the population, approximately 90% Romanians) must be explicitly defined in order to avoid misinterpretations and possible negative consequences regarding inter-ethnic relations.

The discussion of the Local Public Administration Law in the actual Romanian Parliament initiated several debates on whether minority languages may be officially used in public institutions. The Local Public Administration Law not only decentralizes public administration, but also gives ethnic minorities the right to appeal to local authorities and bodies in their own languages in areas where they represent at least 20 percent of the population. Signs can be written in minority languages, and local government decisions can be announced in minority languages, as well. Approximately 11,000 towns and villages are estimated to fall into this category. Rather than making any languages other than Romanian official, the law simply allows for the adoption of local provisions

25. *Identification of the proportion and socio-cultural characteristics of the Roma population from Romanian penitentiary system* Ioan Durnescu and Cristian Lazar, 2000.
26. Article 1.

regarding respect for minority languages, as that is contained in the European Charter of Local and Regional Languages of the Council of Europe. [27]

III. Methods and Means of Collecting and Processing Data Relating to Minorities

There is a mix of methods for collection and processing of minority data, depending on the type of the research, agency, purpose of the research, etc. All the actors involved — governmental agencies and non-state bodies alike — must respect the anonymity and confidentiality of data.

The collection of data is made by using a combination of methods. In the case of opinion pools questionnaires are used. Researchers use scientific sampling methods that appeal to the information contained in the electoral lists of names and addresses, census data concerning the distribution of minorities across the country, former lists of data subjects, etc.

Also, researchers appeal to information gathered from local leaders, teachers, priests, etc. The subjects are usually reached in their home and they have the right to accept or not the questioning.

An important debate relates to the issue of self-identification versus hetero-identification of the data subjects. For example, during the survey run by the Research Institute for Quality of Life Bucharest on the situation of Roma in Romania, several Roma leaders accused the researchers of non-ethical behavior and even racism. The problem was that the identification of the Roma families included in the survey was based primarily on hetero-identification and not self-identification. The problem still remains and researchers tend to combine the methods in order to avoid sensitive situations.

The following principles are taken into consideration during research in order to protect information privacy and ensure data protection. The principle of *voluntary participation* requires that people not be coerced into participating in research. Closely related to the notion of voluntary participation is the requirement of *informed consent*. This means that prospective research participants must be fully informed about the procedures and risks involved in research and must give their consent to participate. Ethical standards also require that researchers not put participants in a situation where they might be at *risk of harm* as a result of their participation. Harm can be defined as both physical and psychological.

27. Document signed but not yet ratified by Romania.

There are two standards that are applied in order to help protect the privacy of research participants. Almost all research guarantees the participants *confidentiality* — they are assured that data appropriate for identification will not be made available to anyone who is not directly involved in the study. The stricter standard is the principle of *anonymity*, which essentially means that the participant will remain anonymous throughout the study — even to the researchers themselves. Clearly, the anonymity standard is a stronger guarantee of privacy, but it is sometimes difficult to accomplish it, especially in situations where participants have to be measured at multiple time points (e.g., a pre-post study).

There are standard procedures in social research for the verification of data accuracy, quality and compatibility. The basic methods used are field verification, telephone verification, cross-questioning, data comparison, etc. For the comparative research and the compatibility, the surveys are using the same type of key words, concepts and coding system.

Usually the terminology used in case of registration of ethnic data is accurate, not coded. The case of Roma is somewhat different. Two terms are used in their case: Roma and Tigan (Gypsy), the last one having a clear pejorative connotation.

Ethnic Monitoring in Britain*

Michael Banton

To act successfully against racial discrimination it is necessary to identify policy objectives that can be attained within reasonable periods of time. This is eas-
iest when systematic data are available about the nature of the problems. The
policies can be implemented best when their impact can be monitored in ways
which enable those responsible to measure progress and pinpoint obstacles. This
need for relevant information is recognized in the General Guidelines for
reporting adopted by the United Nations Committee on the Elimination of
Racial Discrimination.[1] It states the importance of the numeric ethnic characteristics of the different countries with respect to the enforcement of the
International Convention on the Elimination of All Forms of Racial
Discrimination. It argues that "if progress in eliminating discrimination based
on race, colour, descent, national and ethnic origin is to be monitored, some
indication is needed of the number of persons who could be treated less
favourably on the basis of these characteristics." Finally it requests all states to
collect information "on mother tongues as indicative of ethnic differences,
together with any information about race, colour descent, national and ethnic
origins" in their censuses.

The use of a census for these purposes is often unacceptable in African
states. In Europe and North America the problems are less acute, but it may
still be difficult to secure agreement on the categories to be used in collecting
the information. The USA uses racial classifications on birth and death
certificates, and has long used the census to collect data on race and ethnicity,
yet some features of the classification are currently matters of controversy.
One difficulty is that the group names, which are used in everyday life, do not
combine to form a consistent system. Another is that increasing numbers of
persons have multiple ancestries and some want to be accorded a "multiracial"

* This text was originally published in *Diskriminering i arbetslivet — normativa och deskriptiva per-
spektiv. Ett symposium i Sigtuna 22 juni 1999*. at pp 40-53. Stockholm: Socialvetenskapliga forskn-
ingsrådet. We are grateful to the Swedish Council for their permission to republish it.

1. For the exact wording see Michael Banton "Ethnic Monitoring in International Law: the Work
of CERD" in this volume. pp.60 – 61.

identity.[2] A census has to serve wider purposes than the monitoring of racial and ethnic discrimination. Although the United Kingdom's history of attempt-ing to record the ethnic affiliation of individuals has been much shorter, it has encountered comparable problems. Experience in the UK may be of interest to some readers in other European countries, and it is for their use that this note has been designed. It suggests that the elaboration of a procedure for the collection of appropriate data, and the securing of public acceptance for it, takes the better part of a generation and may never be complete because the categories may have to be modified as circumstances change. Disputes about the most appropriate categories, and names for them, reflect some wider and fundamental issues about social identity.

Records of Birthplace

Questions about the nature of the records kept on differences of ethnic ori-gin first attracted attention in Britain in the mid-nineteen-sixties. The children of immigrants from South Asia had special educational needs (e.g., with respect to language teaching) and were concentrated in particular localities, so the Department of Education tried to ensure that no school had more than thirty per cent immigrant pupils.[3] For the purposes of data collection immigrant pupils were defined as:

a. Children born outside the British Isles who have come to this country with, or to join, parents whose country of origin was also abroad and

b. Children born in the United Kingdom to parents whose country of origin was abroad and who came to the United Kingdom within the previous ten years.

Children from Northern Ireland and the Republic of Ireland, and children of mixed immigrant and non-immigrant parentage were specifically excluded. Attempts were also made during these years to prevent undue concentrations of immigrants in particular municipal housing estates, leading an official commit-tee to insist:

2. Edmonston, Barry, Joshua Goldstein, & Juanita Tamayo Lott eds. (1996) *Spotlight on Heterogeneity. The Federal Standards for Racial and Ethnic Classification*. Washington DC: National Academy Press. pp.38-39.
3. Rose, E. J. B. et al. (1969) *Colour and Citizenship. A Report on British Race Relations*. London: Oxford University Press. pp. 265-73.

"Adequate records are essential not merely to counter charges of discrimination and to demonstrate that justice is being done, but also as an inte-
gral part of management and policy-formulation." [4]

When the Race Relations Act 1968 extended the prohibition of racial discrimination to employment, housing, and education, it implied that those
responsible in these fields would have to introduce better forms of record-keeping.

In 1975 the Home Office committee on Race Relations Research commented on the limitations inherent in records based upon birthplace (evident in the
ten-year cut-off point in the Department of Education definition and in the
exclusion of children of mixed ethnic origin). It discussed the possible use of
expressions in common usage, such as "coloured," and other possible forms of
self-classification, such as "ancestry or descent" or "country of origin." It concluded that the development of an appropriate categorization would have to
depend upon the testing of alternatives. [5] With respect to particular fields, the
Committee reported that "we do consider that the keeping of records of employees by racial origin should be regarded as one facet of good employment practice"; "This Committee endorses the Cullingworth recommendations that
records should be kept and used by local authorities"; and "the abandonment
within the education system of any systematic collection of data by racial origin
would be undesirable." The Committee asked the Office of Population Census
and Surveys (OPCS) [now Office for National Statistics] to give consideration
to some further suggestions.

By this time other institutions were exerting influence, notably the House of
Commons Select Committee on Race Relations and Immigration (SCORRI)
which was established in the 1968-69 session of parliament. The first private sector employer introduced the ethnic monitoring of its personnel in 1967. The
Race Relations Board, concerned with its responsibilities under the 1968 Act,
began to advocate monitoring despite strong opposition from both employers
and unions. [6] Some local authorities collected data on the numbers of immigrant
residents to support their claims for additional financial support from the central government. Government ministers told the civil service unions in 1976 that

4. Cullingworth, Barry (chairman) (1968) *Council Housing: Purposes, Procedures and Priorities*. London:
HMSO. paragraph 423.
5. *Race Relations Research. A Report to the Home Secretary by the Advisory Committee on Race Relations
Research*. (1975) London: HMSO. paragraph 35.
6. Sanders, Peter (1998) "Tackling Racial Discrimination" pp. 36-52 in Tessa Blackstone, Bhikhu
Parekh & Peter Sanders eds. *Race Relations in Britain. A developing agenda*. London: Routledge. pp.
38.

action on this front was required and a study was commissioned from an inde-pendent body of the procedures and possible hazards in introducing ethnic mon-itoring in the civil service. In 1981 the Minister submitted a memorandum to SCORRI on the race relations policy of the Civil Service Department. Proposals for a monitoring survey were set out in a 1981 report from the Cabinet Office (which made no mention of the ethnic categories to be employed for record-keeping). Ethnic monitoring in the civil service started in 1989, SCORRI's 1981 report on Racial Disadvantage having given additional impetus to this and sim-ilar initiatives.

The 1976 Race Relations Act established the Commission for Racial Equality (CRE) (in place of the Race Relations Board) and provided that the Commission might propose a code of practice to assist in the elimination of discrimination in employment. The Minister, if he approved of the draft, might lay it before Parliament, and, if there was no objection within a prescribed period, it could then be issued as an official code. If its recommendations were not observed, this might result in a breach of the law. The first such code was drafted in 1978 and, having received the approval of a new government, was issued five years later. When, in 1985, the CRE reviewed the working of the Race Relations Act, it recommended that the Minister should be given a power to prescribe the keeping of records of the ethnic origins of employees and that the Commission should have a power, within these limits, to require that copies of these records be submitted to it. No action was taken on these recommendations. In 1992 the CRE undertook a second review of the working of the Act and recommended that a statutory requirement of ethnic record-keeping be laid on all employers within categories prescribed by the Minister. No mention was made of the categories to be employed. No statu-tory requirement has been imposed, but it may be in an employer's interest to keep such records for use in contesting any claim of discrimination.

A Police Racial Identity Code

Increased concern about racially-motivated attacks in the streets, primarily upon blacks and Asians, prompted a Home Office survey in 1981, which con-cluded that their incidence presented a significant problem. It led four years later to the adoption nationally of a definition of a racial incident to be used by the police and prosecutors:

"any incident in which it appears to the reporting officer or any investi-gating officer that the complaint involves an element of racial motivation

255

or any incident which includes an allegation of racial motivation made by any person."

Racial incidents were to be classified using what was first called a racial identity code but is now referred to simply as an identity code. For readily understandable operational reasons, the police classification was to be based not on country of birth or upon the self-assigned ethnic origin or origins of the victim but on that person's visual appearance. At first this used seven categories: white-skinned European/ dark-skinned European/ Afro-Caribbean/ Asian/ Oriental/ Arab/ Unknown, but when monitoring of a wider range of contacts with members of the public became mandatory in 1996 this was simplified to use four categories: White/ Black/ Asian/ and Other. Record-keeping had to allow for circumstances in which there was more than one victim involved in the incident. According to the report of the *Stephen Lawrence Inquiry*[7] this definition is poorly understood by many police officers. The use of the words "racial" or "racially-motivated" is said to be inaccurate and confusing because all humans belong to one race. Therefore (*sic*) a new definition is proposed: "a racist incident is any incident which is perceived to be racist by the victim or any other person." The government has accepted this definition for use in the initial recording of incidents.

Records of Ethnic Origin

The divergence between the objectives of ethnic monitoring and the description of the population underlay the controversy, which arose when the OPCS drafted a form for use in the national census of 1981. It would have asked everyone to state the country of birth of his or her father and mother, then to assign himself or herself one of ten racial or ethnic groups identified by national names like African/Indian/Pakistani, etc. The universality of a census is threatened if members of the public object to the labels by which they are invited to identify themselves and decline to fill in the form, so surveys were conducted to test the acceptability of selected names. Some Asians preferred to be identified by their religion, while there were people from the West Indies who insisted that their children should be recorded as Black British rather than according to their parents' countries of birth. Though the proposed question did not employ the then contentious expressions "white" and "black" as names for categories, its inclu-

7. Cm 4262 (1999) *The Stephen Lawrence Inquiry*. London: The Stationery Office.

sion was nevertheless vetoed by the Prime Minister at a late stage in the preparations.

SCORRI (by this time a subcommittee of the Home Affairs Committee) reverted to the issue when it selected "Ethnic and Racial Questions" as the topic for its 1982-3 session.[8] In its report, the Committee recognized that many people would not like being faced with the question "Are you white?" but concluded that if it were first explained that such information was needed to combat racial disadvantage, most white people would be willing to tick the appropriate box. Having reviewed the results of tests conducted by the OPCS it recommended a form of question based on "Are you white... black... of Asian origin...?", followed by "Other groups" with the last three categories split so as to produce seventeen subdivisions.

The prevailing controversy about the use of the name "black" was reflected in the 1983 election campaign when the Conservative Party displayed posters of a respectably-dressed young black man with the caption (in capitals) "Labour says he's black. Tories say he's British." The text at the side of the poster began "With the Conservatives, there are no 'blacks', no 'whites', just people. Conservatives believe that treating minorities as equals encourages the majority to treat them as equals." In the debate about the question proposed for the 1981 census no-one objected to the wish of some individuals to call themselves black. The snag was that if a scheme was to allow some people to identify themselves by color, then others would have to be classified by color even though they objected to this. Behind the resistance may have been a suspicion that the adoption of color names would be a step towards the "one drop of black blood" doctrine current in much of North America, whereby a person with one black grandparent and a fair complexion would nevertheless be accounted black. Suspicion of proposals to use "black" as the name for a category was also the stronger because of a move which had started at the end of the nineteen-sixties, and had been encouraged from the political left, to count as black all non-whites, including persons with ethnic origins in South Asia.

The CRE was subject to conflicting pressures on the question of the categories to be used for monitoring purposes. Its problem was eased in late 1988 when, in an important statement, the government announced its plans for the 1991 census. As part of that census a question was posed under the heading "ethnic group," saying "please tick the appropriate box" and offering as alternatives: White, Black-Caribbean, Black-African, Black-Other, Indian, Pakistani, Bangladeshi, Chinese, Other. The CRE recommended that employers and oth-

8. Banton, Michael (1985) *Promoting Racial Harmony*. Cambridge: Cambridge University Press. pp. 88-92.

ers utilize the same nine-point scheme, while adding, as it has always done, that this was not the only possible classification, and that in some circumstances sub-divisions of the "white" category might be desirable. Many other bodies adopt-ed the census scheme.

If there is to be a census question of this kind, then members of some groups, like the Irish, demand the opportunity to identify themselves using the name of their choice. As part of the 2001 census[9] the government intends to use slightly different questions in England & Wales, in Scotland, and in Northern Ireland, so as to take account of local needs. Residents in England & Wales will be asked "what is your ethnic group?" and will be offered five divisions, each subdivided: (a) White: British/Irish/Any other; (b) Mixed: White and Black Caribbean/White and Black African/ White and Asian/Any other mixed back-ground; (c) Asian or Asian British: Indian/Pakistani/Bangladeshi/Any other; (d) Black or Black British: Caribbean/African/Any other; (e) Chinese: Chinese/Any other. It is also proposed that the 2001 census in England & Wales, and in Northern Ireland, should include a question on religion. The Home Secretary has spoken of the desirability of "recording groups, such as Muslims and Sikhs, who identify themselves primarily with their religion."

A system of five categories and sixteen subdivisions is too complex for most monitoring purposes. The names used in everyday life will often fluctuate; for example, persons of mixed ethnic origin may prefer to describe themselves as "half-and-half" or by using a hyphen, like Scottish-Pakistani. The category names used for the census, for the monitoring of employment, and in every-day talk, all interact, in that popular usage can affect the acceptability of cen-sus categories, which, in turn, acquire an official character, and this, if it does not create too complicated a scheme, may make them suitable for ethnic mon-itoring.

The Lord Chancellor's Department (which is responsible for the Courts Service) started to promote ethnic monitoring late in 1987 when the Lord Chancellor spoke of the need to appoint more black magistrates and announced that the result of a survey would be published. The author wrote to ask why the Lord Chancellor had used the adjective "black" to include Asians, and was told by one of his officials:

"There was a great deal of discussion preceding the decision to use the word 'black'. What prompted the adoption of that word is that it was used by the National Association for the Care and Resettlement of Offenders

9. Cm 4253 (1999) The *2001 Census of Population*. London: The Stationery Office.

in its report entitled *Black People and the Criminal Justice System*. We were thus responding in kind."

A major study to compare the sentences imposed on white and non-white persons convicted of criminal offenses in the Crown Court was commenced shortly afterwards. Immediately after publication of the findings, the Lord Chancellor announced that ministers were considering the collection of statistics to assist those engaged in the administration of criminal justice to avoid unlawful discrimination. In May 1993 he added "The Home Secretary and I have asked our officials to look at how best we might go about introducing a co-ordinated system... We aim to monitor systematically all stages between arrest and sentencing..." Ministers and their officials were agreed about the need for monitoring, and its value. So police forces were required, from a date in 1996, to supply an ethnic breakdown of all arrests, cautions, prosecutions and certain other statistical returns, and this is being progressively extended to court proceedings, sentencing, and the probation and prison services. The extension may not be fully effective until a new and uniform computer system is operating. One consideration is that some prosecutions (e.g., for TV license evasion) are initiated by bodies which do not presently record ethnic appearance. A pilot study [10] was unable to complete an analysis of court decisions because information on ethnic appearance was not always being transferred adequately to court records.

In implementation of section 95 of the Criminal Justice Act 1991, the Home Office has published statistics on race and the criminal justice system annually since 1992. For statistics of police action, pre-trial procedures, and trials, they make use of the visual classification of persons as recorded by the police. For the probation service they rely upon ethnic self-assignment using the standard four categories followed by the question "Where would you say your ethnic group comes from?" For the prison population, classification is a combination of self-assessment by the prisoner and observation by the prison officer, using the nine Census categories.

Implementation

The process of persuading either public or private bodies to undertake the systematic collection and use of ethnic records can be lengthy. By 1977 very few local authorities had even considered, let alone introduced, any scheme for mon-

10. LCD (1997) Ethnic *Monitoring of Defendants Appearing at Leicester Magistrates Court 1995*. Research series 11/97. London: Lord Chancellor's Department.

itoring the allocation of the housing at their disposal. Yet though many technical questions about how to implement such a policy remained unresolved[11], the principle was no longer contentious. Nevertheless, by 1985 only two dozen local authorities were operating proper schemes. The position was similar among local education authorities. In the course of the nineteen-eighties the health and social services institutions started, as equal opportunity employers, to record the ethnic origins of their staff. The monitoring of the ethnic origin of National Health service in-patients began in 1995 while many local social service authorities, wanting to monitor the delivery of their services, started about the same time to record the ethnic origins of their clients. Monitoring of persons appointed to serve on public bodies began in 1991.

In 1985 nearly 100 large or medium size private sector companies told the CRE that they had either started the ethnic monitoring of their personnel or were about to do so. The Employment Department sponsored a substantial study, from 1989, of twenty-two employers who had developed ethnic monitoring and represented "best practice."[12] This covered nine public sector organizations (three fire services, two local authorities, one health authority, one police force, one transport facility, and one administrative institution) and thirteen private sector companies (four manufacturing companies, four financial institutions, three service organizations and two retail companies). All had found something of value in the practice of ethnic monitoring. Most were ready to recommend it to others. There were still many problems, not least over the categories to be used, but the organizations displayed a clear commitment to further development. This study has since been supplemented by others, including one of HM Customs and Excise.[13] A compendium of good practice includes an account of the use of ethnic monitoring in the equal opportunities strategy of a retail organization employing 30,000 people in which the managing director explained "After all, if you can't measure it, you can't manage it."[14] The accumulated evidence also testifies to the high degree of preparation and training which is needed to make a success of this sort of exercise.

Some of those who have no objection to ethnic monitoring in principle nevertheless maintain that it would not be appropriate in their organization because

11. Hammond, Robert (1977) "Ethnic records for local authority housing" *New Community*, 6:105-11. pp. 105.
12. Jewson, Nick & David Mason et al. (1992) *Ethnic Monitoring Policy and Practice: A Study of Employers' Experiences*. Research Paper no 89. London: Department of Employment.
13. Moore, Robert (1997) Positive *Action in Action. Equal Opportunities and Declining Opportunities on Merseyside*. Aldershot: Ashgate.
14. Wrench, John (1997) European *Compendium of Good Practice for the Prevention of Racism at the Workplace*. Dublin: European Foundation for the Improvement of Living and Working Conditions. pp. 43.

of what they regard as its special character. If there are grounds for believing that racial discrimination is occurring, the CRE can conduct a formal investigation; then, if discrimination is found, it can either reach a legally-binding agreement with the organization concerned about remedial measures or issue a non-discrimination notice. For example, it was not until 1986 that the Army decided to introduce monitoring, and then at the recruitment stage only (it had been asked about this by the House of Commons Defence Committee as well as the CRE, and had postponed action awaiting information on experience in the Civil Service). Representatives of the CRE met the Minister to argue the need for the monitoring of postings and career development, to introduce equal opportunity training, and to disseminate information on the investigation of complaints of discrimination and harassment and the resulting disciplinary action. During the following years there was a series of exchanges between the CRE, the parliamentary committee, and the Minister, some concerning individual cases of discrimination and harassment. This led to the CRE's decision in 1994 to conduct a formal investigation into recruitment and transfer to the élite Household Cavalry. The findings were published two years later together with details of an agreement reached with the Ministry of Defence on a comprehensive five-year racial equality Action plan.

The first findings from the ethnic monitoring of police patrolling concluded that police forces consistently stopped and searched more black people than white people or Asians, but were less likely to caution black people (as an alternative to recommending their prosecution). When police figures were checked against those from the British Crime Survey it became apparent that many racial incidents were either not reported to the police or not recorded as such by them. In 1997-8 it was still the case that black people were five times more likely than white people to be stopped and searched by the police. To similar effect, the Crown Prosecution Service reported that in the year 1997-98 the police identified as racial incidents only 37 per cent of the cases which, in the view of the prosecutors, should have been so identified. There were nearly 1,300 cases containing admissible evidence of racial motivation and in nearly one-third of cases the court stated that a higher sentence had been imposed in view of this evidence. Figures such as these are regarded as specially relevant when the central government's inspectors carry out their annual inspections of police forces. Judges and magistrates also receive special training on the ethnic minority issues that may arise in both their criminal and their civil jurisdiction.

Discussion

British experience can be represented as a sequence in which institutions and voluntary associations seek to persuade the central government that the implementation of their policies will require better record-keeping. Ministers encourage these developments and policy within their departments is developed in an incremental fashion. A wider range of the public becomes persuaded that, though they do not like the proposals, some sort of monitoring is needed. The effective administration of any ethnic monitoring scheme depends upon public support because it constitutes an additional labor for staff who usually feel that they already have more than enough work. It also makes demands upon individuals who do not wish to assign themselves to ethnic categories, believing that to do so is to legitimize an improper kind of classification. They insist that people should be assessed on their merits and not on physical attributes or the way they choose to lead their private lives. Yet once a scheme is introduced, public acceptance tends to grow (for example, popular acceptance of the arrangements for monitoring religious identification in employment in Northern Ireland increased over the four years 1989-93 from 64 to 91 per cent among Catholics and from 42 to 64 per cent among Protestants). So ethnic monitoring functions as a way of changing the culture within institutions by stimulating individuals to take explicit account of things which, if left implicit, might well have been neglected.

This process can be accelerated if ministers capitalize on events, which have caught public attention. One such was the murder, in 1993, of a black student, Stephen Lawrence. Suspects were identified but the evidence assembled by the police was insufficient for a successful prosecution. The scandal attracted press publicity and led to the establishment of a public inquiry. [15] Implementation of many of the inquiry report's seventy recommendations, such as targets for the recruitment, progression and retention of ethnic minority staff, will depend upon effective monitoring. On 23 March 1999 the Home Secretary described the action planned "to realise the broader vision of an anti-racist society." The measures would extend beyond the police to cover the recording of, and reporting upon, all racist incidents in schools. An annual report on progress is planned. The inquiry report described what it called institutional racism in the police; it contended that comparable failings could have been found in education, housing, and across the public sector. Policy changes in these fields will also depend upon effective monitoring.

15. *The Stephen Lawrence Inquiry*. op.cit.

The most contentious feature of the monitoring scheme that has been adopt -
ed in Britain is the black/white division, which has spread from the other side of
the Atlantic. There is some concern that that the legitimation of this distinction
may strengthen any assumptions that blacks and whites are different in nature,
and that this could limit the freedom of persons of mixed descent to make their
own identity choices. Had the UK lain, for these purposes, within the French
rather than the US sphere of influence, the outcome might have been different.
On the other hand, it is clear that these categories now have a wide measure of
public acceptance, that the adoption of ethnic monitoring is bringing into the
public realm a mass of information about progress towards equality right across
the social spectrum, and that it is helping identify the areas where further action
is most desirable.

In other European countries there may at present be insufficient popular
support for the keeping of records of the ethnic origins of individuals. Yet if the
governments of these countries are to fulfil their obligations under the
International Convention, they need to monitor implementation of their anti-
discrimination policies. Records of countries of birth will be of diminishing util -
ity as more children are born in the country of settlement. Records of mother-
tongues will be useful in only a limited range of circumstances involving indige -
nous peoples and national minorities. Governments will have, firstly, to com -
mission experimental studies on the lines promoted by the ILO[16] in order to
monitor implementation, while, secondly, if their courts are to adjudicate upon
allegations of unlawful discrimination, the burden of proof will have to be laid
on the respondent to furnish the kinds of information needed to ascertain
whether the aggrieved person has been treated less favorably than persons of
different ethnic origin.

Update

Since this document was drafted there have been important developments.
The Home Secretary has published his Action Plan and Employment Targets.

The Action Plan[17] opens with a statement of a Ministerial Priority for the
Police Services: "To increase trust and confidence in policing amongst minori -
ty ethnic communities." It states that the process of implementing, monitoring

---

16. Bovenkerk, F., M. J. I. Gras, & D. Ramsoedh (1995) *Discrimination against Migrant Workers and
Ethnic Minorities in Access to Employment in the Netherlands*. International Migration papers 4. Geneva:
International Labour Office.
17. Home Office (1999) *Stephen Lawrence Inquiry. Home Secretary's Action Plan.*

and assessing the Ministerial Priority should include ten Performance Indicators, seven of which depend upon the collection of statistics of ethnic origin.

The Employment Targets[18] cover the recruitment, retention and career progression of ethnic minority staff in all institutions for which the Home Secretary is responsible, including the police, the prison service, the fire service, the probation service and the Home Office itself. The targets reflect the relative size of the local ethnic minority population as recorded in the Labour Force Survey. For example, the uniformed section of the Fire Service is set a national target of 7 per cent. At present the ethnic minority representation amounts to 1.1 per cent. The targets are set at 2 per cent for the year 2002, 3.2 per cent for 2004, and 7 per cent for 2009. The under-representation of ethnic minority personnel at senior officer level in all the services is recognized as a serious imbalance. The Inspectorates for the four main services will review the implementation of the monitoring process and the performance of these services in moving towards their targets.

Race Equality in Public Services[19] describes the ways in which, by performance management, progress will be measured in economic activity, education, health, law and order, housing, local government, lottery funding, the voluntary and community sector, and in the government's own performance.

Acknowledgement

Mr. Michael Head and Mr. Keith Abbott kindly commented on an earlier draft of this note.

18. Home Office (1999) *Race Equality — The Home Secretary's Employment Targets. Staff Targets for the Home Office, the Prison, the Police, the Fire and the Probation Services.*
19. Home Office (2000) *Race equality in public services — Driving up standards and accounting for progress.*

IV.

Conclusion

Counting or Numbering?
Comparative Observations and Conclusions Regarding the Availability of Race and Ethnic Data in Some European Countries

Iván Székely

The aim of this paper is to point out some common characteristics and major differences in the law and practice of some European countries, based on the country report chapters of this volume, and also to formulate some conclusions and recommendations regarding the problems discussed in the previous chapters.

The six revised country reports resulting from the Ethnic Statistics and Data Protection project provided the basic information for the present comparative observations. This information was later completed with factual data from other available public sources, especially regarding the legislative situation in certain countries.

The sample of countries cannot be seen as either comprehensive, or representative; and thus it can be used for quantitative analysis only with limitations. It serves, however, the purposes of mapping a relatively broad range of problems and concepts; for setting up a sort of catalogue of issues in the field. It can serve consequently as a basis for formulating certain conclusions and proposals for future action in the area of availability of race/ethnic data, or at least for inspiring their future formulation. This has already been partly realized in the country reports.

General Observations

In comparing the reports from the six European countries (Bulgaria, Czech Republic, Germany, Hungary, Latvia, Spain - each reflecting its specific social, political and legal traditions) it can be observed that the legal situation regarding the handling of data is more or less the same in these countries, at least on a general level. On the other hand, there are great differences in the context of the problems, their social significance, conceptualization and practical management.

The similarity in legal provisions and institutions can be attributed to several reasons. As Colin Bennett[1] discovered as early as the 1980s, technology con-

---

1. See "Different Processes, One Result: The Convergence of Data Protection Policy in Europe and the United States". *Governance*, Vol. 1, No. 4, October 1988; summarized in "What is Policy Convergence and What Causes it?" *British Journal of Political Science*, Vol. 21, No. 2, April 1991.

vergence in the area of data processing resulted in a certain *policy convergence*. This policy convergence has led to the formulation of, *inter alia*, the basic principles of data protection, then the establishing of international conventions, the preparation of guidelines and directives in the field, and, as a third level, this convergence was to be reflected in the similar structure and provisions of national laws. A related reason is the necessity of legal compatibility within the EU, which obliges not only member countries to implement common provisions in their domestic law, but, indirectly, candidate countries as well. The newly democratic countries, especially, face formal and informal pressure to import ready-made Western solutions: to enact laws, to build in provisions in their already existent laws, to make declarations. Another reason for legal similarity is that the (old and new) democratic countries have signed or ratified a more or less similar, standard set of major international human rights conventions and, consequently, implemented and promulgated them in their national law. These existing means can provide real legal guarantees, but can also serve as fig leafs to hide deficiencies in proper data handling or in implementing an effective anti-discrimination policy.

It is worth noting that the first part of the country reports (answers to the legal questions) contain the most thorough and lengthy analysis while the third part (practical methods and means) is the shortest and the most general in each report and resulting study. It can be interpreted as a result of the authors' field of interest: they supposedly have broader information and knowledge on the legal situation than on data collecting and processing methods; the latter would require more of a sociological approach and a knowledge on survey methodology. Another possible explanation is that there are very few methodologies and procedures worked out especially for handling ethnic and other sensitive personal data that have been applied in practice.

More remarkable is that the discussion of issues relating to the protection of personal data is predominant as compared to that relating to minority rights or the availability of ethnic statistics. One reason for this inequality is the composition of the questionnaire itself which began with questions relating to general legal provisions on personal data and included questions on ethnicity and data on ethnicity (as special cases of data handling) later, with less emphasis. The other reason, however, is more general: the law on data protection is much more detailed than that on minority rights or the special provisions on the availability of ethnic data, if any; the legal hierarchy in the former field is more complete and structured, its regulation is formulated in a more precise way.

Constitutional Rights

Table 1 comprises the formal occurrences of fundamental rights relating to data availability, privacy and minorities in the constitutions of the countries sur-veyed. Such a compilation, however, can be regarded only as a general illustra-tion of the range of fundamental rights: on the one hand because it does not show the real content and limitations of rights, their modalities, differences in legal traditions and legal systems as a whole; on the other hand because certain denominated rights can contain or implicate other, not enlisted rights which shall be interpreted as such according to a decision of the constitutional court. Without deeper analysis it is apparent from the table that a standard set of basic rights can be found in almost every constitution, especially in those of the new democracies.

Table 1. Constitutional rights

Rights and limitations	Bulgaria	Czech Republic	Germany	Hungary	Latvia	Spain
DP/self-determination	yes	yes	—*	yes	—	yes
Private life	yes	yes	—**	yes	yes	yes
Freedom of religion	yes	yes		yes	yes	yes
Freedom of opinion	yes	yes		yes	yes	yes
Freedom of expression	yes	yes	Yes	yes	yes	yes
Freedom of information	yes	yes	—***	yes	yes	yes
Freedom of research	—	yes	Yes	yes	yes	yes
Equality/non-discrimination	yes	yes	Yes	yes	yes	yes
Cultural autonomy	yes	yes	—	yes	yes	yes
Language use	yes	yes	—****	yes	yes	yes
Prohibition of ethnic parties	yes	—	—	—	—	—

* The provisions of the Constitution shall be interpreted as the constitutional right to information-al self-determination (The 1983 landmark decision the German Federal Constitutional Court, see chapter on Germany).
**Only: inviolability of the home.
***Only in the Constitution of the State of Brandenburg.
****Mentioned among the equality provisions.

International Conventions

Similarly, the countries have signed, ratified and/or implemented the relevant international conventions and directives, so the lack of these cannot be the reason for the differing approach and practice in the field of availability of ethnic data in the countries surveyed.

In Table 2 the most fundamental general human rights treaties are not included (these are generally ratified in all democratic countries); the listed ones are: the Data Protection Convention of the Council of Europe,[2] the Data Protection Directive of the European Union,[3] the Framework Convention for the Protection of National Minorities of the Council of Europe,[4] and the International Convention on the Elimination of all Forms of Racial Discrimination of the United Nations,[5] and the date of their signature, ratification or entry into force, where applicable.

Table 2. International Conventions and Directives

	Bulgaria	Czech Republic	Germany	Hungary	Latvia	Spain
CoE DP Convention*	–	signed (2000)	1981/1981/ 1985	1993/1997/ 1998	signed (2000)	1982/1984/ 1985
EU DP Directive	–	("implemented" in DPA)	EU member	adequate status 2000	–	EU member
CoE Framework Convention*	1997/1999/ 1999	1995/1997/ 1998	1995/1997/ 1998	1995/1995/ 1998	signed 1995	1995/1995/ 1998
UN-ICERD	1966	1993	1969	1967	1992	1968

*signed/ratified/entered into force

The Council of Europe Framework Convention and the ICERD have been implemented in the domestic law of the countries surveyed (Latvia only signed it). As far as the Data Protection Convention is concerned, only Bulgaria has not as yet joined it; even the Czech Republic and Latvia - two countries representing the newest wave of data protection legislation - have already signed it.

2. Convention for the Protection of Individuals with regard to Automatic Processing of Personal Data (European Treaty Series No. 108), 1980.
3. Directive 95/46/EC of the European Parliament and of the Council of 24 October 1995 on the protection of individuals with regard to the processing of personal data and on the free movement of such data.
4. European Treaty Series No. 157 (1995).
5. Adopted in 1965.

Implementing the EU Directive is obligatory for European Union member states only. The landscape is more diverse here: only Germany and Spain are members of the EU and even Germany still has to implement certain provisions of the Directive in its federal data protection legislation. Hungary, however, officially received the so-called adequate status in 2000. This means that regarding transborder flow of personal data, Hungary is considered to have an adequate level of protection of personal data as compared to the EU member countries. Drafters of the new data protection laws have already built the provisions of the Directive into the new pieces of legislation even in the candidate countries. The Czech report refers to the EU Directive as "implementation," although the Directive should be formally implemented only by EU member states.

Independent Supervisory Authorities

With the exception of Bulgaria each country has a general ombudsman, as well as a data protection commissioner (or persons or organizations with similar functions). Information commissioners, and especially an independent supervisory authority for minority rights cannot be found in these countries, with the significant exception of Hungary and partly Bulgaria. In Hungary - following the Canadian model of the Information and Privacy Commissioner - the function of an information commissioner is integrated with the Parliamentary Commissioner for Data Protection and Freedom of Information (DP-FOI Commissioner). The Hungarian Parliamentary Commissioner for National and Ethnic Minorities is one of the two existing national examples of an independent authority of such a kind in the field of minority protection. All the three Hungarian parliamentary commissioners informally call themselves "ombudspersons." In the case of the DP-FOI Commissioner the author has a critical opinion of this approach: according to his competence and powers defined by the law, the Commissioner, when establishing this new institution, could have and should have extended the range of his core activities from retroactively investigating individual complaints to proactively influencing the framing of big information handling systems in state and private sector alike.

The Hungarian report extensively refers to certain separate and - exceptionally - common recommendations of the two parliamentary commissioners regarding minority issues. Although the recommendations of the commissioners are not binding, they are regarded as highly important and the majority of the recommendations, especially those of the DP-FOI Commissioner, are implemented.

In Bulgaria the National Council on Ethnic and Demographic Issues (NCEDI) was established by the Council of Ministers in 1998 as a body for consultation, co-operation and co-ordination between the government institutions and non-governmental organizations to design and implement the national policy with regard to ethnic and demographic issues and migration. Although the January 2000 report of the Monitoring Committee of the Council of Europe acknowledged the NCEDI's achievements in several important areas, the Bulgarian report in this book notes that one of the obligations of the council is to enforce the 1999 Framework Program for Equal Integration of Roma in Bulgarian Society, yet "no measures have been taken to implement it so far." The European Union's recent report on the candidate countries[6] points out that "the administrative capacity of the NCEDI to implement the program remains low, and the limited financial means allocated for implementation make effective performance of its task difficult."

Table 3. Independent supervisory authorities

	Bulgaria	Czech Republic	Germany	Hungary	Latvia	Spain
DP Commissioner or organization	–	DP Office	DP Commissioner	Parliamentary Commissioner **	DP Inspectorate	DP Agency
FOI Commissioner or organization	–	–	–*	Parliamentary Commissioner **	–	–
Minorities' Commissioner or organization	National Council on Ethnic and Demographic Issues	–	–	Parliamentary Commissioner	–	–
General ombudsman or organization	–	Ombudsman	Ombudsman	Parliamentary Commissioner	National Human Rights Office	Ombudsman

*In the State of Brandenburg: DP and FOI Commissioner.
** Parliamentary Commissioner for Data Protection and Freedom of Information.

Aside from actual deficiencies in their operation, such institutions with their "soft" competence, quasi case-law logic, moderating and facilitating activity, can play a significant role in closing the gap between the mere legal provisions and practice, providing orientation in the field of conflicting rights and interests, and advancing the development of methods and means applicable in practice.

6. Regular Reports from the Commission on Progress towards Accession by each of the candidate countries, November 8, 2000.

Domestic Law

Table 4. Elements of national legislation

	Bulgaria	Czech Republic	Germany	Hungary	Latvia	Spain
DPA	(Bill)	2000	1977 (new Bill)	1992	2000	1999
FOIA	2000	1999	(only 3 States)	1992	1998	1992
Citizens' Registration Act	1999	2000	1987	1992	1998	1957
Statistics Act	1999	1995	1987	1993	1993	1989
Minorities Act	–			1993	1991	

At the national level, data protection Acts can be found in every country sur-veyed, with the exception of Bulgaria. However, Bulgaria has a DP Bill submit-ted to the National Assembly and, once adopted, will likely follow the interna-tional standards, thus reflecting the general trend of policy convergence. Germany belongs to the first wave of DP legislation beginning in the 1970's, and Hungary with its law enacted in the early 1990's to the second one. The other countries belong to the latecomers and enacted their data protection acts in 1999 or 2000. Germany however, where the first DPA was enacted in the State of Hessen in 1970, and whose Federal DPA (1977) served as an early model for the first wave of data protection legislation, still has to adopt an important provision of the EU Directive, namely the guaranteeing of special safeguards for the pro-tection of sensitive data - among others, data relating to racial/ethnic origin. [7]

The policy - or legislative - convergence can be seen in the area of Freedom of Information legislation, as well. FOI legislation, with its Swedish tradition from the 18th century and the USA Freedom of Information Act from the 1960s, has a much longer history than DP legislation. Here Hungary and Spain belong to the relatively experienced countries while Latvia, the Czech Republic and Bulgaria have more recent laws. Germany, one of the European strongholds of administrative secrecy, after decades of legislative attempts, succeeded in enact-ing general FOI laws in three of its States and only has federal legislation relat-ing to the accessibility of environmental information (1994).

The activities of the state statistical services are regulated in law in each of the countries surveyed; the newly democratic countries introduced new statistical

---

7. The latecomers' advantage is that they could already follow the provisions of the EU directive - sometimes simply copying them into their national DPAs - while the old systems, although they work well, have to be modified and adjusted to the common European norms.

Acts in the 1990s. All countries have a Citizens' Registration Act, which regulates the sources, content and accessibility of the central population registers. In Germany, the population register is decentralized in local self-governments and there is a strict separation of informational powers between statistics and other areas of state administration. Thus personal data collected for statistical purposes cannot be used for other administrative purposes, according to a 1983 decision of the Constitutional Court.

A separate Act on minority rights, however, can be found only in two of the countries, Hungary and Latvia. The Latvian Act "on unrestricted development of national and ethnic groups of Latvia and the rights to cultural autonomy" of 1991 is very short and contains only basic statements, while the Hungarian Act on the rights of national and ethnic minorities of 1993 contains numerous detailed rules, as discussed in the Hungarian report.

Such an overview can provide only a very general picture of the legal situation. The listed elements of national legislation are only expectable standards of the legal regime of a developed, democratic country. There are many interrelated provisions in different levels of national legislation and regulation, and the *practical possibilities* of handling personal and statistical data relating to ethnic origin considerably depend on this interrelatedness. For example, the mere fact that a separate Minorities Act exists in a given country[8] is not a decisive factor with respect to the effectiveness of minority protection and the system of minority registration - see the differences in the content of the Hungarian and the Latvian Act and those in the registration of minorities.

This paper is not intended to give a detailed comparative legal analysis of these interrelated provisions. Anyway, one could not simply compare the provisions of national legislation, or only within a limited sphere of validity, even in such a well-defined field as handling ethnic data, since - despite all legislative and policy convergence - the legal system, the legislative traditions and the legal techniques used in the countries in question result in different networks of rules, exemptions, procedures and principles.

An exact analysis of such networks would not only exceed the framework of this volume, but it would partly misinterpret its purpose. The reason for this is, on the one hand, that the lack of ethnic statistics requires mostly practical solutions and not abstract comparative legal analyses; on the other hand, experience shows that state politics, with similar declarations and general legal guarantees,

---

8. On the homepage of MINELRES (Minority Electronic Resources, directory of resources on minority human rights and related problems of the transition period in Eastern and Central Europe, *www.riga.lv/minelres*) a compilation can be found on minority-related national legislation. From the countries surveyed in this project, Bulgaria, Hungary and Latvia are included in this list.

can lead to completely different results (see for example the difference between Hungary and Latvia, discussed below).

Problems and Countries

The country reports and the resulting papers in this volume, beside describing the legal situation and practice, point out some specific problems regarding the availability and use of ethnic data, individual and statistical data alike. The reader can find papers with a basic immanent criticism towards non-availability of such data, while others seem to judge the existing regime of data handling as more or less adequate. Although both public awareness and practice of using ethnic data are different in the countries surveyed, the gravity and the judgement of certain problems largely depend on who prepared the report. If the author is an advocate of minority rights and anti-discrimination policy, he/she naturally emphasizes different approaches than in the case when he is an independent supervisor of protection of personal data.

The problems mentioned in the country reports can be divided into two main categories:

(a) no or not enough ethnic data for desirable purposes, and

(b) ethnic data used for undesirable purposes.

The first category is obvious— these problems inspired the Ethnic Statistics and Data Protection project itself. Problems belonging to the second category mainly refer to the use of ethnicity-related personal data in police or in the criminal procedure or for the purposes of prevention of crime, but other aspects were mentioned in the reports, as well.

With respect to the first category of problems, the Bulgarian report emphasizes that even data resulting from the censuses is not reliable, and it has never been reliable in the field of ethnic statistics. The reason behind this is twofold: first it is the fact that people from ethnic minorities (mostly Roma), being afraid of social stigmatization and other undesirable consequences, do not indicate their ethnicity or indicate a desirable ethnicity in census questionnaires. The second reason is of methodological nature: the changes introduced between the 1992 and the 2001 censuses made certain categories of ethnic data incomparable, thus breaking longitudinal series of statistical data. The report also refers to a 1993 parliamentary declaration stating that in the 1992 census data from the Blagoevgrad district did not reflect the demographic structure of the population (Bulgarian-speaking Muslims were categorized as Turks).

The Hungarian report mentions the problem of defining Roma for research purposes: there are arguments in favor and against all the three existing method-ologies (self-identification, judgement of the researcher, judgement of the envi-ronment). The Bulgarian report indicates the lack of racial and ethnic data in the National Unemployment Service or the National Health Fund, and speaks about this as an "indirect abuse" that prevents authorities from taking measures to alle-viate poverty or combat racial discrimination. The Czech report also points out critically that self-identification of census subjects does not necessarily reflect reality. The Hungarian report notes that the special rights and forms of state support for minority education would require reliable ethnic data and this requirement seems to be contradictory to the ignorance of the state with regard to the ethnic or national identity of its citizens.

As for the second category of problems mentioned, the criminal category of "Gypsy crime" or "minority crime" as a basis for false interpretation and preju-dice is mentioned in several reports. Even in Germany where legal rules are the strictest in this respect, and where, for historical reasons, any form of state reg-istration of ethnicity is forbidden, the Bavarian police are still keeping a registry of persons involved in criminal investigations, which indicates their Sinti or Roma ethnicity. In Bulgaria a standard statistical form is used for recording the ethnicity of perpetrators and suspects, on the basis of the authorities' judgement. The legal and ethical grounds of this registration practice is questionable. Also, in the Czech Republic the Ministry of Interior collects data on the ethnicity of suspects, based on the official's judgement. The lawfulness of such a registration, along with similar governmental databases is also questionable, especially in the light of the new data protection legislation adopted by the Czech Republic.

The Spanish report describes three cases recently reported in the press: local police departments are illegally collecting ethnic data (together with data on color, accent, sexual orientation etc.) and maintaining files on "suspicious peo-ple." These files have not been destroyed despite the explicit call of the Data Protection Agency. In other cases the Agency could not prove the existence of the files, despite the strong suspicion that they existed. A somewhat related Spanish example of keeping illegally collected data in police archives is the case of the registry of "social deviants" set up during the Franco regime. Although after the 1995 reform of the criminal code this registration was terminated, the documents are still in the police archives containing information on "socially dangerous" people, such as Roma or homosexuals.

Among the other cases mentioned in the reports regarding the use of ethnic data for undesirable or questionable purposes, is the practice of the Bulgarian secret services, who are reported to collect data on people's ethnicity and reli-

gious affiliation "for purely discriminatory purposes." As opposed to the opinion presented in the Bulgarian report on the lack of ethnic data in unemployment registers, the Hungarian report describes the casual (unlawful) indication
by the state employment offices of the Romani ethnicity of their clients. Beside
the unlawfulness of this practice - i.e. to record someone's ethnicity without his
knowledge and consent - the result is quite unfavorable for unemployed Roma.
To the contrary of the expectations of some Hungarian Roma leaders who think
that declared Romani ethnicity is advantageous for unemployed people, in practice it is a serious drawback for the people registered in the state employment
databases because of the existing discrimination and stigmatization towards the
Roma in the labor market. Similar abuses of data on Roma are reported in the
Czech study. In the Czech Republic "extremely precise figures" were available
and presented at an international conference, on Roma housing, on questionable
legal grounds. Among the measures triggered by the wave of emigration of the
Roma, Czech Airlines registered "information on the ethnicity of the travelers,"
namely whether they were Roma or not. This clearly discriminatory practice was
allegedly introduced at the request of British immigration officers. In the
Hungarian report the contradiction between the indirect minority registration
in connection to the educational grants and the availability of the parents' written (voluntary) declarations is pointed out.

Latvia represents an altogether different category. As a historical response to
the Sovietization and the resettling of ethnic Russians in Latvian territories, the
new Latvian State introduced a comprehensive policy towards minorities. The
"institutionalization of ethnicity" targets ethnic Russians who constitute the
most important minority in present-day Latvia. According to the Latvian report,
there are not just specific problems in the use of ethnic data, but there is a whole
package of problems: the state system of using ethnic data itself is fundamental-
ly problematic from both human rights and minority rights aspects. In this country everyone is obliged to have an ethnic record in the population register and in
censuses; this data is registered in the personal identification documents.
Nationality does not depend on self-identification but on the ethnic origin of the
individual's parents and grandparents. The granting of citizenship is based on
the nationality record, and without citizenship even the fundamental services of
a modern society are hard to access (about one quarter of the population is still
denied Latvian citizenship).

The above show that, beyond the authors' differing views and priorities, the
objective profiles of the countries in the field of handling of ethnic data have
significant differences. Germany can be considered to be at one end of the scale:
for reasons of history and the resulting legislation and practice, there is no eth-

nic registration, and practically there is no statistical data on minorities at all. At the other end of the scale, in Latvia, ethnic registration is compulsory and personal data on ethnicity affects the everyday lives of individuals. Hungary, perhaps somewhere in the middle range, has a relatively well worked-out sys - tem of both informational and minority rights; still the lack of careful harmo - nization results in practical problems in the interrelated enforcement of these rights.

Counting or Numbering.
Some Conclusions and Recommendations

As it can be learned from the mapping of the legal situation, it is not explicit - ly forbidden to collect, store and use data, even personal data, relating to eth - nicity in the countries surveyed.[9] Statistical, or irreversibly anonymized individ - ual data on people's ethnic belonging - if available - can be used for scientific and statistical purposes, or, in general, for purposes not connected to the individual data subjects. Minority organizations and churches, within the scope of their activity, may register their members. In general, personal data can be collected and used on the basis of informed consent of the data subjects.

In practice, however, it is not easy to meet all the legal requirements and ensure all the safeguards laid down in national laws and international documents. With special regard to the - formal and substantial - sensitivity of ethnic data, it is not simple to guarantee the *free*, *express* and *informed* consent of the individual - the three basic attributes defined in the EU directive. Furthermore, it is nec - essary to guarantee a continuous legitimacy of the use of ethnic data; an "isolat - ed" consent in one single point of the procedure is not enough.

However, the mere mapping of the legal situation does not throw light upon whether

(1) the rights which should be protected, granted and enforced, are of "col - lective" or individual nature; i.e. rights that people are entitled to have only in a community as its declared members, or as individuals; and when these rights are violated, the violation affects people only as members of a community or as individuals,

and

(2) for the protection of these rights (of whichever nature) data on the indi - viduals or data on the communities is needed.

9. Portugal was not included in the survey. In this special case the Constitution itself contains a gen - eral provision which prohibits the use of personal data relating to, among others, religious beliefs.

In the author's view, protectors of minority rights, even if they intend to pro-tect the rights of a *community*, or fight against its discrimination, should always respect the dignity and self-determination of the *individuals* concerned. The implied individual rights and freedoms include not only those related to their eth-nicity but also those granted for everyone, with special regard to informational rights and freedoms. Besides, these goals can be reached by using statistical data, or individual data that is not connected permanently to the data subjects.

As has been mentioned earlier, the missing data is necessary to avoid dis-crimination or facilitate preferential treatment. However, the reader should be aware of the experience reported from different countries: avoiding the use of ethnic data relating to individuals, or even to communities, does not necessarily mean avoiding discrimination. Indirect discrimination is always possible in the case of communities which can be defined by other, not-ethnic parameters, and in which a certain minority constitutes a dominant proportion (for example, Roma in certain marginalized populations).

On the other hand, preferential treatment does not necessarily require the use of personal data. It is possible to *count* the members of a community without *numbering* them, i.e. without recording them individually in files, registries or computer databases. In such cases it causes no special harm, for example, if not only Roma but other poor people are given support or aid as well. The practice of "counting *versus* numbering" is interrelated with questions of self-identifica-tion. Within a certain (probably estimable) margin it should be tolerable if some people declare themselves belonging to a certain community only in the hope of receiving preferential treatment.

*

In the debates concerning the issue of gathering ethnic data some implied illusions also emerge. One of them is the illusion of the Good State, in other words, the belief that the ruling majority of state and society alike is basically act-ing as a benevolent welfare institution and the only role of data on ethnicity is to provide a potential tool for helping minorities. Although this description is over-drawn, and certainly few people are totally convinced of this idealistic role, the positive aim (to provide factual data for an effective anti-discriminatory policy) can somewhat divert the attention from the double-edged nature of ethnic data.

One should never forget the classical examples of abuse of data on ethnicity such as the post-war deportation of ethnic Germans from Hungary. In that case the already archived 1941 census sheets were reused in 1945/46 to determine who had declared him- or herself an ethnic German and, consequently, whom to expatriate. Those who say today that this is an unfortunate historical event which can never return, should not overlook what has recently happened in Kosovo, just a few hundred kilometers from some of the countries examined in this volume. There, in the first period of the war, masses of ethnic Albanians were expelled and stripped of their documents and other proofs of identity in order to make their return difficult or impossible. Thus an unusual (but unfortunately, easily executable) abuse of ethnic data was committed: people's ethnicity and data connected to their ethnicity was the basis of the attempts to delete them from essential registries that serve as the proof of the citizens' entitlement for rights and services in the modern state.

Another illusion implied in the debates is that a proper legal and institutional framework equals its proper operation. This problem should be taken into consideration and carefully balanced when discussing the popular issue of introducing the ombudsman's institution in countries of the region: this function is especially dependent on the person's qualities. If you provide narrow competence to this institution, its impact can be negligible. If you provide wider competence to it, a wrong person can cause great harm, can damage the prestige of the whole institution.

Therefore what protectors of minority *and* informational rights should really trust in, is not a central legal or institutional element, or a strict legal and administrative hierarchy, but a network where everyone has his or her own role: lawyers, independent supervisors, NGOs, demographers and sociologists, informaticians, the representatives and organizations of minorities - and, most of all, the data subjects themselves.

The significance of the legal guarantees, however, should not be underestimated. These are necessary but not sufficient conditions for exercising rights related to the use of ethnic data. Beside high level declarations, constitutional provisions and legislative acts, a series of detailed legal regulation as well as internal rules, guidelines, ethical codes, best practice documents should also be formulated. These pieces of regulation and self-regulation should be worked out in cooperation with representatives of different sectors and professions concerned: minority groups, NGOs, information experts, researchers, the state statistical organizations, commissioners or ombudspersons (if available), local self-governments, even churches.

*

There is another level of cooperation which is needed for solving methodological problems: working out practical data handling solutions. Here the

280

knowledge and experience of experts from the legal, sociological and information processing fields should be integrated. In the course of such a cross-disciplinary teamwork it is advisable to take the following principles and methods into consideration.

The safest method is to record *statistical* data on ethnicity from the beginning of data collection. This meets the fewest legal obstacles and implies the lowest potential danger to individual data subjects. The latter is not the case with groups of people: the use, disclosure and publication of data on ethnic groups also require careful consideration. A geographically or physically located community - for example, pupils of a school - can be a target of atrocity itself.

In order to record reliable statistical data of high resolution, the researcher might need the help of local "interface" persons as data suppliers. The best such data suppliers are members, leaders or representatives of ethnic groups, minority organizations or communities, or other trusted persons, for example school directors in districts with minority population. Naturally, the quality of the data highly depends on the data supplier's interest, the proper communication of research purposes and the foreseeable impacts of data collection, and the fair relationship between data supplier and researcher.

Sometimes data relating to *individuals* is needed. This kind of data can be reliable and anonymous at the same time: these criteria are met by data recorded without identifiers.[10] Such a technique results in individual but not personal data sets. A good example for using such individual data sets is the 2001 census in Hungary, where - as a result of the extensive negotiations between the DP-FOI Commissioner and the Central Statistical Office - not even the census sheets contain personally identifiable data.[11] Instead the comprehensiveness and quality of data is ensured by other reliable statistical methods. (The questionnaire also included questions on ethnicity; answering those was voluntary.)

If legal and ethical requirements (e.g. free, express and informed consent, the right to inspect, alter or delete one's own data, continuous legitimacy of data handling) are met, it is also possible to collect *personal* data relating to ethnicity. However, as soon as the purpose of data collection allows it, the data should be anonymized, i. e. irreversibly deprived of the identifying details. It should also be guaranteed that no *personal* data recorded for statistical or research purposes can be used by the state administration.

---

10. Besides name, date and place of birth, social security number and other similar natural or artificial identifiers, data can be regarded as identifying if it can be related to a specified or specifiable person; for example, the occupation indicated as "the director of a [given] primary school."
11. It was argued that by combining the unidentified individual data it is still possible to trace back to the data subjects. Even if this is true in certain cases, the positive approach of designing the census deserves appreciation.

A useful method for "temporary anonymization" is storing separately the identifying data from other individual data. This might be necessary in cases when the researcher or data controller has to return to certain data subjects, for example for making interviews, or carrying out a longitudinal research or monitoring. In such cases the connection between identifiers and other data should be reestablished *temporarily*, only for the time which is necessary to identify the data subject again, or to add new data to the existing record.

The connection between the identifiers and the rest of the data is technically realized by means of "connecting codes," namely numbers or alphanumerical codes which unambiguously identify a given person *in a connection* between two databases or two segments of a database. As a guarantee of fair and lawful handling of personal data, it is advisable to store the two database segments at different responsible data controllers, or at least to store the connecting codes (the keys to join up the two or more parts again) at a trusted third party. This solution can be regarded as a "key escrow system." The best option, however, from the data protection point of view, is that the keys are deposited with parties where the personal (ethnic) data in question is *a priori* available - close to the source. The reason is that one should not neglect the possibility that, in an unfortunate scenario, the independent keeper of the key would be forced or compromised, and the re-joint ethnic database containing personal data could be used for wrong purposes, for example, segregation or persecution of members of ethnic communities.

Another important task is to guarantee the methodological coherence of time series in the long run. Whenever a new aspect or a new classification system is introduced, it is essential to ensure the compatibility of the old system with the new one, even if the latter contains more criteria for processing and analysis. If the old and new data sets do not use the same categories or units, the data should be transformable from one system to the other. Without such a coherence the quality of measuring temporal processes or estimating future trends would be unacceptably low for serious research.

Throughout the debate concerning collection of ethnic data a potential confrontation emerged between two human rights protecting societies: data protectors and minority rights protectors. In other words, not only rights can compete in abstract legal theory but also their committed advocates in real life. Although it is not possible to perfectly eliminate all potential collisions of competing rights and interests, the aim is not to conflict but to find mutually satisfactory solutions in practice. Hopefully the issues raised above will contribute to this process.

Appendix

The Questionnaire
Outline and List of Questions for Country Experts

I. Legal Framework

1. General overview on the rights and freedoms of information and commu-nication— particularly on the protection of personal data and on information self-determination (major legal guarantees, regulations on sensitive data, pre-conditions of linking databases, special features of handling data in academic research).

2.
a) Do individuals have the right of access and review their personal data, including personal data about ethnicity?
b) Can individuals have access to others' personal data, including personal data about ethnicity?
c) Do individuals have rights of access to information about communities or other groups?
Please distinguish, where applicable, differences between individual rights of access with respect to a) information stored by the state and b) information stored by non-state bodies.

3. Do individuals have rights to request/demand altering or deleting data or other records being kept about their person (including data on ethnicity)?
If so, are there limitations concerning what data can be altered or deleted, and is ethnicity included among "deletable" information?

4. What legal sanctions are available for abusive storage, transmission and/or use of information?

5. Is there a difference in the legal regulations concerning data collection by state authorities and by private actors? Please provide details, quoting laws.

6. What rules apply for the transmission of data? Are authorities allowed, for

example, to pass personal information about individuals across state lines/share information with neighbouring states? Under what conditions?

7. The connections, overlaps and contradictions between the two former fields, i.e. minority rights and data protection.

8. Is there an independent supervisory authority for the protection of minority/data protection rights, and with what kind of authority?

9. Is there a public registry or archive where individuals can review data being stored about themselves by the state?

10. A brief summary on the special regulations on personal data registration including census data and central population registries.

11. How are the international legal documents in the given areas observed, and do they have a binding effect? (international organizations that the country belongs to, international human rights documents signed and ratified in the given country, special agreements that the country signed in this field — e.g. Council of Europe Convention on Data Protection, what CE recommendations does the country follow, how do the EU regulations have an impact in the given country in this field).

12. Legal regulations resulting in discrimination, although the provisions may not be prima facie discriminatory.

13. Decisions of the Constitutional Court or Ombudsman's recommendations, concrete cases regarding the availability and/or use of race statistics. Court decisions, interpretations, legal statements. Please provide examples of court decisions which have made use of race statistics, i.e. cases of discrimination in employment, education, etc., where the court has referred to the number of applicants/the number accepted/the number rejected by race.

14. Please give any examples of any law, regulation, internal government departmental directive or other legal norm, which mentions in any way (authorizing or prohibiting the use of) race or ethnic statistics. Please note any conflicts in the legal regime.

15. Future prospects, possibilities for legal reform in the field.

II. Data on Individual Members of Minority Groups
and Minority Groups as a Whole and
the Uses of such Data and Statistics in Practice

1. An overview on the registration of data on minorities, including registries based on law, registries of churches, religious communities, minority based interest groups, local-self-governments, associations etc. Are there illegal data registries? Compulsory and voluntary provision of data — what fields? The quality and major characteristics of registered data. (Please provide information as to the existence or non-existence of race statistics in the police or other law enforcement agencies, government, employment offices, housing agencies, schools, offices of equal opportunity, monitoring, etc.)

2. How and who can use the data in the registries?

3. What are the positive effects of the existence of the registries and of using their data?

4. Are we aware of any data abuse regarding minorities (both in the legal and illegal realm)?

5. What kinds of statistics have been produced on the basis of the registries?

6. Census
a) Data gathering: how are respondents asked to provide information on their ethnicity (if they are at all)?
i) Is there a "checklist" system or a blank space, to be filled in by the respondent?
ii) Are respondents allowed to have more than one ethnicity (hyphenated), or are categories fixed?
iii) Are language and ethnicity split or merged?
iv) Can persons specify an ethnicity that is not officially recognized?

Where possible, please provide the exact formulation of census questions relating to language and ethnicity.

b) Have all or parts of censuses ever been rendered invalid as a result of public non-participation/civil disobedience?

c) Census data processing and reporting:

i) how is the above information processed?

ii) are certain categories listed in the census collapsed (melted into one, e.g. "others") for the purposes of reporting data?

iii) how do authorities classify information?

iv) how do they report persons who have listed more than one ethnicity, a non-official ethnicity, etc.?

7. Non-census:

a) What official bodies are known to keep statistics on ethnicity?

b) Are these known to be stored and used centrally? Or is their centralized usage only a matter of speculation?

c) Have authorities ever used non-census statistics on ethnicity publicly/non-publicly? Which authorities have done this? Please cite examples, as comprehensively as possible.

d) Have authorities distributed ethnic statistics to private entrepreneurs?

e) Have authorities renounced publicizing ethnic data, but not renounced storing/using it? (Please include source).

f) What non-state bodies are known to have gathered/stored/distributed/published race statistics? For what purpose? How comprehensive have these been?

g) Where authorities and/or non-state actors are known or suspected to keep data on ethnicity, is the descriptive terminology accurate (i.e., the name of the ethnic group) or coded?

h) Where authorities and/or non-state actors are known or suspected to keep data on ethnicity, is ethnicity a proper noun or a qualifier?

8. Has anyone ever been tried/convicted for crimes related to the gathering, storing or distributing data on ethnicity? Is there case law on data protection in the use of ethnic data? Civil and criminal law suits in this respect and their publicity in the press.

9. Major debates and arguments (in government, media, academia, and NGO-s) on using data on minorities.

10. What provisions have been made, in law or in practice, for the inclusion of minority groups — especially minority groups historically burdened by discrimination — for participation in decision making about the gathering, storage and use of data on ethnicity?

III. Methods and Means of Collecting
and Processing Data Relating to Minorities

1. What methods and primary data are used for collecting and processing minority data by researchers, government agencies, and civil organizations? (personal data directly from the data subjects, personal data from persons other than the data subject, personal data from existing databases, individual but not identifiable data, available statistical data, data derived or aggregated from other available data, data based on estimations, etc.)

2. How do the interviewers reach potential data subjects in case of personal interviews or data collection?
   – using name and address lists? (where do they obtain the lists from? on which legal ground? how do they select the sample?);
   – using information from intermediaries? (community leaders, schoolteachers, neighbors etc.);
   – using stochastic methods?;
   – using their personal knowledge and contacts?

3. What other methods and techniques have been proposed and discussed (advantages and disadvantages from both legal and ethical aspects, as well as from the aspects of the quality and reliability of data processing)?

4. What kinds of guarantees are used for protecting information privacy/ ensuring data protection (e.g. making personal data temporarily or permanently anonymous; connection codes to separate identifying and ethnical data of the data subjects; Privacy Enhancing Technologies (PETs), especially in computerized data processing)?

5. How do data controllers ensure data quality and compatibility (for internal coherence and comparative research)?

6. Which are the relevant — national or international — surveys in this area? Which methods were used, what were the results and how were the results used?